The Best of John Russo!

HOW TO MAKE EXCITING MONEY-MAKING MOVIES combines the best of my three books on movie making, which are known as Bibles of the Industry. They are the books Quentin Tarantino was referring to when he said my books guided him through his first complete movie. I was also told by Scott Moser that these books guided him and Kevin Smith through film school and the making of their first movie! I am pleased to have helped many, many young filmmakers to jump-start their careers. And I want to do the same for you!

So, read and study what I have written. You probably won't find a better way to invest in yourself than to make a start with HOW TO MAKE EXCITING MONEY-MAKING MOVIES.

"I made a movie I didn't finish. Then I read your books, took notes and made charts, and that's what guided me toward my first complete movie."

– QUENTIN TARANTINO

Books by John A. Russo published by
BURNING BULB PUBLISHING:

Novels
The Academy
The Awakening
The Booby Hatch
Black Cat
Dealey Plaza
Limb to Limb
Living Things
Night of the Living Dead

Non-Fiction
How to Make Exciting Money-Making Movies
How to Make Your Movies Look Professional

Most Burning Bulb Publishing books are available at special quantity discounts for bulk purchases for sales promotions, premiums or fund raising. Special books or book excerpts can also be created to fit specific needs.

For details, write to our marketing department at info@burningbulbpublishing.com or via standard post at Burning Bulb Publishing, P.O. Box 4721, Bridgeport, WV 26431

How to Make Exciting Money-Making Movies

JOHN A. RUSSO

Burning Bulb
PUBLISHING

How to Make Exciting Money-Making Movies
by **John A. Russo** / Edited by **Gary Lee Vincent**

Burning Bulb Publishing
P.O. Box 4721
Bridgeport, WV 26330-4721
www.BurningBulbPublishing.com

Cover designed by Gary Lee Vincent with licensed elements from Fotolia.com (55626218) and CanStockPhoto.com (csp22303014).

Second edition (Black and white ed).

Paperback ISBN: 978-0692385531

Printed in the United States of America

Library of Congress Control Number: 2014957997

"Movies seemed to be the best way to combine the writing and the sensory. I had unconsciously figured this out when I got my first camera in Vietnam. I was shooting stills between rainy seasons. I bought a Super-8 when I got back, then went up to 16mm, and then Godard happened, doing incredible new things with film. It had to be movies."

– OLIVER STONE

Author's Note
MOVIE MAGIC

MOVIES AFFECT large masses of people—as art, as entertainment, as a method of wide-scale dissemination of fact and opinion. Making movies offers a means of involving the mind and body in creating something that will have a direct and powerful effect on those who see and hear it.

Because modern communication is the lifeblood of our culture, many persons nowadays feel a need to know how motion pictures are made and marketed. More and more people have jobs that require them to produce film, to supervise production, or at least to be knowledgeable enough to effectively employ the talents and services of motion picture specialists.

If you are a critic writing about film, an advertising exec who recognizes the merits of film in selling products, services and ideas, a home-movie enthusiast, a film investor, or simply an enjoyer of films, this book will enlighten and entertain you. It was written primarily for those who have a consuming desire to *make* movies. But it is also for everybody who aspires to a deeper and broader understanding of the art and craft behind "movie magic."

John Russo

CONTENTS

Part I: Conceptualizing
1. Story Anatomy
2. Coming Up with Exciting, Hard-hitting Concepts
3. High Concept Versus Low Concept

Part II: Writing
4. How to Come Up with a Strong Plot
5. Making Characters Live and Breathe
6. Outlining
7. Fleshing It In
8. Collaborators, Re-writers, Tinkerers and Meddlers

Part Ill: Selling
9. The Deal Makers
10. Making Contacts
11. Packaging your Project
12. Staying Power

Part IV: *Heartstopper*--An Object Lesson
13. Pitching a Hot Concept
14. Developing the 30-Page Outline into a 500-Page novel
15. Whittling the Novel Down to a 90-Page Screenplay
16. The Production Gets a Green Light
17. Using the Screenplay as a Recipe to Direct the Movie
18. An Overview of Movie Distribution

Part V: Dirt Cheap Production

19. El Cheapo Shooting, Editing and Finishing
20. How to Write a Good Dirt Cheap Script
21. Hire to Hire Low Cost Actors
22. How to Hire a Low Cost Crew
23. How to obtain Cheap Props, Costumes and Locations
24. How to Shoot on a Short Schedule
25. How to Avoid Getting Raked Over the Coals
26. How to Distribute Your Own Movie

Part VI: Interviews

27. Clive Barker
28. Wes Craven
29. John Landis
30. Joe Dante
31. Rick Baker

Appendix 1: Sample Pages from *Heartstopper / The Awakening* Novel Outline, Novel and Screenplay

Appendix 2: Sample Distribution Agreement, Investor Agreement, Freelance Player Contract, & Release Form

Part I
CONCEPTUALIZING

"If you or I don't do good films, somebody else will take the money and make bad ones. They'll make some jumped-up, tin-pot, wanking piece of fascism like Top Gun."

– ALEX COX, director

"Given the cost of movies today, and the cost of marketing movies, my view is that the only real audience to pursue is the young audience. Young moviegoers are less critical, and they're more susceptible to an advertising blitz."

– PETER GUBER, producer

"Never, never try to scope the market. If you say, they want science fiction so I'll write science fiction, or they want mysteries so I'll write mysteries, you're doomed. You've got to write what you're passionate about. Otherwise you'll produce juiceless, flavorless fiction."

– DEAN R. KOONTZ, writer

1
Story Anatomy

EVERY MOVIE MUST tell a story. And our goal as filmmakers is to tell stories that captivate millions of people. So let's begin with an analysis of exactly what a story is.

According to my desk dictionary, a story is a narrative or recital of an event or series of events, whether real or fictitious, intended to entertain a reader or hearer or viewer. A story line is the rough plot of a film, play, or novel.

Fine. But there are good stories and bad stories. Stories that are witty, and stories that are boring. Stories that work, and stories that simply fall apart.

In order to put one together and make it stand up straight, make it walk and talk and do all that entertaining it's supposed to do, we have to understand the basic anatomy. So let's get it on the table and start dissecting.

BASIC STORY ELEMENTS

Every story is composed of five basic elements:
- Time
- Place
- Setting
- Character
- Plot

Time, of course, is the chronological placement of the story—the month, day, year, or historical period. Sometimes we need to get very specific about *time;* for instance, we may have a story of political intrigue taking place on November 22, 1963, the day that

President Kennedy was assassinated, and the events could not logically take place on any other day. Other times it serves us well to be very general about chronology; we may need to know only that the story takes place "sometime in the distant future."

Place is the general geographical location—the city, state, country, or planet (or even the supernatural plane, such as limbo, heaven, or hell) where the story occurs. Again, sometimes extreme specificity is called for, such as the name of an exact country or city. Other times we may locate the story more generally, such as "in a major city," or "in a deep forest," or "on a hitherto undiscovered planet."

Setting refers to specific details of scenery and background— the look and feel of the day, the weather, the outdoor or indoor location—any and all factors that may contribute to the *mood* of the events we are going to relate, including other events that may have already happened or are impending. For instance, we could have a story taking place "in the middle of a violent storm, in a ramshackle house without plumbing or heating, in the heart of an urban ghetto. After the death of a street person."

Character refers to the human or nonhuman personages who are going to populate the story. There are stories about humans, and there are stories about animals, and there are stories about animals that act like humans (and *vice versa)*. There are even stories about creatures that never really existed or whose existence is quite speculative, such as unicorns, ghosts, vampires, goblins, angels, devils, and werewolves.

Plot is the chain of events, incidents, or situations in a story. A plot and a story line are roughly the same thing; they may be thought of as the skeleton of a story. A plot is not really a living, breathing story, any more than a skeleton is a person. A plot is a sketchy outline of what is going to happen, without many of the rich, involving, entertaining details fleshed in.

The plot is not always the most important element of a story either. Sometimes character and/or setting take precedence and intrigue the audience more than the story line does. TV's *Columbo* mysteries were driven by the quirkily fascinating detective character played by Peter Falk. And Stanley Kubrick's *2001: A Space Odyssey* appealed enormously to modern audiences because of the imaginative setting that it so wonderfully and seemingly authentically explored.

BASIC STORY STRUCTURE

In order to have a good story, the five basic elements—time, place, setting, character, and plot—have to be well balanced and skillfully woven together. The story needs to have a strong point of view, an unerring sense of direction, a dynamic pace, and exquisite timing. Edgar Allan Poe, a master storyteller (and pioneer in the writing of chillers and thrillers), helped establish the basic structure of a good story:

- Prelude
- Conflict
- Climax
- Denouement

The *prelude* is the beginning of the story, the calm before the storm. Here we are usually made aware of time, place, and setting, and some if not all of the major characters are introduced. Sometimes the pace here is disarmingly unhurried, putting us off-guard, so that we will be hit harder when the action becomes fast and furious. Other times the "calm before the storm" is not so calm at all—the story opens with a bang and keeps right on pounding at us.

The *conflict* is usually introduced early, though it may be suspensefully delayed. The conflict is the struggle between different characters, or of characters against natural or supernatural forces. Finding out how this struggle will be resolved is what keeps us watching a movie or turning the pages of a book, and it may be prolonged through twists and turns and various complications, till we are biting our nails and writhing with suspense.

The *climax* is the high point of the conflict, the point at which action and suspense are at their maximum, and the outcome is in the most doubt.

The *denouement* is the outcome itself, the resolution of the conflict, the solving of the puzzle. At the end of it, the characters' lives are changed, sometimes to their liking and sometimes not. They may find love and happiness, or they may not even survive. Either kind of ending can be apropos. If we are not to insult the audience's intelligence, we may find that an unhappy or shocking ending is the only kind that makes sense.

MAKING A STORY MAKE SENSE

Nothing will lose an audience faster than having gaping holes in the logic of a story. There is no excuse for sloppy craftsmanship. Every good story must be constructed with three important criteria in mind:

- Unity
- Coherence
- Emphasis

Unity is the welding together of the parts of a story, each contributing to the other and furthering the whole; harmony, as opposed to inadvertent discord; oneness of purpose, thought, spirit, and style.

10

Coherence is the logical cohesion and connection of story elements; believable motivations and interactions between characters and events.

Emphasis is the marshaling of action, dialogue, and all story elements toward the enhancement and embellishment of the story, so that its meaning and purpose may be made clear and its impact fully realized.

The storyteller's craft is a disciplined one. And unity, coherence, and emphasis are the benchmarks of that craft. Dramatic incidents must have reasons for occurring, and must be interdependent and intertwined. Problems must not be solved too easily, or in an unrealistic way. Once we understand a character, he must continue to behave within the parameters of his own psychology, and must not suddenly do something that we wouldn't expect of him and couldn't logically rationalize. We must not bend the story's characters to our whims merely to facilitate some bizarre twist of the plot.

Generally speaking, it's all right to get your characters into trouble by the use of coincidence, but coincidence should never be used to get them *out* of trouble. The use of coincidence and certain uses of magic (even in stories of the supernatural) are too easy, too facile, and make the audience feel cheated—and rightly so.

As I mentioned before, Edgar Allan Poe helped establish the principles of good story telling, and he must have known what he was talking about, because today his stories are still being made into successful movies, even though they were written over 150 years ago. In 1990, the world's leading horror directors, Dario Argento and George Romero, collaborated on a movie called *Two Evil Eyes,* an anthology of Poe stories. A modern critic has said, "Poe's stories are miracles of precision. Each word is in place. Every sentence is constructed with the aim of contributing sharply to the ultimate and clearly envisioned effect."

11

The key point here is that Poe was always after an *ultimate and clearly envisioned effect.* In other words, he had a strong central premise or theme in mind, and then he remained true to that theme from beginning to end. If we wish our own stories to be strong and substantive, we must adhere to that same principle.

THEME AND CONCEPT

In order to come up with stories that can truly fascinate and excite people, we must think first and foremost in terms of *theme* instead of plot. Many people have difficulty doing this, because they don't fully understand the difference between theme and plot. A plot is what happens in a story. A *theme* is the philosophy behind what happens—the issue, the meaning, the vital question that the story explores.

The plot takes the characters from A to B to C. The theme makes people *care* about where they started from in the first place and where they're going to end up. A dynamic theme elevates a plot, giving it a reason to exist and a precious chance to become a story that deserves to be told. In other words, the theme should guide the plot and should come before it, in the sense that the plot should arise out of vital issues that concern you and cry out to be explored. So, if a plot falls into your lap without a theme, you should invent one for it, to rescue it from utter triviality.

William Shakespeare often borrowed plots and stories from other writers who came before him. Most of those writers are long forgotten. But Shakespeare's plays and sonnets will probably live forever. It is because his works dealt in subtle and complex ways with important, universal themes—questions of life and death, honor and dishonor, love and hate, courage and cowardice, loyalty and love. Whether you want to write the great American novel or produce a hit horror film, you should remember that no matter how full of action or danger the situations are that you put your characters into, people won't care very much if they don't care a whole lot about the ideals and principles that the characters embody and the ideas they are going to explore.

The milieu in which those characters and ideas are going to operate, and all the nuances, innuendos, and ramifications of that milieu, comprise the story's concept. The dictionary definition of *concept* is a mental image; a generalized idea formed by combining the elements of a story into a unified whole.

When theme and concept come together, then we have a genuine *idea* for a story. And the idea crystallizes so that we can all see what the story is intended to be and can determine whether or not to become excited about its possibilities.

To illustrate this point, let's consider the following three movies:

The Bridge on the River Kwai
Alien
The African Queen

What in the world could *Alien* have in common with those other two pictures? After all, the other two are both commonly thought of as "grand old classics" and "high examples of motion picture art," occupying in most people's minds a pedestal to which a horror/science fiction film need not aspire. Well, the answer is that they have the same theme as *Alien* does: the indomitability of the human spirit, the triumph of courage and persistence in the face of seemingly impossible odds.

The indomitability of the human spirit is a theme that has been explored again and again and again. *Alien* chose to do it aboard a spaceship; *Bridge on the River Kwai* in a Japanese prison camp during World War II; *The African Queen* aboard a ramshackle riverboat at the outbreak of World War I. In 1990, *Alien* was given the highest award in its genre—it was inducted into the Horror

Hall of Fame along with *Psycho, The Exorcist,* and *Night of the Living Dead.*

Why was it so successful?

Theme and concept had a whole lot to do with it. *Alien* was basically an old-fashioned ghost story set in a brand-new milieu. The concept was to take an indomitable heroine and strand her in outer space, where she must pit all her physical, mental, and emotional resources against an extraterrestrial monster that just happened to be one of the most unique and terrifying monsters ever created.

Right away, it's a concept that we can get excited about. And the concept is wed to a universal theme. Time, place, and setting are extraordinary. The labyrinthine bowels of the spaceship are a deliciously spooky environment for nerve-racking suspense and shocking twists and turns of plot. The leading human character, Ripley (played by Sigourney Weaver), is a beautiful, dynamic "woman of the nineties," with great appeal for audiences at that time. And the leading nonhuman character, the alien, is fiendishly conceived—not only is it clever, intelligent, and bloodthirsty, but it keeps changing form, and each transmogrification is more terrifying than the last, so that we never know exactly what kind of creature we will be confronting next, and just when it seems we may have found something that works against it, the same thing may not work next time.

Alien is an excellent example of an artful combination of winning story elements. That's what all of us are striving for. So let's start digging in and learning the things that will give us a chance to achieve similar success.

2
Coming Up with Exciting, Hard-hitting Concepts

SO YOU LIKE to make movies. Fine. But what are you going to make them *about?* This is a soul-searching question for everybody in the business. And to be successful, to have an impact, everybody has to answer it in his or her own unique way. And the answer has to be *marketable.*

Stephen King said once that he was lucky because he happened to have a marketable obsession: an obsession with things suspenseful and scary. He puts his obsessions on paper, and they earn millions of dollars.

For most people it's not quite so easy. And of course it's not really as easy for Stephen King as the above paragraph makes it sound. It's one thing to have an obsession. It's another thing to do the hard, involving work that fleshes the obsession out and makes it leap off the page or the screen to scare millions of people the same way it scares *you.*

Most of us have to constantly rack our brains and be on the lookout for the rare burst of inspiration that will lead to a marketable idea. In this chapter, I'm going to tell you how to make those bursts less rare. I'm going to help you open up some resources for good ideas and for the development of those ideas into concepts that can be sold.

I'm assuming here that you're interested in coming up with your own ideas. But even if you're not—that is, if you plan on producing or directing other people's screenplays—you've still got to be able to recognize a marketable concept when you see one.

And you've got to be smart enough and shrewd enough to guide other people through the writing, rewriting, and general brainstorming and hassling that it takes to turn the concept into a finished script that a bank might finance and a distributor might buy.

Many chillers and thrillers have basically the same theme as *Alien* does. But that doesn't mean that any movie can be successful so long as it involves courageous characters battling tremendous odds. We've already seen that *Alien* had much more going for it. Its outstanding concept and the clever story elements married to that concept excited studio executives enough to pry loose a big budget and land a first-rate director, cast, and production staff with the ability to deliver a well-executed picture that got raves from critics and sold millions of tickets worldwide.

Being able to come up with concepts like that is what separates the highly successful professional from the also-rans in the entertainment business. The successful professional has an instinct for what will capture the popular imagination and can perceive when the time might be ripe for exploitation of a particular theme, slant, or trend.

In order to fully develop these kinds of instincts and perceptions, you've got to:

1. Know and understand the kinds of ideas that have succeeded and failed in the past.

2. Have a deep curiosity and keen insight into current events and trends of thought.

3. Be able to wisely project your efforts into the future.

Rest assured that you don't need a crystal ball to do any of the above. All you need *is* the willingness to learn about the world you live in—the day-to-day world and the world of entertainment, which explains, enlightens, and elucidates the so-called "real" world.

UNDERSTANDING THE PAST

The oldest and best advice that is given to would-be writers is, "Read, read, read. Read the best that has been written. Read everything you can get your hands on." Would-be filmmakers have a similar task. We must see movies. Lots and lots of movies. Particularly, but not exclusively, we must see movies in the genre that we wish to work in. By knowing what has been successful in the past, and by understanding why, we gain insights into what might succeed now.

We have seen that *Alien* was a futuristic haunted house story. Well, *Rooster Cogburn* was a Western *African Queen*. In both cases, somebody saw that a formula that had worked well in the past could be transposed into a different time and setting, and would work well once again. There is nothing wrong with taking an old concept and giving it a new twist, a fresh slant. In fact, some filmmakers make a living from redoing the hits of the past in a modern way. Peter Bogdanovich exhibited a real flair for capturing the essence of the quirky travelogues and comedies of the thirties with his hit movies *What's Up, Doc?* and *Paper Moon*. And Brian De Palma, with a script by Oliver Stone, remade the classic *Scarface,* by using a modern-day drug dealer as the central character, rather than the original lead character based on prohibition-era villain Al Capone.

But De Palma didn't have a simple rip-off in mind. He wanted to offer up a comparison between crime lords of the past and crime lords of the present, not only as they exist in real life but as they have been portrayed on screen. He wanted people to ask themselves some hard questions, such as: Have we glamorized these arch criminals too much? Were the gangsters of the twenties and thirties somehow "cleaner" and more honorable than the ones we have now? Are even the criminals getting worse, as our society decays around us? Or were they always much more reprehensible

17

than the romanticized, media-purveyed image of them that we have allowed ourselves in large measure to accept as fact?

In perceiving these kinds of issues, we can see that there was a concept behind the remaking of *Scatface* that imbued the project with a sense of purpose, a sense that the remake could be worthwhile. The new film and the old film were like mirrors, bouncing images back and forth at each other, and illuminating both the past and the present.

The point is that the past is there, and all of us can learn from it and build on it, not just slavishly copy what has been done before. All of the great storytellers, the great directors, have a lot to teach us. We can learn from their work what clicks and what doesn't click, and by knowing what has already been done, we have a better chance of recognizing a wonderfully original idea when one comes along.

Even the not-so-great writers and directors can teach us something. Ernest Hemingway once said that bad writers exist to give good writers ideas. He wasn't trying to encourage plagiarism; what he meant was that a bad writer might have an idea that doesn't work, either because it's a bad idea or because it wasn't executed properly, but it might inspire a good writer to think of a better idea or a better style of execution.

After all, wire was just wire till somebody cut off a short piece and bent it into a paper clip.

Happy accidents might occur if you're willing to let the whole wide world of ideas be your playground.

Night of the Living Dead was a movie concept that took some old themes and old concepts and bent them into a brand-new shape. When we made that picture, zombie movies had been made before, but none of them had been smash hits. Zombies weren't considered heavyweight fright material like Frankenstein, Dracula, and the Wolfman. The zombies in the old horror movies didn't really do much other than walk as if they were in a trance and

18

occasionally strangle somebody or heave somebody against a wall. They moved so slowly you could easily get away from one of them if you were out in the open instead of trapped in a locked room.

What we did was give the old zombie legend a new twist. We made our zombies into cannibals—eaters of human flesh. Suddenly they were way more dangerous, way more terrifying. If a zombie bit you and your brain wasn't destroyed, you *became* one of them. And in our movie there were *lots* of them. They were weak and slow-moving as individuals, but they had strength of numbers on their side.

These new slants struck at some primal fears that exist in people the world over. One of the strongest fears that people have is the fear of death—and the living dead, the zombies, are the fear of death magnified, because they represent death that never ends, and a "life after death" that nobody really wishes to have.

Conceptually, what we had done was cross the zombie myth with aspects of the vampire and werewolf myths to come up with something new.

And zombies are dangerous even when the sun shines.

A nice shot of the cast from the original 1968 version of
Night of the Living Dead. Photo courtesy of Image Ten, Inc.

KEEPING CURRENT

Good story ideas can be found anywhere and everywhere. But you have to be consciously looking for them, and you have to be dogged and relentless about it. In many ways, it's not even hard work. It's part of the fun and excitement of being deeply interested in life and having the drive and zest to understand it and experience it fully.

Somebody said once that the unexamined life really isn't worth living. So, take a keen interest in everything around you. Both your lifestyle and your artistic potential will benefit.

What does this mean in practical terms?

Well, in my own case, I spend about $700 a year on publications. I read motion picture trade magazines, so I can stay up-to-date on what's happening in the industry, both in a creative and in a business sense. And I subscribe to a dozen popular magazines, so I can keep myself aware of newsworthy developments in art, science, literature, politics, etc.

I don't read all this material from cover to cover; I'd never have the time.

I scan it, and read in detail the stuff that strikes me the hardest. I take special note of vibrant or charismatic people, new scientific discoveries or cultural trends, and current fads or fancies that I might find interesting or amusing or even scary and dangerous. Since I work in the realm of horror, some of these "scary and dangerous" developments in the real world might inspire a story idea.

For instance, one day a few years ago I read an article about brain implants. I learned that a doctor at Yale was implanting platinum electrodes in people's brains and connecting them to battery-powered remote-control devices that enabled him to elicit just about any physical or emotional response that he wished from them. He was advocating that all human beings should have these devices implanted at birth, so that we could engender a more

20

peaceful and productive society. I immediately filed this article and began to do more research. The file grew and grew. And eventually it led to my novel *The Academy*. Conceptually, I think of it as a *Rosemary's Baby* of technology. Technology gone awry is the evil in the book, to my mind a much more plausible evil than witchcraft. In my novel, some of the students in a school for gifted children in Manhattan have been given brain implants without their knowledge, and the experiment isn't working out so well.

In addition to doing a lot of reading, I also watch quite a bit of television and listen to the radio. I want to know what's going on as a concerned citizen of the world, and of course I'm also always primed for story ideas. I watch all of the TV news magazines like *60 Minutes* and *20/20*. And I also watch any specials that deal with paranormal experiences, bizarre occurrences, unexplained phenomena, etc., etc.—good fodder for the mind of a horror writer.

Although the supernatural is fun to tinker with and explore—and I've done it in quite a few of my books and movies—I don't really happen to believe in it very much. Somebody asked me once how I could write about it, then. Well, do you think Lewis Carroll really believed in Wonderland? Did James Barrie believe in Peter Pan? Did Jonathan Swift believe in Lilliput? Fantasy is a useful tool for exploring reality. I had a great deal of fun playing with the vampire myth—twisting and bending and contradicting it, and giving it some shocking and humorous new slants—in my novel *The Awakening* and the movie based on that novel, *Heartstopper*.

But what really scares me is the wrong or dangerous directions that our society goes in sometimes. The lawlessness, the lack of respect that people have for one another, people bashing each other's cars or shooting at each other on the freeway, serial killers, maniacs who gun down children in school yards. As I said before, technology gone awry. The possibility of misusing knowledge; misusing it grotesquely, even fatally. All the things that human beings do or may do that have the potential for terrible destruction.

21

These kinds of concerns will hopefully give a sharp perspective to my work. So, when I choose story material out of the huge volume of material that I digest, I'm out to elaborate upon this perspective—to point out some of the things that scare me or trouble me, and get people thinking about them—instead of just going along with a dangerous technology or an insidious trend, looking only at its benefits and failing to see its warning signs.

In January of 1991, Academy Entertainment released a movie based on an original screenplay and novel that I wrote, which was partially inspired by a TV news segment. The movie was *Voodoo Dawn,* about a serial killer who fancied himself to be a voodoo god.

This project got off and running one afternoon when Bill Links (producer of *Deadtime Stories* and *They Bite)* phoned me and said that he had seen a news segment on TV about a crazy man who had captured and murdered two children at a motel; the kids were unlucky enough to be staying in the room right next door to the killer, who was supposed to be a deranged Haitian, possibly a "boat person" irresponsibly released from a mental institution. Coincidentally, I had seen the same segment, and it had shocked and appalled me. Bill Links said that something like that could be turned into a low-budget movie, and he knew somebody who would probably finance it. While we talked, I slid open my file drawer, and told Links that I had been collecting articles about voodoo sorcerers and modern-day cannibalism, and that kind of background would apply perfectly to a serial killer from Haiti, where voodoo is *the* main religion, and all sorts of gruesomely primitive superstitions still abound.

Links and I quickly worked out a deal involving his company, Trio Films, and the eventual production company, Bedford Entertainment, and I wrote an original screenplay developed from the ideas that we talked about plus the ideas in my file and considerable additional research. (By the time the movie got made, two other writers had chipped in, and the finished result doesn't bear much resemblance to what I wrote originally, although the voodoo serial killer is still there. And I got paid pretty well for my efforts.) *Voodoo Dawn* has been distributed successfully overseas for the past few years and is also available in the United States.

By always being on the lookout for story material and by using the methods I've described, I always have ten or fifteen ideas in my file, in various stages of development. Sometimes a file is only a tentative title and a smattering of articles. Other times it may contain a preliminary treatment. As time goes on, I keep adding to the files till I have enough there to start outlining a story and developing characters.

That way, if a producer, distributor, or book editor calls with a certain story slant in mind—or if he's looking for something but doesn't know exactly what—I have plenty of ideas and many, many viable concepts that I can hit him with. A professional isn't a one-shot wonder. If you want to succeed in this business, you've got to be prolific, and you've got to be ready to deliver the goods at any given moment.

PROJECTING INTO THE FUTURE

Today's hot gimmick is tomorrow's old hat.

One of the reasons it's tough to impress anybody by copying what's already out there is that by the time you see a movie, the idea, the pitch, the concept that caused it to get made are already probably at least three years old. A lot of water has already gone under the bridge. It takes, usually, at least a year to make a movie, from preproduction to finished print. Then, it may take quite a few months, and sometimes years, to get it into distribution. And remember, before it even went into production, the script had to be written and rewritten and all the aspects of the project hashed and rehashed until some studio or other decided to give it a green light.

That's why it's often futile to try to imitate a current hit. You're going to be a dog chasing your tail if you keep trying to jump on other people's bandwagons.

It's best to be original—a leader instead of a follower. As I've pointed out, that doesn't mean you can't learn from what's already been done and build on it, to your advantage. But whatever you do, try to bring to it your own fresh perspective, your own unique slant. Try to turn your own ideas into the thing that's going to be hot *tomorrow*.

Sometimes two or three horror movies will come out and none of them will do any business, or a big-budget horror flick with high expectations will be a box-office bomb, and studio execs will be saying, "That's it, horror is dead, nobody wants to see horror anymore, the horror flick is as dead as the Western." Well, I say that's the best time to write a horror film. Or to start making one. Because by the time you get it onto the market, the cycle will have come full circle again, and people will be looking for horror movies. And if you happen to have one of the few that's available . . .

Of course you can't always count on everybody to be as perceptive as you are. Sometimes you can come up with a forward-looking concept, even a potentially seminal concept, that you just can't sell. What's really frustrating is when your own associates or agents are the obstacle, and you can't even get past *them,* let alone pitch the concept to a potential buyer. Or when you've written a script for an idea that you just *know* is hot, but nobody will give you the money to make it. I wrote a treatment for a movie about near death experiences five years before *Flatliners* came out, but my agent told me to forget it. My screenplay for *The Majorettes* was written before *Halloween* was made and could have been the first of the slasher movies, but an investor pulled out of the project after we already had it into preproduction, so we had to scrap it for several years, and when it finally got made it was accused of being an imitator.

What am I supposed to do about stuff like that? Cry? Become bitter? No, I'm afraid it's just the breaks of the game. Every professional working in the business has a dozen of those kinds of hard luck stories, and we don't even usually talk about them, let alone cry in our beer. The only reason I mention them here is to show you that if you let stuff like that get you down, you'll never succeed. You have to simply go on and hope for better luck next time. I know quite a few talented, creative people who were discouraged early in their careers by a few rejection slips or a couple of near grabs at the brass ring, and they're not writing books or making movies anymore. Instead they're unhappy and full of self-pity.

Several times when I've been writing a book or screenplay, I've found out that either somebody else is writing something in a similar vein, or else something similar is already out on the market. The reason this happens is that we all live in the same world, we're all plumbing that world for marketable ideas, and the same themes or concepts that excite me or you are quite likely to excite somebody else. Or lots of somebody elses. That's what we're hoping for, isn't it? Only we want to be first with the goods and first to collect the paycheck.

To give yourself the best chance at the prize, you must develop your own particular talents to their fullest, work from your own worldview, concentrate on what interests and excites you, and be true to your vision. Then, even though you will be using methods used by all professionals everywhere, your stories and movies will bear the unmistakable stamp of originality.

3

High Concept Versus Low Concept

WHEN WRITING A novel, your imagination is virtually unrestrained. For the cost of a ream of paper, you can take your readers on a trip to Mars—or to the local garbage dump. But that same difference in locale, in a screenplay, would mean the difference between a movie that could cost $30,000,000 versus one that could be shot for under $1,000,000.

Movies cost a fortune. According to the October 1990 issue of *Premiere* magazine, the average cost of a feature movie in 1989 was "a whopping 30 percent higher than in 1988 and an unthinkable 250 percent higher than in 1980. By comparison, grocery prices increased by about 40 percent over the same period."

The average cost of a studio feature is now $23,500,000. One of the major reasons for the spending spree is the studios' penchant for so-called "high-concept" movies. *Batman* with its $50,000,000 budget, was a high-concept movie; it returned $250,000,000 domestically, and another $150,000,000 overseas. *Sex, Lies, and Videotape* is a low-concept movie; it cost $1,100,000 and returned $30,000,000. Of the two pictures, the low-concept one was the most profitable if we look only at *percentage* of profit.

But in *profit dollar volume,* the high-concept movie dwarfed it. How much would you rather have in your bank account? The $29,000,000 in net profits earned by *Sex, Lies, and Videotape,* or the $350,000,000 in net profits earned by *Batman?*

Doesn't take a genius to figure that one out, does it?

26

The studios aren't going to flush the $29,000,000 down the toilet. But it's small change to them. They figure that people aren't going to come out of their houses in droves to see anything that's not high concept. The studios feel that they have to spend big to win big. And when a low-concept movie like *Driving Miss Daisy* tops $100,000,000 at the box office, they consider it a fluke. And they can't live off flukes. They need a more predictable formula. And they go on believing that one can be found. And right now the panacea is "high concept."

So, what are the differences between high concept and low concept?

High-concept movies cater to the notion people have that when they come out of their houses to spend seven dollars for a ticket and another two or three dollars for soda pop and popcorn, they had better be buying something *big*. Bigtime spectacle, bigtime action, and bigtime stars. Bigtime directors, too. Bigtime fad, bigtime craze. The kind of thing everybody is talking and reading about and dying to see.

Low-concept movies are generally low budget, although nowadays the studios tend to consider anything under $10,000,000 *low* when just ten years ago that kind of layout was merely average. The reason low-concept movies are so "cheap" is because they don't involve spectacular settings, costumes, props, or special effects. No bigtime stars, either; or at least no big-money stars. Sometimes a bigtime star will make it possible for a low-concept movie to get made by taking a cut in salary, from his usual $10,000,000 a picture back to a measly $3,000,000. The best low-concept movies are usually pushing ideas rather than pizzazz. They deal in intimate relationships between engrossing characters, rather than in flamboyant displays of charisma and gloss.

I don't mean to sound sarcastic, merely flippant. I appreciate both high-concept and low-concept movies, I really do. High-concept movies need not be shallow. *The Godfather* (Parts I, II and III) were high-concept movies that had plenty to offer on every level. While the worst low-concept movies succeed in achieving shallowness along with all their other liabilities; and sometimes they actually *aim* for shallowness—the many teenage sex comedies, some of them quite successful at the box office, are good examples.

In the "chiller and thriller" category, two examples of successful low-concept movies are *Child's Play* and *Night of the Living Dead.*

To facilitate discussion, let's list the high-concept ones for comparison:

Poltergeist
Die Hard
RoboCop
Star Wars
E.T.
Raiders of the Lost Ark
Alien
Ghost

Raiders of the Lost Ark was high concept all the way; George Lucas and Steven Spielberg made one of the most entertaining spectacles of all time by taking all the most exciting themes and concepts from the Saturday serials that had thrilled millions of people in their heyday, elaborating upon them, and rolling the whole ball of wax into one bang-up big-budget movie. Some of the other movies on the list—like *Poltergeist, Die Hard,* and *Ghost*—probably wouldn't be considered high concept if they weren't loaded with spectacular stunts, awesome pyrotechnics, and fabulous special effects.

With the studios in this big-spending mode, you can see that if you succeeded in selling a high-concept project, you'd certainly make a lot of money. But your chances of having anything to do with a project, beyond selling a treatment or script, would be almost nil—if you didn't already have a big name. You wouldn't get to be the director or producer. You wouldn't get to be a technical adviser. You probably wouldn't even get to be a gaffer or a grip, even if you wanted to. But if the movie became a megahit, you'd become a hot screenwriter, and you could probably sell another script for big bucks.

Fine, you say. You can live with that.

But the problem is how to make that first score.

Well, let's not lose sight of the fact that quite a few low-concept films in the chiller/thriller category have made a big splash and have helped launch bigtime careers. Some excellent examples are Wes Craven's *Nightmare on Elm Street,* John Carpenter's *Halloween,* and Joel and Ethan Coen's *Blood Simple.* In order to crack into the business, you might do well to aim for that level of production. Especially if you have visions of producing or directing your own movie.

The way I handle the problem is that I try to develop some properties in the high-concept mode and others in the low-concept mode. I even write some screenplays that would be given a high-concept treatment if made through a major studio, and yet I could do a good job of producing and directing those same projects if I had to scale back and do them on a low budget with independent financing or through a smaller independent distributor.

After all, making a low-budget movie doesn't mean that the movie has to be paltry or flat, devoid of thrills or impressive effects. In lieu of hard currency, ingenuity and hard work can accomplish a great deal. In my book *Making Movies,* I illustrated in detail how to make a successful movie on $200,000, using *The Majorettes* as a case history. In that film we managed to have some impressive pyrotechnics at an unbelievably low cost just by finding the right people to do the job. We blew up a car, a van, a house trailer, and two motorcycles—for a total cost of $4,000. When you are making a low-budget movie, you have to do everything possible to pull it up by its bootstraps and make it look like it cost more.

The trailer, car, and motorcycle we blew up in my movie, *The Majorettes.*
Photo by John Russo.

Sometimes it is even possible to transform a high-concept movie into a lower-concept movie without losing all the pizzazz. Just for fun, let's consider how this might have been done with *Alien.* Well, what were the biggest cost factors in this movie? The setting and the special effects. What if we decide to give up one of these high-concept aspects, and hang on to the other? For instance, we could decide not to have the movie take place in outer space. We could bring the alien creature to earth, and devise some inexpensive way of getting it here. We could even maybe do some shooting at the Kennedy Space Center, implying that the creature was brought back as a stowaway on a space shuttle. Now, where does the creature end up? We need a place that might come close to matching the spookiness of a spaceship. How about some kind of underground mine? Maybe even one that could be made to look like a laboratory of some sort? I don't know for sure if that would work. Suppose it doesn't? Maybe we should just have the space creature stow away again in a space scientist's car, and he brings it home to his apartment complex. Now everybody who lives there is in mortal danger.

You get my point? The lower-concept variation is already starting to sound pretty exciting. And it would cost a lot less to pull off than the original idea did. It would probably even make money. But not as much money as the original. Not nearly as much. Because the idea of putting that incredible mutating creature on a spaceship was just *perfect,* and I'm glad nobody tinkered with it and sold it short.

HIGH-BUDGET THRILLS

If you are going to work in the chiller/thriller genre, then you must strive to chill and thrill audiences to the max, no matter how much money you have in your budget.

The nice thing about writing a high-concept screenplay is that the sky is almost the limit as far as what you can write into it. You can almost have the same unlimited freedom as you would have if you were writing a novel. I say "almost" because I don't think you would want to write a movie script that would cost $300,000,000 to make.

In any event, you don't need to hold back very much on wild, nutty, expensive incidents if you are thinking high concept from the jump. But remember, even if you somehow get $40,000,000 to spend on your extravaganza, it doesn't mean that success is guaranteed. Mega-budget flops like *Ishtar* and *Heaven's Gate* amply demonstrate that point. Top talents like Dustin Hoffman, Warren Beatty, and Michael Cimino weren't immune to failure.

Neither was George Lucas: consider the crash landing of *Howard the Duck.*

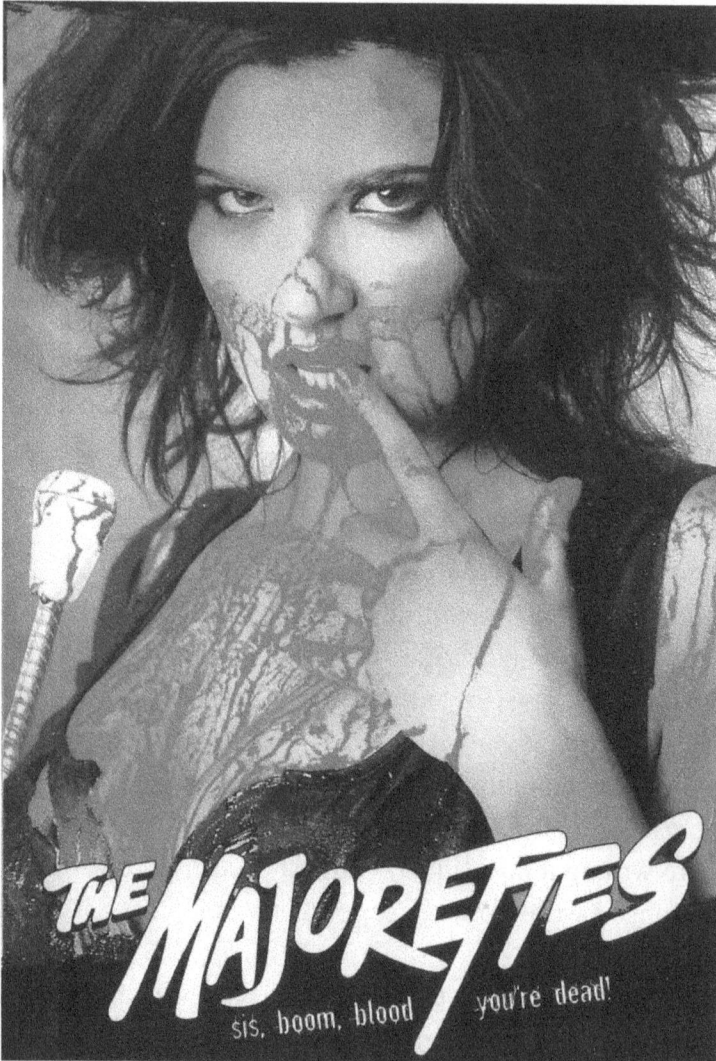

*The Majorettes **DVD Cover (primary version). Cover designed by Shriek Show 2003. Photo by Ward Boult.***

Success isn't measured by how many dollars you have to work with, but by how well you make the dollars work. You not only have to have a great concept, but it has to be well tailored to your particular budget, and it has to be shrewdly and skillfully pulled off. That means all the elements have to click—the director, the cast, the camera and lighting crew, and all the support people, especially those responsible for production design, costuming, locations and sets, stunts, animation, makeup, and special effects.

In other words, everything that contributes to the ultimate look, feel, and *style* of your picture has to be carefully considered and well integrated within the overall concept. If you can achieve this, then if the concept was right to begin with, and if it's executed without serious flaw, the finished product ought to make people stand in line to buy tickets.

Die Hard is an example of a high-concept thriller packing a hard wallop in every department. The plot is simple: one man going up against a gang of terrorists and defeating them despite enormous odds. It could have been a low-concept movie if the logistics—the cast, location, and special effects—were kept as simple as the plot. But Bruce Willis, one of the world's top box-office draws, was brought in as the star. The picture was set in a metropolitan skyscraper instead of a modest building in a small town. And the skyscraper was destroyed (at least on film)—smashed up, blown up, and set on fire. In a low-concept movie, only the people would have been destroyed, with the use of fake blood, bullet squibs, etc.—all dirt-cheap special effects compared with the cost of seeming to destroy a skyscraper.

The presence of Bruce Willis not only took the budget up (he gets at least $7,500,000 a picture) in the casting category, but made it possible, and necessary, for all the other budget categories to rise. Now everything had to be first class. The picture was now marketable in a big way. So it had to promise and deliver a big payoff to distributors, theater owners, and customers domestically and abroad.

Whether you are thinking high concept or low concept, you have got to bear in mind that you will hardly ever land a major star for a low-concept film. In fact, it is very tough to land even a minor star for a low-concept film. Minor stars don't like to think of themselves as minor, and even if they are, they have no intentions of staying that way. So they're always looking for first-rate properties that can build their careers, and they hate to waste their time with anything less.

Now, there are certain big-name directors and big-name actors who like to do projects of strong social importance, even if they have to battle for the chance. For example, Oliver Stone and Tom Cruise teamed up to do *Born on the Fourth of July,* based on the true story of Ron Kovic, a soldier who became a quadriplegic due to wounds suffered in Vietnam. But Stone and Cruise had to fight long and hard to get financial backing for this picture; it took them ten years to finally get it made. What chance would it have had without their support?

Bearing in mind that you will eventually have to land a strong, capable cast, and maybe even a major star, for whatever movie you desire to make, then it behooves you to come up with a concept and write a script that contains one or more powerful, interesting, meaty roles that a worthy actor would want to sink his teeth into. Otherwise, the concept might not be packageable and might be doomed before it even gets off the ground.

LOW-BUDGET THRILLS

Welcome to the land of ingenuity.

If you are planning on making a low-concept, low-budget movie, you are facing a wonderful challenge. I don't say "terrible," I say "wonderful"—because the process is not only tough but exhilarating and potentially tremendously rewarding. You're in good company, too. People like George Romero, Brian De Palma, Francis Ford Coppola, John Carpenter, Sam Raimi, and Wes

Craven all went down the road before you. And look where they are now.

Low-budget thrillers generally exploit two primary ingredients: sex and violence, while big-budget thrillers usually exploit two primary ingredients: sex and violence. Surprised you, didn't I? You thought I was doing to say something different. But think about it. There's as much sex and violence in the high-concept James Bond films as there is in *Psycho, Halloween,* or *The Texas Chainsaw Massacre.* But the sex and violence in low-budget films probably stands out more in the minds of highbrow critics and blue-nosed would-be censors because it isn't surrounded by the gloss and *savoir faire* of a 007 epic.

Does that mean that sex and violence are what made the low-budget hits successful? Not necessarily. They were just two of the major ingredients in the recipe. Sex and violence were also two of the major ingredients in *Hamlet,* by the way. These things just seem to excite a great many people. Sometimes they're used simply to titillate, and sometimes they're part of a serious attempt on the part of a playwright or filmmaker to try to understand or illuminate the erotic and aggressive aspects of human nature.

Just because you're making a violent, sexy low-budget movie doesn't mean it has to be a piece of worthless trash. *Blood Simple* was a sophisticated, intriguingly complex murder story, and it was pulled off with unique flair and cinematic style. The movie had people hanging on the edge of their seats to find out what was going to happen next. According to *Newsweek,* the Coen brothers made the plot up as they went along. "You paint yourself into a corner and then have to get out of it," said Joel Coen. "We figure if the authors don't know what's going to happen next, the audience couldn't possibly know."

The thing that most successful films have in common, whether high concept or low concept, is a good *story.* And that's the one thing that needn't cost you anything but ink and paper. If you're going to make a low-budget thriller, make sure you start out with the best story you can develop. One that makes people want to keep turning the pages. In chillers and thrillers, people confront sex, violence, and death—vicariously. And it's fun being scared. It's fun getting that charge of emotion and adrenaline in a relatively safe way.

So make sure that the people who see your movie are going to have fun.

Give them the excitement and twists and turns that they crave.

Films like *Night of the Living Dead, Halloween,* and *The Texas Chainsaw Massacre* prove that you can structure a concept with low-cost elements—small cast, inexpensive logistics, etc.—dealing with just a few characters in a terrifying situation, and if it's skillfully written and executed, it will appeal to audiences in a big way. One thing those three films have in common is that the monsters were *people.* In other words, no attempt was made to come up with any sort of weird, expensive creature, let alone one with the complexity and sophistication of the creatures in high-concept films like *Alien, Predator,* or *The Abyss.* This eliminated the need for expensive makeup, sculpturing, animation, or special effects. And that's why there are so many low-budget movies dealing with psychopathic killers—the filmmakers simply can't afford to portray a menace that would be more costly.

However, I know a filmmaker from New Jersey, Warren Disbrow, who wrote a script involving a fantastic monster, and he shot, directed, and edited the movie himself on a budget of less than $50,000. He succeeded in selling the movie, called *A Taste for Flesh and Blood,* for home video distribution. Warren and some of his friends and associates happen to have learned the sculpting, casting, and special makeup skills necessary to build a pretty awesome-looking monster. So they didn't have to make just another slasher film.

Therefore, even if you don't have much money, it doesn't mean that you must do some trite imitation of somebody else's work. Try to come up with a fresh perspective. A new slant. Then your movie will have a shot at decent distribution. People might pay to see it. It might even get good reviews. But if you try to just rip off what has been done before, filling your story with uninteresting or unappetizing characters getting gruesomely murdered one right after another, nobody will take it very seriously and it won't boost your career.

TELEVISION THRILLS

Some kinds of thrills are prohibited or constrained not by lack of money, but by the exigencies of the medium in which they will be viewed. I'm talking not only about television, but about the different kinds of television: network, cable, home video, and pay-per-view.

Despite the outcry against gore and violence in movies (promulgated by groups such as the National Coalition Against Violence in Television), according to an article in *TV Guide,* "TV is crawling with ghouls, vampires, psychos and things that go bump in the night." The article goes on to point out that shows dealing with sci-fi, fantasy, and the supernatural are now drawing bigger audiences than other kinds of syndicated programs.

Then it lists and describes then-current thriller/chiller series, among which were:

Dracula: The Series
Swamp Thing
Monsters
Tales from the Darkside
Saturday Nightmares
The Hitchhiker

37

Tales from the Crypt
Alfred Hitchcock Presents
Ray Bradbury Theater
Dark Shadows

An impressive list. And these are only the series. The article goes on to describe genre TV movies like *Stephen King's It, Psycho IV: The Beginning;* and *Not of this World.* Plus the many, many films that started out as theatrical releases and eventually went into successful TV syndication, like *Carrie, The Island of Dr. Moreau, Village of the Damned, The Birds,* etc., etc.

Television in all its formats has become an outstanding marketplace for movies. Just a few years ago, the average budget for a TV movie was only about $800,000, but nowadays lots of features are being made by HBO, Cinemax, and USA on budgets of $4,000,000 to $8,000,000. This is happening because the cable networks have to keep their subscribers happy, and they can't do it anymore by simply buying up theatrical releases. Also, by the time the cable outlets can get their hands on a theatrical release, many people have already seen it, not only in the theaters but on home video and on free television. Original presentations by HBO, Cinemax, USA, and others represent a determined effort to keep subscribers tuning in and paying their monthly subscription fees.

Now, obviously, if you want to penetrate this market, you have to come up with the kinds of concepts that can play on television. You have to furnish the chills and thrills without swamping people in blood and violence.

Although you can get away with "stronger stuff" on cable than on network TV, I wouldn't rely on this to continue to be the case. Censorship groups and concerned viewers are stepping up the pressure on producers and sponsors to keep toning down the mayhem.

The result, according to the aforementioned *TV Guide* article (by David Lieberman), is that "TV horror may be returning to its roots—when psychological terror and subtlety had more impact than an ax to the head. At the same time, today's practitioners of the genre have added a new element—humor—that humanizes and allows us to empathize with the creatures they've conceived."

If you intend to sell to television, you have to come up with concepts and plot elements that rely on cleverness and restraint, not just slam-bang action and blatant violence. For that matter, even when creating a concept for a theatrical release, you must bear in mind that the movie will eventually have to be reedited for television. If you have twenty minutes of gore, mayhem, and foul language that must be taken out of a ninety-minute feature, you're going to end up with seventy minutes of TV movie—and nobody will buy it. It might not even get distributed theatrically, because distributors have to rely on eventual television sales to amortize their investment.

And if there aren't going to *be* any television sales . . .

You get the picture. But I hope you don't get to keep it—on the shelf—in your own home.

Part II
WRITING

"The number of readers required to turn a book into a bestseller is far less than required to turn a movie into a blockbuster. In the publishing world sales of 500,000 hard-covers would make a superstar, but 500,000 admissions to a mainstream film is a drop in the bucket."

– RICHARD KOBRITZ, producer

"It's only the writer who gets gang-banged in this business. You never see two directors or two cameramen on the screen. The writer puts everybody to work, but he's the disposable commodity."

– STEVE SHAGAN, screenwriter

4

How to Come Up
with a Strong Plot

I'M GOING TO teach you the easiest way I know of to come up
with a tight, exciting, well-constructed plot and mold it into a hard-
hitting screenplay for a chiller or thriller. It's the method I always
use in my own writing, whether I'm working on a book or a
screenplay.

So that you can learn by example, in this and succeeding
chapters I'm going to take you step by step through the writing of
my screenplay *Voodoo Dawn*. In Chapter 2, I told you how the
project got a push as the result of a conversation between me and
Bill Links, after we both had seen a news story on television. After
Bill and I beat some ideas around over the phone, I was left with
the lonely task of coming up with a concept, developing a plot, and
writing a screenplay.

So I immediately turned on my word processor, right?

Wrong. First I had to gather a lot of background material and
do a lot of hard, careful thinking, all geared toward shaping my
initial thoughts, my rough ideas, into something that could become
marketable.

DOING MY HOMEWORK

As I mentioned, I already had some articles on voodoo and
cannibalism in my file, so I reread them and started taking notes,
and continued to gather and read research material. I already had
decided that the killer in my story would be a Haitian, probably an

illegal alien, and so I read articles about the "boat people" who were arriving illegally in Florida at that time, and I also read up on Florida in general, since that state was the logical setting for the story. In fact, it was a pretty spooky, exciting setting because Florida was in the throes of a tremendous crime wave, due not only to the drug trade but more especially to a crazy deal made between Cuba and the United States that allowed Castro to empty his prisons and insane asylums and send us all his loonies and cutthroats.

I knew that voodooism and Haiti were of course strongly connected with the zombie myths, but I didn't really want this new script to be a zombie story—in other words I didn't want to keep playing directly off the success of *Night of the Living Dead.* I wanted to break new ground. Therefore, in doing my research, I was on the lookout for a germ of an idea—a nugget—that would give a fresh slant to whatever I would write.

Finally, in a book called *Mysterious Monsters* by Daniel Farson and Angus Hall, I came across what I noted as an excellent description of a man buried alive. This article and others that I found later showed me that it was possible for bodily processes to slow down, resembling death, so that a man could be buried and then supposedly "brought back from the dead" sometime later. In other words, there could be a real basis to the belief in zombies.

So, perhaps I could have the killer in my story be found drowned on the beach (as happened to many of the boat people), and he could come out of his grave later in a particularly scary sequence. This would have the power of a supernatural occurrence without actually *being* supernatural—because if the killer was a so-called voodoo sorcerer, familiar with the trance-producing drugs that the sorcerers use, he could have drugged himself before his boat went down. His "magic powers" could all have perfectly mundane explanations—but, being insanely warped by his superstitions, he could believe he was "chosen" anyway. He could be convinced that he was a *loa*—a voodoo god.

I found in my research that the most feared of the voodoo gods is Chango, the god of fire, lightning, destruction, and death. So I chose this name for my sorcerer. He calls himself Chango, though his real name is Hector Chanfray, and he is the descendant of the Hector Chanfray who in real life was a hero in the fight for Haitian independence from France.

So far, what was shaping up pretty well for me was my basic theme: the conflict between reality and superstition, the warping of a human being by a destructive system of supernatural beliefs. This particular theme is a favorite of mine. I like to keep reminding people that many of the worst evils in society, from the pathological behavior of certain individuals to the mass hysteria of the Inquisition and the Holocaust, stem from ignorance, superstition, and the controlling of men's minds by charlatans and demagogues.

Links and I had discussed that this would be a script for a low-budget movie, an attempt to come up with a villain perhaps as striking as *Friday the 13th's* Jason or *Halloween's* Michael. So far I kind of liked the Chango character and I was pretty sure I could develop him in a wild, frightening way.

However, at this stage, even though I had some interesting ideas taking hold, I still didn't have a firm concept. I still needed to answer some hard questions: What does Chango *do* once he comes back from the dead? If he kills people, *why* does he do it? What makes him any different from all the other killers in a dozen other slasher films?

REFINING MY CONCEPT

I started toying with the fact that voodoo dolls play such a strong role in the popular conception of voodoo. But I wanted to stay away from the trite, hackneyed thing—pins stuck in a doll causing pain, disease, death. I didn't want my premise to depend on magic. I wanted something legitimately scary but not hokey.

What if Chango wasn't the only one washed up on the beach? Suppose six of his followers drowned with him, and they're all buried in a paupers grave, and Chango comes out of the grave first? Then what would he do? He'd try to bring his henchmen "back to life."

How would he do this?

It dawned on me that he could set about constructing a life-size voodoo doll. How? By murdering six people and taking a body part from each one: two arms, two legs, a torso, and a head. When he buries the "doll" and then resurrects it, his followers will come alive. Not really. But Chango *believes* that this is so. And so, as the audience begins to see him stitching the first body parts together, an aura of grisly suspense takes hold.

Now I was happy with my theme and concept. The conflict between reality and superstition would be played out against a landscape of modern-day horror, as scary as today's news headlines.

THE PLOT THICKENS

By working things through to this stage, certain plot elements already were apparent. What I had so far could be summarized as follows:

Voodoo Dawn is the story of Chango, a voodoo sorcerer fleeing prosecution for cannibalism in Haiti, who is washed up on a Florida beach with six of his followers, all of them apparently dead from drowning. But Chango doesn't stay dead. He comes back to life, by trickery that seems like actual magic, and sets about killing innocent people in the vain hope that he can cause his followers to arise and . . .

And what? Who exactly does he kill? Who discovers it? Where exactly do the killings happen? Does Chango get away with them? Or does somebody figure out what he is doing and why? Not only that, but does somebody figure out that these killings are being committed by someone who's supposed to be dead?

The poster for foreign distribution of *Voodoo Dawn* portrayed Chango wielding his whip and machete, a severed head at his feet.
Courtesy of ADN Associates, Ltd.

To deal with all of the above, I needed to invent more characters, major and minor ones, and more twists and turns of plot. I had to make everything build to a climax and a suitable denouement.

It seemed obvious that if seven dead bodies were going to be found on a beach, the cops would come into the story right away. Okay. How about a couple of detectives? I came up with the names of Vince Dawson and Clint Jones, two detectives, one white and one black. I figured that since Chango was the bad guy and had to be black if he was a Haitian voodoo priest, I ought to balance things by having at least one good guy who was black.

Through the eyes of Dawson and Jones, the details of Chango's horrible crimes would be revealed, and much of the plot would unfold.

I needed somebody to discover the seven drowned bodies, and I wanted this episode to start the script off with a bang. Somewhere along the line, I had read an article about children being kidnapped and cannibalized in Haiti—and I figured it would be ironic if the dead *bokor* (sorcerer) were to be found by an old man and his grandson, both Haitians, but in this country legally—but familiar with rumors of Chango's deeds in their native land, and scared to death of him. I decided that the boy, Jean, would find the bodies, and the old man, Silvio, would recognize Chango and try to behead the corpse to prevent the *bokor* from coming back to life. But a policeman stops him from doing this. And Dawson and Jones are called upon the scene.

I further decided that Silvio and Jean would go to the cemetery that night to perform a ritual to try to keep Chango from arising. But Chango would arise and kill them both, cutting off the old man's arm and cannibalizing the boy.

Now the serial killings are set into motion, and Dawson and Jones have a powerful motivation to stop the killer.

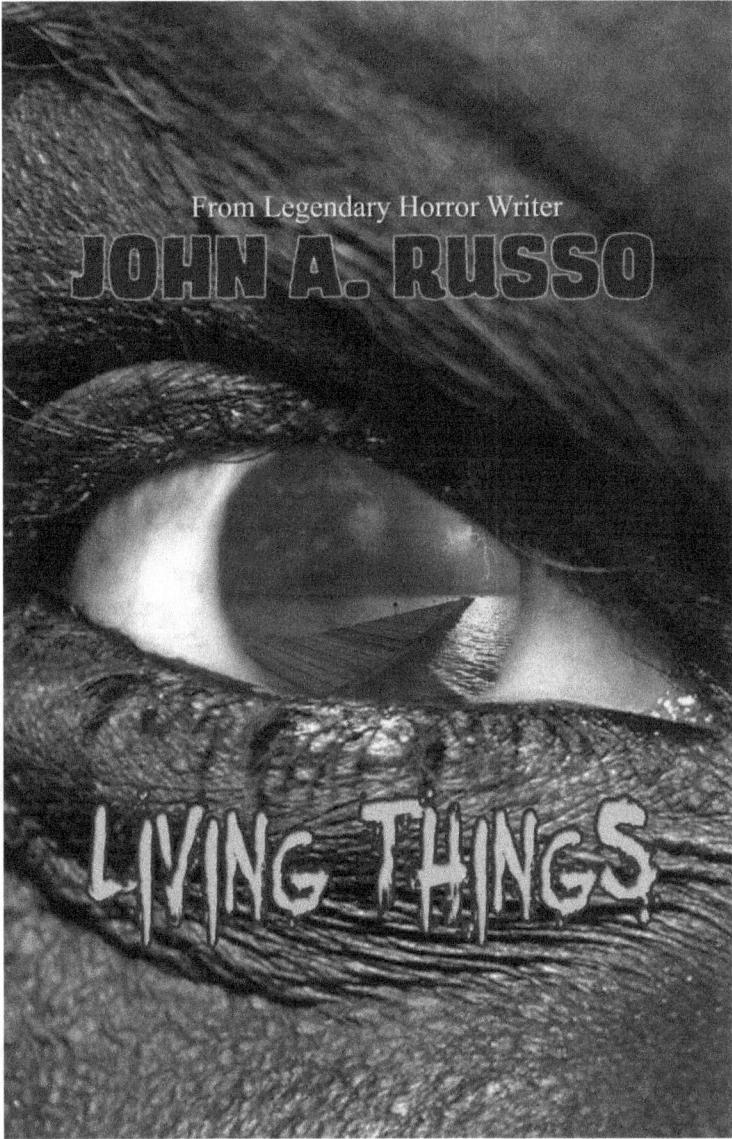

Voodoo Dawn **was eventually adapted into a full length novel called** *Living Things. Cover courtesy of Burning Bulb Publishing.*

But they don't know much about voodoo. So they don't know exactly what they're fighting. They need someone to teach them— and the audience—some of the "niceties" of sorcery and voodooism.

49

So, I invented Dr. Martha Lewis, an anthropologist specializing in Haitian culture , who sponsored Silvio and Jean when they came to this country. Naturally she would have to identify their bodies after Chango kills them. So naturally she would meet Dawson and Jones and be questioned by them. And she and Dawson could begin to fall in love.

To make the plot even tighter, I decided to establish that Silvio was the caretaker of some beach cottages owned by Martha Lewis. He had just finished cleaning and repairing one of the cottages because Martha's daughter and son-in-law were coming down from New York to vacation with two other couples, and they were going to stay at the cottage.

Now I had six more potential murder victims—all tied to one of my central characters, Dr. Martha Lewis.

Tony Todd (above) not only played Ben in the 1990 remake of *Night of the Living Dead,* but also played Chango in *Voodoo Dawn.* Note: Chango's name was changed to Makoute by the time the picture got made.

So the murders would go on, right at the beach. And in a boat shed Chango would be performing his rituals and stitching body parts together.

And Dawson would stay in touch with Martha because he's infatuated with her and because she's the "voodoo expert"—and eventually the two of them would figure out that Chango must have drugged himself with Zombie Cucumber (an actual substance that the *bokors* use) and he must be taking body parts to build a talisman.

Martha tells Dawson that the ritual for the Reclamation of the Dead must take place at the site where they're buried. So the two of them go to the cemetery at night to stake it out and stop Chango, and there, in a suitably spooky place, our action-packed wrap-up takes place.

Now we have a fairly strong *skeleton* of a plot. It still has to be developed further, though. Turn the page, and let's keep working.

5

Making Characters Live
and Breathe

ONCE YOU HAVE decided the general character types that you need in order to make a story line work, you've got to start thinking about those characters in depth and researching and perhaps interviewing people who fulfill similar roles in real life so that you can make your fictional characters seem just as alive and real. Just as hateful, lovable, despicable, or endearing, too. In other words, your characters have got to be capable of eliciting strong emotions from an audience—strong feelings of empathy or fear or whatever you happen to be after.

I not only collect articles that might give me thematic and conceptual ideas, I also collect articles about interesting people. Some of these people help me flesh out characters for my novels and screenplays. Generally, writers try to observe and understand on a deep level the people that they come into contact with in everyday life, and pattern their fictional characters after charismatic people they already know. But when you can't do the whole job that way, you must resort to the same tool we've already been using: research.

In the case of *Voodoo Dawn,* I gathered together articles about Haitian refugees, political figures, historical figures, etc. I was particularly interested in the *houngans* and *bokors*—*the* voodoo priests of white and black magic. But I also wanted to steep myself in the *feel* of Haiti—the cultural mix and political and economic climate that could engender and maintain the voodoo religion and produce a phenomenon like the boat people. I wanted to know what should be going on in the *minds* of the Haitian characters I had to develop, not only the empathetic characters but the evil ones.

It would have been helpful if I could have traveled to Haiti, but this low-budget project couldn't justify the time and expense. So I did the next best thing. I interviewed an attorney whose business took him and his wife to the Haitian capital, Port-au-Prince, fairly regularly. I found out about the lawyer by telling a few friends and associates about my project and asking if they knew anyone who could help out, and my insurance agent set up a meeting with the attorney. From him I gained many insights. I remember that he talked extensively about the Tonton Macoutes, the paramilitary gang of thugs used by "Papa Doc" Duvalier, President for Life of Haiti, to torture and terrorize the populace.

Once I completed my research, I was able to start making background notes on my key characters. Using the notes from my file, I'll show you how I proceeded. For the sake of simplicity, let's divide the characters into two groups: empathetic and non-empathetic.

EMPATHETIC CHARACTERS

These are the characters that we want the audience to care about and identify with, in a positive way. If the audience doesn't care about the people we are going to put into jeopardy, our story will fail miserably no matter how clever our plot happens to be or how much slam-bang action we fill it with.

If we are going to care deeply about people, they must exhibit appealing personality traits and they must have personal histories that interest us and make us sympathize with them. They must not be self-absorbed; they must care about others. They must be warm and loving. They need not be beautiful, clever, witty, or unusually charming—but this being the movie business, sometimes it helps to invent a few characters who *are* that way.

Bear in mind, though, that in real life none of us are perfect. Perfection would probably be boring. Our fictional characters, even (and perhaps especially) the empathetic ones, should have some of the flaws and foibles that make us human. And they're allowed to make mistakes. When they do the wrong thing in certain situations, or when they do nasty or careless things, as all of us do sometimes, we should be able to still care about them and hope for the best. After all, isn't this the way we treat our loved ones in real life?

Here are my preliminary sketches of the empathetic characters in *Voodoo Dawn:*

Silvio Narbonne. A withered old man, a Haitian immigrant, brought to this country on a visa gained for him by anthropologist Dr. Martha Lewis. Silvio's son and daughter-in-law were newspaper reporters imprisoned and killed by the Tonton Macoutes for "crimes against the regime." Prior to their imprisonment, they used to help Martha Lewis gain access to interview subjects and research material for her books. Silvio is very religious and superstitious; a living example of what someone once said about Haiti, that "it is 90% Catholic and 100% voodoo."

Jean Narbonne. Silvio's grandson, seven years old, a wiry, resourceful boy with a tinge of sadness always in his demeanor because of what was done to his parents by the Tonton Macoutes. Full of energy, he's almost too much for his aged grandfather to keep up with.

Dr. Martha Lewis. Professor of anthropology at Braxton State College in Braxton Beach, Florida. A bright, attractive, ash-blonde widow, age forty-four. She and her husband, also an anthropologist, used to travel and do research together, but he died a long, agonizing death from multiple sclerosis a few years ago. Now Martha travels and writes on her own, continuing to specialize in Haitian culture. She has a daughter whom she loves very much, but the daughter lives in New York and rarely visits. Martha would like to convince her to move to Florida, but restrains herself from meddling too much. She also secretly wishes that her daughter's marriage would produce a grandchild.

Lieutenant Vince Dawson. A police detective, about fifty years old. A tall, tough-looking man with a lined, cynical face and cold, steely eyes. Divorced after twenty-two years of marriage, he keeps paying the tab for his son and daughter to stay in college in South Carolina, even though they never write or phone unless they need something. Under his rough exterior, he's kind and considerate, and he has a wry, flippant sense of humor—which he needs to see him through the grisly aspects of his job as a homicide investigator.

Lieutenant Clint Jones. Dawson's partner on the police force. About fifteen years younger than Dawson, but just as tall and tough-looking. Also with a kind interior. Also flippant and witty. Also divorced—a common way for police officers' marriages to end, but made even more common nowadays because of the horrendous crime wave that started in the late seventies and is still going on—putting terrific pressure on wives and husbands because of the long, hard hours on duty and the constant fear of death and disaster.

One thing I was after in sketching the backgrounds of Dr. Martha Lewis and Lieutenant Vince Dawson was to make them *available* for each other, so that a romantic relationship could develop. He's divorced, and her husband has died. Vince and Martha are both lonely. He's a tough man doing a hard job, but he's not hard on the inside; and he's intelligent—so it's not totally out of the realm of possibility that a college professor like Martha might be attracted to him.

To illuminate Martha's personality and her needs still more, I invented another character for her to interact with:

Albert Scanlon. A mild-mannered, slightly effete English professor whose wife has left him. Martha has been dating him off and on, but their relationship is basically platonic. Martha's daughter and Albert's daughter have been trying to encourage Martha and Albert to marry—it would relieve the young people of responsibility for the "old folks." But Martha doesn't really want to marry Albert; she can't help comparing him with her deceased husband, who was a bold adventurous man—filling their anthropological field trips with zest and energy.

Notice that, through Albert, we can reveal that Martha is attracted to strong, capable men. This gives us even more reason why she might be attracted to Dawson, even though their occupations and educational backgrounds don't seem to match so perfectly.

Also , because of the presence of Albert Scanlon in the script, I was able to write in another important minor character: Albert's daughter, *Mary Ann.* She knows that Susan Crandall and her friends from New York are going to be at the beach cottage, and she goes out to pay a visit because she and Susan are friends and conspiratorial matchmakers.

And Mary Ann becomes one of Chango's early victims.

NON-EMPATHETIC CHARACTERS

Just because we might dislike or even hate them, it does not give us license to make our non-empathetic characters any less human than the others. They still have to be *real.* That is, they still have to seem as if they *could* exist, even if intellectually we know that they don't exist except in the realm of fantasy, like the creatures and villains in *Alien, Halloween,* or *Raiders of the Lost Ark.* It's not enough to make your key villain look ugly and make him do ugly, horrifying things. He ought to have whims, quirks, motives, and desires—in other words, a strong, believable *personality*—just like the other characters.

In *Voodoo Dawn* I had only one active villain—Chango. His followers were all dead, drowned on the beach, never to arise, despite all of his macabre, misguided efforts. Here are my preliminary notes on him:

Chango. A descendant of Hector Chanfray, a sorcerer and leader of the Haitian people in their struggles against French colonialists and slave traders. His real name *is* Hector Chanfray, but he has taken the name of the voodoo god of fire, lightning, thunder, and death. He's almost seven feet tall and built like Arnold Schwarzenegger. His hair is in dreadlocks, with little ceramic gargoyles hanging from the braids. Lightning bolts are branded into his pectorals. His cheeks are tattooed with small serpents. Tattoos and scars in the shape of skulls, claws, and daggers dot his massive thighs, forearms, and biceps. He is a former Tanton Macoute—one of Papa Doc Duvalier's brutal, terroristic bodyguards. He speaks only Creole, and wails his chants and rituals in an eerie, keening dialect that frightens the audience—not only because of the chilling sound but also because they don't understand any of the words—which is a mystique that many esoteric religions and superstitions rely on.

Now, because of the glut of slasher films already on the market, I wanted to do everything I could do to make Chango unique. Already he had an eerie motive for his killings and dismemberments that I felt was a stronger and clearer motive than what was usually found in these types of movies. But I also wanted to give him some unique weapons and accoutrements. I decided on a voodoo drum with a head of human skin, a bull whip with a spiked lash, and a machete with a handle of human bone.

Also, remembering that Chango was said to cannibalize children, I added one final grisly touch. Around his neck he wore a thong necklace with a pouch containing the severed finger of one of his young victims.

These details would enable me to create some suspense in the finding of the seven drowned bodies. We don't just stumble on them, flat out. First, little Jean Narbonne spots the drum bobbing in the ocean. He wades out to get it—and jumps back, mistaking the whip coiled inside for some kind of large snake. He runs back to his grandfather. And he and Silvio together discover the bodies. But Silvio doesn't know one of them is Chango till he opens the leather pouch—and the severed finger drops onto the sand.

Thus, you can see how character development contributes powerfully to development of plot. Every pertinent detail interacts with all the other details, helping to create desirable symmetry and substance within your overall design.

VICTIMS

Let's go on to a discussion of a character subcategory that particularly applies to chillers and thrillers. I'm talking about victims. The people who are going to "get it." Well, sometimes they don't end up getting it, but we think that they might, and so they help keep us in suspense while they're showing us, through the danger they're in or the horrible things they encounter, just why we should be scared and who or what we should be scared of.

Victims shouldn't just be cannon fodder. They have to live and breathe just like the other characters, so that we will give a hoot when they stop living and breathing.

In the worst of the slasher films, a group of teenagers, pretty much interchangeable one with the other, because they all have about the same personality or lack of it, gets bumped off one by one by somebody or something. The somebody or something might even be a unique and genuinely terrifying presence. But, unfortunately, we fail to care much about the kids because they're a bunch of vapid airheads whom we'd leave off our invitation list if we wanted to throw a nice banquet. They don't have deeply felt convictions or worthwhile goals. Usually all they want to do is party and have a good time—and these paltry intentions are interrupted by terror. But the impact of the terror is diluted by the triviality of the characters who are being terrorized.

In *Voodoo Dawn* I wanted to create some victims that the audience would care about. Silvio and Jean, the first two people that Chango would kill, had some strong motivations—first they tried to behead the *bokor,* and when the cops prevented them from doing this, they would go to the site of the mass grave to bury the *bokor's* voodoo implements—his whip, drum, and machete—and say prayers that might prevent him from arising.

Now, what about the other potential victims? They were going to a beach cottage, but that didn't mean that they had to have nothing but partying on their minds. Instead of the usual gang of teenagers, I decided to make them young business people working in ad agencies and art houses in New York. Susan and Barry Crandall would invite the two other couples to her mother's cottage to outline a serious proposal: that they should all quit their jobs and band together to form a new agency.

To give further dimension to the story, I made one of the couples black: Carl and Shelly Beck. Shelly used to live in Florida and still has scars on her arm from being bitten by a police dog during a civil rights demonstration in the sixties. She hates the idea of coming back here, even for a vacation, but the others have talked her into it. She thinks that race relations haven't really improved much, and the crime wave that's been taking place is in many ways worse than anything that was going on years ago, and she has a creepy-crawly feeling that something terrible is going to happen.

VOODOO DAWN

SYNOPSIS

Miles and Kevin, two street-wise young New Yorkers, are on their way to the deep South to spend a few fun days with their college friend, Tony. Lost in the middle of nowhere, they bump into Tina, an attractive but feisty migrant worker.

On their way to Tina's village, they encounter weird, hostile people. Things become even more "hairy" when they discover that the village is in the grip of a mysterious killer. Out of their depth with nowhere to hide, they join forces with Tina and the villagers. Using the black magic powers of a voodoo priestess, they succeed in destroying the killer only to be confronted by his even more sinister creation...

Some of the hapless victims in *Voodoo Dawn*. The synopsis here reflects changes made in my original script by three other writers before the movie finally got made. *Photo courtesy of ADN Associates, Ltd.*

The other couples also have their problems. Susan's husband, Barry, is greedy and callous, and he's secretly set on cajoling a loan of $25,000 from Martha Lewis to help launch the new business. And he intends ultimately to force the others out and take over everything, but for the moment of course he must mask his intentions.

Dan and Lisa Morelli have been trying to have a baby, but Lisa is having difficulty becoming pregnant. When the business proposal is revealed, she is afraid that she and Dan will have to drop the idea of ever having a child, because if they jump into a demanding new enterprise she'll have to keep working—and she'll soon be too old to become pregnant.

My hope was that since my potential victims had the same hopes, fears, and concerns that many young couples have today, I would have a good shot at eliciting empathy from the audience and keeping the audience interested in something besides who was going to be the next character bumped off. The characters would contribute texture and meaning to my subplot involving the decision to be made about Barry's business proposal.

With all my homework done, I now had a good grasp of the basic storyline and who the players were going to be. The next job was to develop a detailed outline of the story, letting the characters carry it along.

6
Outlining

ONCE YOU HAVE a theme, concept, basic story line, and general cast of characters for a screenplay, the next step is to make a scene by scene outline that you can work from in order to write a treatment or finished script.

A *treatment* is an essay-style description of the story and characters, done with a view toward making the concept "come alive" in the mind of the reader, thus whetting his appetite for the eventual finished product. Treatments are usually ten to thirty pages long. They are useful in getting distributors or investors interested in a project, because often they don't want to take the time to read anything longer prior to deciding to become more heavily involved.

I probably already had enough ideas under my belt to do a good treatment for *Voodoo Dawn* at this point. But Bill Links said that he would need a finished script to sell to his prospective partner, Steve Mackler of Bedford Entertainment. So I plunged into it as soon as I had done all the preliminary work I've described.

MY SPECIAL SYSTEM FOR EASY OUTLINING

Now that I've got your attention, let's qualify the word "easy." Nothing in this business is really easy. But my system of outlining makes the process about as easy as it can get. It reduces the task to a formula that works well enough and fast enough that I no longer approach outlining with any great trepidation or fear; in fact I'm always kind of anxious to get into it, once all my homework is done, because here is where I get to experience the fun of being the first person to feel the story truly coming together and looking and sounding (in my imagination) like a viable movie.

I take a three by five-inch notepad, and start writing down every incident I can think of that could happen in my story. Each incident gets its own slip of paper. In the upper left-hand corner of each slip, I draw a little circle. Later I'm going to play with the scenes, moving them around and arranging them into sequences that seem to make sense, and inside the circles I'll start penciling in scene numbers—which may change later as I think of connecting scenes and character involvements and change the order accordingly.

At first each slip of paper may have only a sentence or two on it. But as I think of additional details for the "business" in that scene, I jot down additional notes and the slips fill up with my chicken-scratch writing.

Below, randomly selected for your edification, are transcriptions from five of the scene slips from my *Voodoo Dawn* file:

- Silvio Narbonne and his grandson Jean on the beach with their metal detector. Jean finds a voodoo drum and whip bobbing on the water. Then he and Silvio find seven bodies washed ashore. Picking the dead boat people's pockets, Silvio sees a leather pouch around one's neck. The severed finger drops out. Silvio knows it is Chango. He takes Chango's machete and is about to behead the *bokor* when Patrolman Rudez stops him.
- Chango performs a ritual with drum, chant, etc., over the captured body parts. (He does this after each kill.) We begin to see that he is assembling a "new" body from all the parts.
- Clint Jones discovers that the bloody fingerprints on Silvio's shovel, used to kill Silvio in the cemetery, are

Chango's fingerprints. How can this be, since the *bokor* was supposed to be dead and buried?

- Martha and Vince go to the cemetery to try to trap Chango. Jones, having been phoned by Dawson, or having guessed their destination, is on his way and arrives in time to save the day.

- Mary Ann Scanlon goes to the beach cottage to see her old pal, Susan. No one is there. She strips to her bikini, rubs on suntan lotion, and takes out her sketch pad to while away the time. And she is attacked and killed by Chango, after a wild, frenzied, all-out battle that partially takes place in the water.

Once I accumulate twenty or thirty slips of paper like these, I lay them all out on my desk and start sliding them around and finding a basic order that makes a logical story flow. It is usually pretty easy to see, right off the bat, which dramatic incidents must go near the beginning of the screenplay, and which must come near the end. The middle is trickier. So I must keep experimenting, as if putting together the pieces of a jigsaw puzzle, until the picture makes itself whole. Often, as I said, this involves altering the pieces or inventing new pieces to better connect the ones that already exist.

For instance, it was easy to see that I needed the scene featuring Silvio and Jean on the beach to come first, because I had made up my mind that I wanted the story to start off with a bang, with the intriguing discovery of the washed-up bodies. The idea of giving the old man and his grandson a metal detector came to me when I realized it would be nice for them to have some obvious purpose that had brought them to the beach.

It was also easy to see that Vince and Martha's going to the cemetery to trap Chango would have to come near the end of the screenplay. So I moved it there right away.

But when were we going to see Chango's ritual for the first time—the stitching together of body parts?

Silvio's arm would be amputated in the cemetery, and Chango wouldn't sever another body part till he killed Mary Ann Scanlon (he was going to cannibalize Jean, not amputate the boy's limbs). So, that enabled me to move the slip of paper with the first ritual scene to a position after Mary Ann's death.

At some point Dawson and Jones had to become aware that Chango might not be dead. Fingerprints are considered incontrovertible evidence as to the perpetrator of a crime, so I thought of finding fingerprints on the shovel in the cemetery. But how would Dawson and Jones know they were Chango's—if the police had nothing to compare the fingerprints to?

This problem caused me to jot down two additional incidents on my slips of paper. One was a scene of the coroner fingerprinting each corpse on the beach (as is often done in real life when people are found dead in mysterious circumstances). This was a nice grisly detail for a horror story.

It also inspired the other additional scene I referred to: Dawson on the phone with Captain Armando Raphael of the police station in Port-au-Prince, trying to find out details about Chango. This scene would help get across to the audience the climate of superstition and fear in Haiti, and the police incompetence that enabled Chango to escape to America. Note also that the captain was a (minor) character whom I had not thought of before. It was good to have him in the story as a direct visual tie to Haiti, even though we would probably only see him in his office and would not go to Haiti to film anything or make use of stock footage (although stock footage is sometimes a viable route for low-budget movies to go): for instance, we might make use of a few establishing shots of Port-au-Prince, just for flavor, then dissolve to the police chief.

I kept on working with my slips of paper, putting my jotted-down scenes in workable order. Many of these slips had to do with things that would involve the three couples who were coming to the cottage to be set upon by Chango. I had to show them driving on Florida highways, coming into the town of Braxton Beach, and arriving at the cottage. I had to figure out how to space revelations about themselves that they would make in the course of their conversations.

I also had to decide who would die and exactly when and how, and who would survive. Each of these incidents was a scene note on a slip of paper, with attendant details filled in as they occurred to me. And of course these slips had to be positioned in accord with the others.

When I was finished with this procedure, I ended up with twenty-four slips of paper which, if read in order, would actually tell a fairly detailed story. And I could work from these slips, referring back to my research material and notes when necessary, to write either a treatment or a full-fledged screenplay. Although Bill Links had said he wanted to skip the treatment for the time being, I intended to write one eventually, because treatments are so handy for encapsulating a story and making it into its own "blurb" or sales pitch.

In the next chapter, we'll see exactly how my story line and characters got fleshed in and shaped into a script that could make a good movie.

7
Fleshing It In

NOW I WAS going to take each slip of paper—each scene with its attendant notes—and keep writing, filling in visual and conversational details, till I ended up with my finished screenplay. In doing this, I still had to keep myself open to new ideas and happy accidents. Nothing was carved in stone. Possibilities more exciting or apropos than the ones I had already thought of might occur to me. People and events might interact in unforeseen ways, causing new scenes to be born or old ones to change or disappear. Hopefully all this would be to the better, if I kept my head on straight and did the right kind of job.

Fiction writing is a dynamic process, always in a state of flux and always offering exciting new avenues, from start to finish— and sometimes even afterward. That is, after other people get a chance to read and offer suggestions, or even after the writer distances himself enough to be inspired by fresh perspectives, considerable reworking might take place.

Screenplays have to be essentially *visual* because that's the nature of the medium in which they're going to be produced. In the chiller/thriller genre, although you must strive to create interesting characters with strong, clever personalities, feelings, thoughts, and ideals, the fact is that if you dwell upon the cerebral too much in today's market you're probably not going to get the screenplay sold and produced. So I try to think heavily in terms of images—images that can convey ideas and emotions without long speeches—sight and sound images that feel very exciting to me—and I try to mold those images into shape with coherence and impact.

Once you have a strong outline, if your thoughts and observations are astute and well thought out, and cinematically detailed, and if you have intriguing, well-developed characters in your story, then it kind of takes care of itself. But it only takes care of itself with much consistent hard work alone in your room at the computer.

TWISTS AND TURNS OF THE WRITING PROCESS

Up to this point, as I said, I had wanted *Voodoo Dawn* to begin with a wallop—the discovery of the drowned sorcerer and his cohorts. But now I started to have second thoughts—now I was going to commit ideas to paper, and the imminent need to start putting everything down in a form that would have to *work* made me increasingly troubled. What was bothering me was the fact that if I stuck to my scene layout, I would be making the audience wait a long time to meet most of the characters they'd d be expected to identify with for the major part of the movie. Also, it was going to be tough for the audience to get a feel for the warm relationship between Martha Lewis and Silvio and Jean, if they never got to see her with Silvio and Jean before the old man and his grandson got killed.

Because of these considerations, I made the decision to open the screenplay with the two couples, the Morellis and the Becks, who were driving down to Florida to meet Barry and Susan Crandall at the beach cottage. But the opening montage of on-the-road shots would carry titles and credits and would be scored with ominous music, utilizing voodoo drums and chants. We therefore *know* something bad is going to happen even while we're learning about the people (eventually to become Chango's victims) through con-versation in their station wagon.

Next I went to a scene of Silvio and Jean on their way to the beach with their metal detector, but stopping by at the cottage (the eventual scene of mass murder) to talk with Martha Lewis and be introduced to Barry and Susan. Thus, the relationship among all these key people was established within the first ten minutes of screen time.

Then I went immediately to the beach with Silvio and Jean for the discovery of the bodies and the attempted beheading of Chango—the grisly events that would cause the whole story to take off at a fast pace. Dawson and Jones soon arrived on the scene, and my entire cast of major characters would be firmly established in the audience's mind.

These kinds of transmutations invariably happen during the writing process, even when you're working from a good solid outline. You have to be open to surprises and improvements and have fun with them when they occur. Sometimes whole characters who seemed essential at first end up dropping out of the picture. Other times new characters have to be invented along the way, or your initial conception of them needs to change.

CHARACTERS WHO START WALKING AND TALKING ON THEIR OWN

Sometimes as you get deeply into a writing project, and the characters keep developing and developing and seeming more and more alive, a certain character might not do what you had outlined for him to do. That is, you could *make* him do it (after all, you're the omnipotent writer), but if you impose your will on the character in that way, he'll suddenly jump *out* of character and throw the audience for a loop. Whoops! The character has developed complexities you hadn't bargained for, and now you've either got to remake him from scratch, or else let him do what he wants to do.

If you let him do what he wants to do, which is generally the wiser choice, at that point your plot—and the rest of your outline—

has to change. Usually this is for the better. Now you've got a story that is coming alive in a very special way.

In my initial outline for *Voodoo Dawn,* the scene in the cemetery was going to climax with the capture of Chango. But the character of Chango that I had constructed was too powerful, too evil, too awesome—almost superhuman, in fact—to ever be captured by ordinary mortals. He refused to *allow* himself to be taken. The fight between him and Dawson and Martha in the cemetery turned into a long, involving, tremendously harrowing episode. And Chango would have won—if Clint Jones hadn't arrived in the nick of time to put a bullet in his brain.

Even this didn't kill the *bokor.* He ended up in the hospital on a life-support system, supposedly brain-dead but still breathing. One could almost believe he really did possess supernatural powers and would miraculously recover.

This development put a crimp into one of the key elements I had outlined for the ending of my story. I had wanted Dawson to interrogate the captured *bokor* and find out where the life-size voodoo doll was buried. Chango would pretend to break down and tell, but really he wanted to tell—so the doll would be dug up by the police: the resurrection of the doll would magically cause the resurrection of his six followers.

Obviously, with Chango in a coma, Dawson couldn't interrogate him. How would the cops find out where the voodoo doll was? My solution was to have Martha and Dawson arrive at the cemetery just as Chango was burying the doll. So they already knew where it was. Also, ironically, after the fight in the cemetery Vince ended up in the same hospital as Chango, his arm having been almost torn completely off by Chango's whip. And there Susan Crandall expressed to her mother her own superstitious fear that the *bokor's* evil magic might not die.

Then occurred the final scene: two gravediggers exhuming the life-size voodoo doll made from severed body parts, to take it to the morgue.

They were both nervous and feeling spooky. And they didn't know if they were seeing shadows moving, caused by wind rustling the leaves of the trees, or if the ground itself was shifting over the mass grave—a prelude to the actual arising of Chango's followers. The scene froze for closing credits—making the audience wonder what would have happened next, if the movie had gone on. Or if there were ever to be a sequel.

THE BLURB

One of the tests of a successful piece of mass-market writing is whether or not it can be "blurbed." Can its strong points, its basic slant, be gotten across succinctly and powerfully, so as to "hook" people into wanting to read it or see the movie?

Here is the blurb that I wrote for *Voodoo Dawn* that appeared on the back cover of the original novelization published by Imagine Books:

WHEN THE SUN COMES UP WILL THE DEAD OUTNUMBER THE LIVING?

Seven bodies have washed ashore in Florida, and one of the drowned "boat people" is Chango, the voodoo sorcerer whose leather pouch holds a child's severed finger.

The sorcerer and his six followers have been buried in a mass grave. And prayers have been spoken to exorcise their unholy powers.

But Chango's spirit still prowls the moonlit beaches, taking victim after victim . . . leaving them cannibalized and dismembered.

Too late we find out that parts of human bodies are being used in an insane ritual.

And, come morning, we will face the full-fledged horror . . . the unspeakable terror that is VOODOO DAWN!

When you come up with a concept, a theme, a story line for a chiller or thriller, it is a good idea to try to write a blurb for it. Try even to write a zinger, a one-liner that could go on a movie poster or in a trailer. If you can't do this, maybe the concept isn't focused sharply enough to appeal to a mass audience. And perhaps more importantly, it might not be tight and hard-hitting enough to sell to a financing company.

In this business, you always have to keep marketing factors in mind. That might seem crass and "unartistic" but it's one of the hard facts of life. As I said earlier, a movie can't be made for the cost of a ream of paper. You're asking somebody to have enough faith in your project to cough up thousands and perhaps millions of dollars. So you've got to give him a powerful basis for his confidence.

You've got to believe in yourself. And work hard to make others believe in you, too.

8

Collaborators, Rewriters, Tinkerers, and Meddlers

ONCE YOUR SCREENPLAY is done, you can breathe a sigh of relief. But not for long. Because now it comes under the scrutiny of the people who can help make it fly. Agents. Distributors. Producers and directors. Money people. Even other writers hired by any or all of the above to tinker with your work and try to "improve" it. Sometimes you might welcome their help and other times you might become annoyed or angry. Sometimes you might end up splitting a fee with them when you really don't want to. In any event, you have got to be able to deal successfully with these kinds of people, if you want to build a career in the entertainment business.

COLLABORATORS

Certain projects even start out with collaborators as part of the package. My very first feature film, *Night of the Living Dead,* was a screenwriting collaboration between me and George Romero. We were good friends and business partners, and the arrangement went smoothly. We didn't argue, fight, or even discuss who would do what. We just went ahead and did it, and then we shared the credit. First George and I bashed around some ideas, then he took those ideas and wrote the first half of the story. Then he got tied up with one of the commercial film clients we had at the time, and I wrote the second half of our horror story, based on ideas chipped in by the two of us plus some of our friends and associates. We added a few refinements after we got into production, but basically the movie got made as written.

Too bad all projects don't go as smoothly.

If you choose to collaborate with someone on a screenplay, that's fine, as long as you are on the same wavelength. But remember that "artistic differences" have wrecked almost as many movies as "irreconcilable differences" have wrecked marriages.

Choose your collaborator wisely, and before you do anything together, put everything in writing: who is to do what, who is to get paid how much, how the credit is to be shared, and who is to have top billing.

Once a producer or distributor gets involved with your project, you have automatically gained a collaborator. Sometimes this happens before any screenwriting takes place, as it happened with me and Bill Links on *Voodoo Dawn*. Other times the collaboration is formed and picks up momentum once a producer or distributor acquires a monetary interest in your property.

This is often quite beneficial and is not always to be looked upon with fear and dread. If the producer or distributor is worth his salt, he brings much experience and many shrewd marketing insights to the party. If you are willing to work congenially, with an open mind, your potential for success may be enhanced. On the other hand, if you are blindly stubborn, always insisting that your own point of view is the only correct one and that you are the only true artist, your project may find itself on rocky ground, may never get a green light, or may suffer from your own shortsightedness (pigheadedness) even if it does somehow get produced.

REWRITERS

When a screenplay is commissioned or sold to a producer or distributor, he will always insist upon the right, in his sole discretion, to hire additional writers to do rewrites. Again, sometimes this works out favorably. Other times the writer of the original work hates the outcome and resents sharing credit with someone he feels has butchered his script.

It is almost impossible for any writer who wants to get his material sold to obtain a contract that does not contain a rewrite clause. And it doesn't matter whether the writer is an unknown or a big name. In his book *Adventures in the Screen Trade,* William Goldman said, "I have had some wonderful times in the movie business ... but scratch a screenwriter and you're bound to find some horror stories." Then he goes on to tell about being bumped from projects without being told, having his stuff rewritten without his permission, and having projects canceled right out from under him. Sometimes his first and only clue to any of the above would be the disconnected phone of a director or producer that he had been working closely and supposedly amicably with, right up to the moment the unseen bomb was dropped. And they would do this to him even after he had already written proven successes like *Butch Cassidy and the Sundance Kid* and *All the President's Men.*

My first experience with having a script rewritten by somebody else after it was already sold came with *Return of the Living Dead.* It started out as a collaboration in the first place, between me and Rudy Ricci and Russ Streiner; Rudy was one of the investors in the original *Night of the Living Dead,* and Russ was the co-producer. We developed a script for a spin-off, and sold it to Fox Films for quite a lot of money. But of course there was a rewrite clause, and when Dan O'Bannon (writer of *Alien* and *Blue Thunder)* was hired to direct *Return of the Living Dead,* he did a complete rewrite, partly necessitated by the fact that "straight horror" was supposed to be out of fashion at the time and the distributor wanted to make a horror comedy. I happened to like the movie that Dan made, even though his script was drastically different from the one we had sold to Fox. But, as the result of all these machinations, Dan O'Bannon ended up with the screenplay credit, and Russ, Rudy, and I got a much lesser credit for our "original story." At least we were paid well, and the movie was a hit and is generating some residuals.

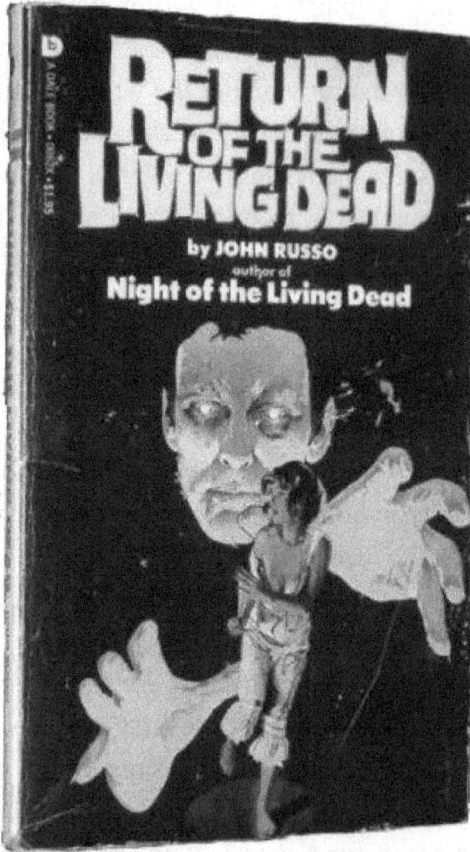

**The original horror version of *Return of the Living Dead*
was published by Dale Books in 1978.**

With this less than exuberant experience under my belt, I tried to protect myself against unwanted rewriters on *Voodoo Dawn*. I was able to negotiate a clause that gave me top billing, even if others were hired to do a rewrite.

I tried to compel the distributor to employ me and me alone to rewrite my material, but he refused to be nailed down that hard.

The net result was that once again the original concept got scrapped somewhere along the line, and the script was completely rewritten by two other people in an effort to make it into an action-adventure instead of a horror movie. The Chango character was weakened and his screen time was reduced. The life-sized voodoo doll came to life in the end. And the people having the "action-adventure" are a bunch of teenagers—just what I had striven so hard to avoid.

If you want to see how my original *Voodoo Dawn* story turned out, you'll have to read my novelization of it, *Living Things*, published by Burning Bulb Publishing, which tells the original story in an elaborated form, and then carries it several years into the future, where Dawson, Jones, and Martha Lewis are still tangling with the voodoo sorcerer they thought was dead.

I'd still like to someday make the movie my way.

AVOIDING TINKERERS AND MEDDLERS

Adventures like the ones above are part of the reason why I like to direct my own films. By working with private financing and smaller distributors, I've been able on quite a few occasions to make movies the way I think they should be made. *Midnight* and *Heartstopper* were projects wherein I was able to retain creative control, but the budgets were small—particularly in the case of *Midnight*—so creative freedom was tempered by financial constraints. But I still think it was worth it. I'm fairly pleased with the way those films turned out, and I enjoyed the challenge of pulling them up by their bootstraps.

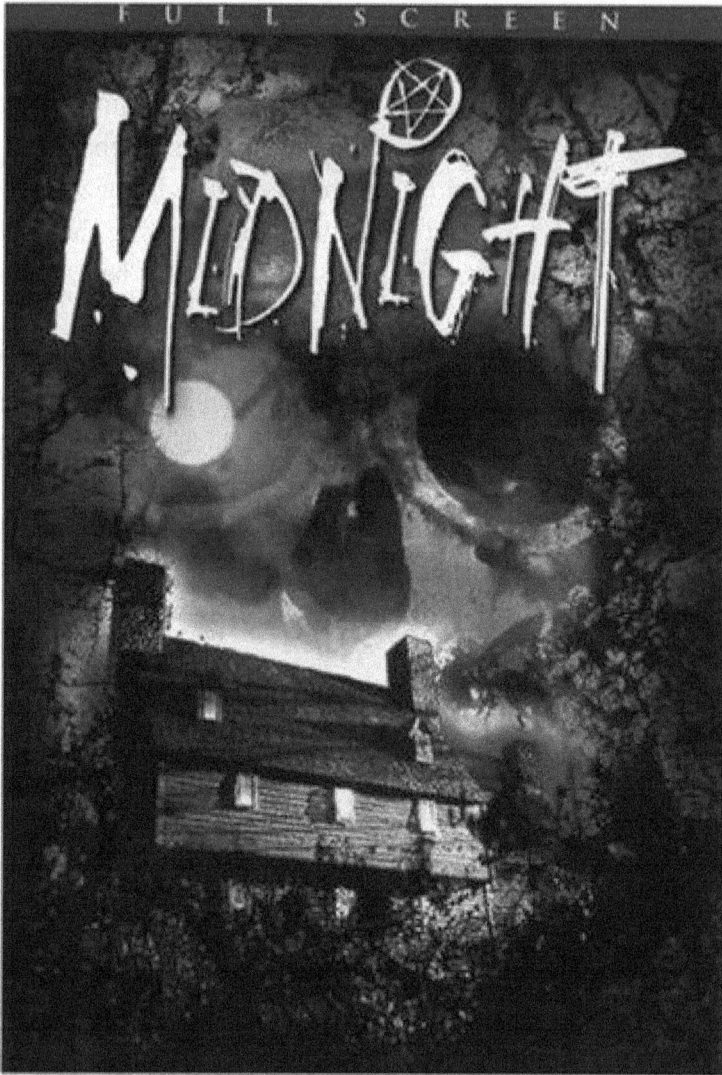

**DVD Cover of *Midnight*. Film written and directed
by John Russo, distributed by Lions Gate.**

You might want to take the same approach. Try to raise money
on your own to get your pet projects produced and distributed. Or
else try to ally yourself with people who believe in you strongly
enough not to tamper too much with your work. This includes your
close friends and associates—all the people you're going to have to

work with to actually get your film made. All too often there are disastrous clashes of ego and opinion in every stage of a creative effort.

Remember, making a movie is *always* a collaborative effort. The producer or director might have strong authority, but he has to depend on many others to share his vision and work wisely to bring it to the screen. Therefore, he must be prepared to work harmoniously with all these people and wisely select the ones with the right mix of talent, discipline and resourcefulness.

So, if you want to stick with your material, all the way from concept to silver screen, you're accepting a tough but exhilarating challenge. Even if you have to do it on a low budget, it's a great joy to be able to work from a script that you wrote yourself to realize your own vision in your own unique style.

Part III
SELLING

"I think all the people involved in market research should be forced to have their wives and girlfriends fill out exit polls when they leave the bedroom. That would be the end of market research."

– DEBRA WINGER, actress

"As long as my agent is making money for me, it's great. I hope I have to pay him a million, because that means I'd be a millionaire nine times over."

– MARK REISMAN, writer

9

The Deal Makers

NOW YOU HAVE a great concept, a great script, but how are you going to get it made into a movie? You might not have to face that question if your project has come tailor-made with a financing/distribution deal, as was the case with *Voodoo Dawn.* But what about subsequent projects? How are you going to continue building your career? How will you avoid turning into one of those show-biz people who don't ever get any work anymore and have to keep telling talk show hosts they're "on hiatus?"

In this chapter, for those who want to crack into "the biz" and *stay* in it, I'm going to discuss the deal makers—agents, business managers, entertainment attorneys, packagers, and promoters who you may have to work with in order to bring your work to the marketplace. In my book *Making Movies,* I gave detailed advice for those who wish to go it alone, either out of desire or necessity—advice about how to make up a budget, raise money, organize and complete a production, and sell it to a distributor. My aim here is to advise you on how to work with the wheelers and dealers who can help you do all of that and more.

AGENTS

Many unpublished writers and aspiring filmmakers believe that if they could only somehow land a good agent, their worries would be over. Fame and fortune would be just around the corner. The agent would tout them, push them, and land big-money writing, producing, or directing assignments galore.

But in the real world things don't usually work out so gloriously.

Tobe *Hooper,* director of *The Texas Chainsaw Massacre, Poltergeist,* and *Salem's Lot,* once told me that no agent ever got him a job. Huh?

Then what in the world do agents *do?*

Well, sometimes they really do land jobs for their clients, but more often they negotiate the deal points on jobs for which the clients have already been sought out. That means the clients, not the agents, have to create the demand for material or services, so that the agents can follow through.

A literary agent doesn't usually sell a client onto a book-writing job; he sells the client's finished book or book proposal to a publisher. A screenwriter's agent doesn't usually sell the writer onto a movie production; he sells the writer's script or treatment to a production company.

Producers and directors, even those with big names like Tobe Hooper, don't have jobs spoon fed to them by their agents, either. They have to go out and create a basic demand for their talent and ability. Then an agent can parlay that demand into a deal. Or at least he can try.

What this boils down to is that if you don't give an agent something to sell besides your scintillating personality, your big or not-so-big name, and your past laurels, then you're going to have a tough time staying busy and paying your bills. Movie stars can sometimes land gigs mostly on "fame and name." Movie-*makers* have to keep on developing marketable projects and turning those projects *into* hits—or at least reasonable successes—in order to stay in demand.

Earlier in this book, you saw how the *Voodoo Dawn* project got started, not by an agent, but by a producer, Bill Links, phoning me and bashing around some ideas. Bill and I already had a good working relationship; he helped sell the *Return of the Living Dead* deal to Fox Films. Once Bill Links, Steve Mackler, and I got together on *Voodoo Dawn,* my agent at the time, Bruce Kaufman of Triad Artists, Inc., helped hammer out the contractual details.

The *Night of the Living Dead* remake worked pretty much the same way. I phoned George Romero and Russ Streiner and asked them to pull together with me to remake our picture. We then had several meetings to discuss basic details of the proposed collaboration. Then George's agent, David Gersh, of the Gersh Agency, and my agent, Bruce Kaufman, got involved in structuring the details of the deal and shopping the project to the major production and distribution companies.

I want to point out that an agent's ability to negotiate makes him extremely valuable to you even if you have to bring the gigs to him instead of the other way around. He knows how hard he can squeeze the studios. He's got up-to-the-minute knowledge of the Hollywood production scene and the interaction between supply and demand. The agent will generally ask for—and get—way more money than you would have dreamed of asking for on your own. And he'll get you "perks" you would have been embarrassed to mention even if you had thought of them in the first place.

The chauffer-driven limo, the big expense account, the first-class accommodations during travel and on location—all of these things and more, the agent will ask for and get. And even if you didn't really want some of them, it's kind of nice to know that somebody is there to see that you get treated as well as other up-and-comers do. In the wild, wacky world of movie magic and escalating budgets, you might as well have your fling on the escalator. The agent will push for as much as he can get for you, and rake off a 10 percent commission, but you'll be very glad to pay it.

Now, even though I've taken pains to show you that an agent can't automatically smooth the path to success for you unless you help him find some of the grease, there are times when agents actually are instrumental in landing gigs for their clients instead of just doing the negotiating. For instance, if an agent knows that a project doesn't have a director yet, he will try to persuade the production company to hire one of the directors in the agency's stable. Or, if the agency is taking part in the packaging of a project, all of the talent in the agency's stable—producers, directors, screenwriters, cinematographers, etc.—may have a shot at getting hired.

Within a major agency like Triad Artists, there are agents who handle actors, agents who handle directors, agents who handle producers, screenwriters, cinematographers, editors, what-have-you. There are agents who specialize in dealing with low-budget production and distribution houses, and agents who specialize in dealing with the majors. There are certain projects where the entire "package" is put together by the agency—virtually all the actors and staff of the project will be furnished by the agency, with the approval of the financing company. This is a golden opportunity for the agency's stable of clients.

But again, if you don't have impressive enough screen credits (even though you may have succeeded in landing an agent—based on the agent's belief in your potential), you will not have much chance of becoming part of a bigtime package at this stage in your career. The agent knows this, and will not even try to sell you onto such a package until you do something to make yourself "hot."

HOW TO LAND AND KEEP AN AGENT

Now, you've got to make yourself hot, or at least a little bit warm, in order to land an agent in the first place.

If you want to motivate an agent to take you on, you've got to convince him either that you are a marketable commodity right now, or that you soon will be. If you have no producing or directing credits, it's an overwhelmingly safe bet that no agent will agree to push you as a producer or director. So you will have to earn some credits before you begin approaching agents.

However, even if you have no screenwriting credits, you may be able to land an agent to represent you as a writer—if you have written an exceptional screenplay. The reason is that the screenplay itself acts as your badge of credibility. A piece of good writing sells the writer of it as effectively as a good movie sells its producer or director.

My former agent, Bruce Kaufman, was recently responsible for selling a first-time movie script for $1,200,000. The script, entitled *The Ticking Man,* about an android implanted with a nuclear bomb, impressed Bruce and others at Triad Artists so much that they devised a tantalizingly clever way to pitch it. On a Friday afternoon, they had messengers deliver to each of twenty handpicked film producers and studio executives a loud ticking alarm clock painted black with a cryptic message on the face: The Ticking Man Is Coming. The script itself wasn't sent out till the following Tuesday, and by then a bidding frenzy had started, resulting in a whopping sale.

Many literary agents and movie agents will read unsolicited manuscripts as part of their continuing quest for fresh, exceptional talent. Through reference sources I will give you in Chapter 10, you can obtain agents' names and addresses and find out which ones are looking for new writers. If you are in doubt, send a query letter—don't just mail your manuscript to them cold.

It is also quite possible to get a book or screenplay sold without going through an agent. Publishers and film production companies also read unsolicited manuscripts. If you get an offer on your own, you can then obtain an agent to negotiate the deal for you. I landed my first literary agent that way. What happened was that in 1973, five years after *Night of the Living Dead* was originally released, I was approached by a book packager who wanted me to write a novelization. But he wanted to take a 40 percent commission, which sounded like a rip-off to me. So I phoned a published writer whom I knew and asked her to recommend an agent. Since the novelization deal already was viable, the agent, Theron Raines, agreed to take me on as a client and try to land an even better deal. The net result was that I didn't need to involve the packager; Theron got me an advance $2,000 higher than I would have gotten, and he took only a 10 percent commission instead of 40 percent.

The advantage that budding writers have over budding producers and directors in the game of landing an agent is that it is much easier and cheaper for writers to give agents something to evaluate and perhaps sell. The raw material that goes into a screenplay (ink and paper) costs peanuts, and the raw material that goes into a movie costs mucho. But just as writers are judged on the quality and marketability of the screenplays they have already written, producers and directors are judged by the quality and performance of the movies they have already produced or directed. It is true that first-time producers or directors are occasionally hired, but even then they usually have attained screen credits on some other level and have made suitable contacts and impressed influential people before getting their big chance. For example, Declan Baldwin, who was our line producer on the *Night of the Living Dead* remake later became the producer on a $14,000,000 movie that George Romero directed titled *The Dark Half,* which is based on one of Stephen King's best sellers. It was Declan's first producing credit—but by that point, he now had twenty movies under his belt, having worked his way up from unpaid intern to production assistant, location manager, unit manager, production manager, and so forth.

If you don't have the patience to climb the rungs the way Declan Baldwin did, then there is still the other viable choice I've already given you: raise money on your own to make your own movie. Sam Raimi, Tobe Hooper, Spike Lee, and George Romero are fine examples of people who have fought their way into the system by attaining success outside of it. Once you make a hit movie, even if you had to do it on a low budget, you should be able to attract an agent.

The thing that helped me and George Romero both was that we write screenplays in addition to producing and directing. So, even though at the early stages of our careers we had only very low-budget movies to our credit, the agents who agreed to take us on were figuring that they could sell our writing even if it might be tough to sell us as producers or directors. It also helped that we are both prolific in terms of the volume of scripts that we write and the number of projects we maintain in various stages of development. Agents don't want to wait forever for a client to give them something to sell. The marketplace is constantly changing, so therefore they need a constant supply of new material to meet the new demands.

There are two key aspects to motivating an agent. One is to get him to take you on in the first place; and the second is to keep him working hard and persistently on your behalf after you become one of his clients.

Once you land an agent, you can't just lie back and wait for him to make you a star. In order for your relationship with an agent to endure, if you haven't registered any sales yet he's got to keep believing that you soon will; and if you have been a breadwinner in the past, he's got to feel that you will keep on landing gigs and earning him commissions. Therefore, you must keep on developing and improving your track record, and keep on involving yourself in projects that recharge the agent's belief in your potential.

This doesn't mean that the relationship should be a one-sided one, with you working hard to please *him* and getting little or no feedback in return. You must have faith—and evidence—that the agent is helping you land gigs (even if you initiate them) and is negotiating good deals for you when the gigs come in. He should be willing to communicate with you promptly and regularly when anything important is in the offing, and should keep you informed as to what he thinks of any projects you submit for his consideration, and what has been the disposition of those projects—in other words, his follow-up. Is he going to submit the project, and to whom? Is he going to help package it? Does he think it has major or minor flaws that should be revamped? Does he think it is unmarketable and should be scrapped?

If you fail to get this kind of input from your agent, you will be working in the dark. He is your liaison with the marketplace. And the relationship with him has to be a two-way street. If it isn't that way, then you will have to consider finding a new agent or going it on your own.

BUSINESS MANAGERS

Many people in the movie business feel that they can't really maximize their chances of success by being represented only by an agent. They worry that an agent won't do enough for them, either because he doesn't believe in them strongly enough or because he's too busy pushing others (with perhaps bigger names) or because his time is split among too many clients. Or maybe because the agent just doesn't have enough clout, for whatever reasons.

People in the biz are always angling for an extra advantage in the clamor for success, and one of the currently fashionable angles is to hire a business manager. The business manager is supposed to help in the scramble for gigs. And he is supposed to be able to do it more effectively than an agent can because he can give a client closer attention and can work with him more intimately to help develop properties, package and promote projects, garner publicity, entice studio support and financing, etc., etc.

When the client and the business manager are on the verge of a deal, the agent is brought into the picture. Then the parties work as a team to ice the deal on favorable terms. The agent might then fade into the background again, till the next deal comes along, while the business manager might stick with the client all the way through the project, even playing some sort of role during production.

Sometimes a writer/producer/director entices somebody to work with him as a business manager to help land gigs, by making an arrangement that allows the manager to produce whatever gigs are landed. The manager takes a prearranged fee (and usually a percentage) of the projects he lands and/ or works on.

ENTERTAINMENT ATTORNEYS

There are lawyers who specialize in the business and legal problems of the entertainment industry, and it is difficult for the ordinary practitioner to match their level of proficiency and understanding of current practices within the industry. So all the major studios, the agencies, and most of the top artists (both in front of the camera and behind the camera) employ these kinds of lawyers, known as entertainment attorneys.

Because they are involved closely with all the players in the movie business, the attorneys have branched into areas beyond their original specialty. Some of them have become agents and/or business managers. Some have gone on to become producers, too.

It is often very helpful to have an agent who is also an attorney. But in cases where the negotiation or interpretation of a contract goes beyond an agent's level of expertise, the agent will seldom hesitate to call upon an entertainment attorney for the necessary input.

When we were getting ready to remake *Night of the Living Dead* in 1990, because of the almost fifty-year history of the original *Night of the Living Dead,* the various deals and contracts were extremely complicated, and my agent put me in touch with an entertainment attorney who scrutinized everything and gave us quite a bit of helpful advice. The chain of formal agreements

AF"O WRITE, PRODUCE & DIRECT EXCITING MONEY MAKING MOVIES

included the one between me, Russ Streiner, and George Romero; the one between me and Russ and Image Ten, the company that made the original movie back in 1968; and the separate agreements that George, Russ, and I had to make with the financing company, 21st Century Films. In situations like this, an entertainment attorney can be invaluable, and can save you many years of grief and loss of income.

Some entertainment attorneys even help package projects, including the writing of offering circulars and prospectuses, and the raising of production financing. They also may get involved with marketing and merchandising offers and contracts. Because of their respected position within the industry, and the many excellent contacts they develop in the course of their work, they can often help the aspiring filmmaker in ways that can equal or exceed the value of their legal advice.

PACKAGERS AND PROMOTERS

We've already seen that sometimes agents and entertainment attorneys can help package and promote projects. But there are some packagers and promoters who have few skills that pertain to movie-making other than packaging and promoting. That is, they don't have the negotiating ability or contacts that an agent has, the knowledge of contractual matters that a lawyer has, or the writing, producing, or directing talent of a filmmaker.

But they want to be in the movie business. They want to be the movers and shakers behind certain projects. And sometimes they're pretty darn good at it.

Tom Fox, who bought, packaged, and sold the *Return of the Living Dead* project, had never before made a film. He was fairly wealthy; he and his family had made their money in the railroad business. He fell in love with the idea of becoming a movie producer, and was bound and determined to become one. So he bought our screenplay, signed up Clu Gulager and James Karen to star in it, and hired Dan O'Bannon to become the director. He left his hometown of Chicago to shop his very first movie package in Hollywood, and eventually landed a deal with Lorimar. Then he became the executive producer of the movie, which became a hit and spawned a sequel. Since then, Tom has produced a couple more films. Now he's an established packager, promoter and producer instead of merely an aspiring one.

A guy like that, with the money and drive to see a project through, wouldn't be a bad ally for an aspiring filmmaker.

The trouble is, there are lots of guys out there purporting to be packagers and promoters, and many of them aren't much better than con men. Trying to decide who's going to be worth working with and who's going to waste your time and money is a tough, debilitating chore. Sometimes they don't just waste your money, they steal it.

Part of the fun of the biz is its atmosphere of hype, hoopla, and hullaballoo. It's harmless enough when all that's at stake is the price of a ticket to a show that turns out to be a rip-off. But when you're *working* in the biz, risking your own time, effort, and livelihood, you must beware of the hucksters, thieves and con men who can take you for a ride and wreck or temporarily derail your career.

So, when you are offered the opportunity of working with an agent, a lawyer, a packager or promoter, be sure to choose one with a good track record. If he hasn't been in the movie business for long, he may not have the track record, but he still ought to have strong credentials and a good reputation going back to his previous area of endeavor. Don't be afraid to check him out thoroughly. Ask for references, and actually talk with them. Be shrewd, and use your own best judgment. And don't do anything on faith; get it all in writing. Remember that if something sounds too good to be true, it usually is.

Keep working to maximize your credentials, so you'll have more and more clout in dealing with the deal makers. Every good script that you write, every good film that you make, whether low budget or not, makes them want to stick with you and help you move on to bigger and better things.

10
Making Contacts

THE DEAL MAKERS aren't going to beat down your door to work with you. You've got to go after them. How do you find them in order to get your script or proposal in front of them? How do you even begin to make them interested enough to read your stuff or meet with you to discuss the project you have in mind? How do you make new contacts when the old ones haven't panned out?

With these questions tormenting your brain, the feeling of satisfaction you experienced when you first conceived of your project is beginning to fade. Your friends and associates are losing interest. Once you were raring to go, but now you don't know what to do next. You are totally stymied. Your career is going nowhere fast.

Rest assured that this is an ongoing problem, not just for the beginner but for those who have already made a mark in the biz. The more credits you have, the easier it becomes to launch new projects—but it is seldom something that happens as easily as falling off a log.

But what about *Voodoo Dawn?* That was pretty easy, wasn't it?

Nope. It started out looking easy. But the movie didn't get made till three years after Bill Links and I had our initial conversation about it. In between times there were plenty of complications—haggling, maneuvering, rewriting, rehashing, including arguments and dissension among the producers, distributors, and financiers—to the point where Bill Links got bought out of the project by Bedford Entertainment before the movie even went into production.

By the time *Voodoo Dawn* got released, I had already made three more movies and published four more books. You see, by now I know better than to put all my eggs in one basket. And I'm always on the move, doing the things necessary to keep my career from bogging down and grinding to a halt.

In this chapter, I'm going to teach you how to keep your own career from bogging down. I'm going to show you how to move in the right direction when you've run out of resources and contacts close at hand and you're trying desperately to get in touch with somebody who can help you lift a stalled project up from ground zero.

PUBLICATIONS AND DIRECTORIES

It's pretty hard to contact an agent, entertainment attorney, packager, or promoter if you don't know where to find one. So, even though this may be elemental for some readers, let's start out with a discussion of publications that are valuable references for filmmakers.

Writer's Market is one that can easily be overlooked. Published yearly by Writer's Digest Books, it is available in most bookstores. It contains names and addresses of literary agents, publishers, and film and tape production companies that are looking for scripts. It also contains articles filled with advice about how to successfully pursue a writing career. If you write books as well as screenplays, you may want to try to obtain a literary agent; many literary agents either try to sell material to the movies on their own, or else they work hand in hand with motion picture agents to do so.

Variety and *Hollywood Reporter* are the main trade publications of the motion picture industry. They will keep you up-to-date on everything that's happening in a business and creative sense. New production and distribution companies are being formed all the time, and old ones are merging, diversifying, or going out of business. From reading these publications, you can develop a pretty good understanding of who these companies are and what kinds of projects they seem to be looking for. *Boxoffice* puts out special issues each year listing theatrical and home video distributors with addresses, phone numbers, and names of officers and key personnel.

It is also a good idea to subscribe to some of the popular movie magazines.

They are filled with useful information about producing and directing, production financing, and the promotion and marketing of screenplays and screen projects. Writers' magazines like *Writer's Digest* and *The Writer* contain monthly updates on the literary and audio/visual markets, how-to articles about all aspects of plot and character development, and columns that specialize in the art of screenwriting and selling.

Of course talent agents, production companies, and motion picture distributors are listed in the Yellow Pages of the cities wherein they reside. And in the White Pages, too. So it's never too hard to at least obtain phone numbers and addresses. The major players are in New York and Los Angeles, but there are also producers and distributors in other large cities. Most states now have film bureaus to try to bring in film productions (because of the huge boost film dollars give to state economies), and these bureaus usually publish directories of local producers, directors, writers, and technicians.

Obtaining a directory from your state film bureau is a good way to find out how to reach people close to you who might become your partners in pushing your own film project.

PROFESSIONAL ORGANIZATIONS

Sometimes it helps to know that you're not alone in your struggle. There are some organizations that you can join as a virtual amateur, and there are others that won't let you in until you obtain professional credits.

I mentioned *American Film* magazine earlier, and the way you obtain a subscription is to join the American Film Institute. With membership in AFI, which costs currently less than thirty dollars per year, you get admission to their seminars and lectures, discounts at selected movie theaters across the country, access to research and reference facilities, and advance notice of and discounts to film festivals. The AFI seminars cover vital aspects of the movie business such as screenwriting, directing, producing, movie financing, and movie distributing.

The Authors Guild, Inc. accepts as full members authors who have published at least one book, and as associate members authors who only have works in progress. Annual dues are on a sliding scale depending upon writing income, but the base dues are sixty dollars. The guild has many membership services, including a health and hospitalization plan. It publishes reports and bulletins full of useful information about publishers, agents, legal issues, tax and business problems of authors, etc., etc.

The Writers Guild of America has two main branches, the east branch and the west branch. Membership can be acquired only through the sale of literary material or employment for writing services. The guild performs many valuable services for members besides negotiating favorable contracts and pay scales with the studios. Manuscript registration, health insurance enrollment, credit union membership, and banking, checking, and credit card plans are available through WGA at favorable rates.

The Directors Guild of America has membership requirements as stringent as those of the WGA.

Both the DGA and WGA publish directories of their members, which may be obtained by writing to the guild headquarters.

The Horror Writers of America is another interesting organization. Published writers are accepted as full members, and non-published writers can become affiliate members. The HWA publishes a membership directory and regular bulletins covering all aspects of the horror business, including advice about agents, publishers, and the markets for books and screenplays.

CONVENTIONS AND FESTIVALS

The various guilds and associations hold conventions and awards banquets which are good affairs to attend for the purpose of making contacts and learning about the book and movie business. If you are a member of one of these organizations, you will find out about these affairs through the membership bulletins. If you're not a member, you can find out about them through ads in the trade publications and on the internet.

Movie conventions are good places to meet celebrities, dealers in chiller/thriller merchandise, established producers, directors, and distributors, fans of the genre, and aspiring writers and filmmakers.

I make it a point to attend as many of the conventions as possible in order to keep my name in front of the fans and meet influential people working in my field. A couple of years ago in Los Angeles, Tobe Hooper, George Romero, Gary Brandner, and I got together and held a panel discussion about the horror genre and our own particular books and movies. It was fun to do, and we got along well and laid some groundwork for potential future projects.

Another fine way to make contacts is to attend the various film festivals held around the world. Lists of these festivals are published on the internet (a good resource for researching festivals is www.Withoutabox.com). There are horror and science fiction film festivals and independent feature film festivals, as well as the more mainstream festivals such as the one at Cannes or at Robert Redford's Sundance Institute. The American Film Market is also an excellent place to meet film people, attend symposiums, and learn the latest developments in the movie business.

Selling the *Voodoo Dawn* novel at a horror convention. The novel tie-in helped raise financing for the movie. *Photo by Bob Michelucci.*

SPRINGBOARDS

Every time you make a good contact, it has the potential of leading to other good contacts. And every time you work on a project, it has a tendency to help you toward other projects. Many times it doesn't even matter if what you're doing at the moment isn't directly related to what you want to do ultimately. By getting out and meeting people and by constantly learning and doing, you are building a foundation that can springboard you toward the kind of success you wish to achieve.

People who stay at home and wait for the big break to come to them will waste their lives waiting. Good things happen to those with the drive and ambition to make their own breaks.

Every project I've worked on, even the ones that in and of themselves weren't so successful, has paved the way toward another project. For instance, back in the early seventies I made a movie called *The Booby Hatch.* It was a very low-budget sex satire, and for two years we couldn't find a distributor. But I kept plugging away, and finally struck a deal with a small New York company, Independent-International Pictures.

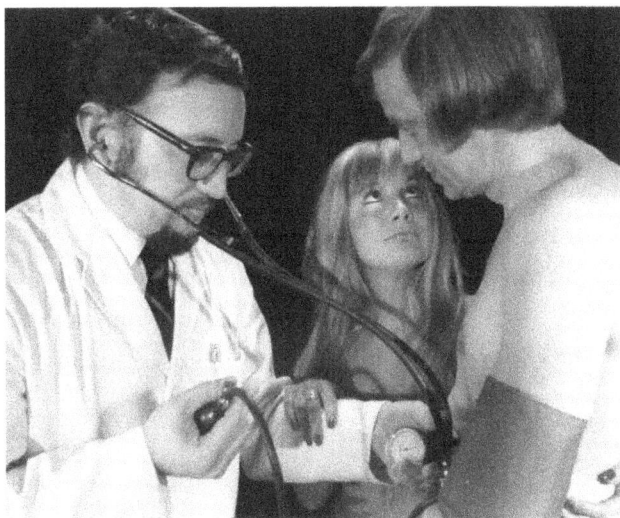

In *The Booby Hatch* I also had an acting part, playing a scientist/doctor.

The Booby Hatch turned a nice profit for them, and I got along well with the officers of the company, Sam Sherman and Dan Kennis.

They hired me to write a screenplay for them, *The Black Cat,* and although they haven't so far made the movie, I was able to sell my novelization to Pocket Books and then to Burning Bulb Publishing for a re-issue.

Then, in 1980, Independent-International helped finance and distributed my movie *Midnight.* It turned a tidy profit in its theatrical release, and sold $1,000,000 worth of videos when it was released on home video by Vidmark Entertainment. I also wrote a novelization, which was a best seller in the United States and has been sold in a dozen foreign countries.

Additionally, through Dan Kennis and Sam Sherman I've made numerous important contacts in the movie business—distributors, agents, reviewers, and other filmmakers. The agent that I previously mentioned, Bruce Kaufman, I met through another agent introduced to me by Sam Sherman.

See what I mean?

Many people told me not to bother making a film like *The Booby Hatch* on a desperately low budget. But at that point in my career, nobody was offering to give me enough money to do something bigger. The choice was to do nothing or to do something. I chose to do something. And I don't have any regrets about that decision.

The trick is to stay busy. Don't fold your hand because you're temporarily discouraged. You can't win the game if you don't play. If you can't sell a screenplay, novelize it and maybe you can sell the book. Then somebody might buy the book to make it into a movie.

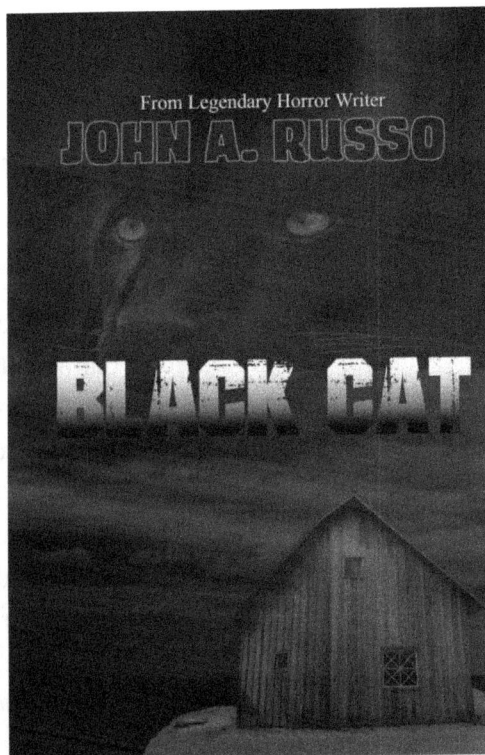

The 2014 cover for *Black Cat*, designed by Gary Lee Vincent.
Courtesy of Burning Bulb Publishing.

If you can't get hired as a writer, producer, or director, try to get onto the crew of a movie production in some lower capacity. That way you'll meet the players. And next time around, if you've done the right kind of job, you might get a chance to move up. John Badham, director of *Blue Thunder* and *WarGames,* used to work in the mail room at Universal. Adrian Lyne, director of *Fatal Attraction and Jacob's Ladder,* used to make TV commercials. Oliver Stone couldn't get hired as a director after he graduated from the NYU Film School, so he had to drive a taxi in order to pay his bills; a few years later he hit it big with *Platoon.*

Don't be discouraged by rejection. Almost nothing in the movie business happens "normally." Stay in the game the best way you can. And refuse to think of yourself as a loser.

11
Packaging Your Project

IF YOU HAVE just a script and your own credentials (or lack of credentials) to sell, the marketplace can seem cold and impenetrable. Miracles like the one Sylvester Stallone pulled off are few and far between. Remember? When he wrote *Rocky,* he insisted that he wouldn't sell the script unless he was also signed to play the lead role, and he stuck by his guns till the studio gave in. So that one great script became his ticket to fame and riches; it led to his becoming not only a star actor but a producer and director, and he's pretty much calling his own shots nowadays.

The key point here, even though we're talking about a fluke, is that Stallone reached high, but he reached for something that was *possible.* He already had acted in some Hollywood movies. And he knew the studio liked his script. So he asked them to let him star in *Rocky.* He did not ask to be the director. He did not try to sell himself as something he had never been before.

If you have a script that you believe in, and you can't raise the money to make it outside the studio system, and you lack the credentials necessary to land a producing or directing position even if a studio buys the script, then you have three ways to proceed in order to prevent the project from dying:

1. Try to sell only the script and give up any thoughts of working on the production.

2. Try to build your credentials by working on other people's productions or on lower-budget productions of your own.

3. Try to package your project, allying yourself with people who have the credentials and/or resources that you lack.

Selling a script, even though you won't be involved in that particular production, isn't a bad thing, especially if it's a major deal. It gets you money, screen credit, and publicity. It's a big boost to your career. Writers often eventually make the shift to producing or directing. If you've written a successful movie, people are willing to believe you might be able to direct one. It's one of the springboards I talked about in the previous chapter.

In my own case, even though I've produced and/or directed seven movies, they've all had relatively low budgets; therefore, if I write a screenplay for a movie that would require a high budget, I have to realize that my agent will probably not be able to sell me as producer or director (although he will certainly try). So, I deal with this problem by writing some scripts that I am looking to sell outright to the major studios, and some that I am looking to produce or direct myself.

Working on other people's productions to build your credentials is a fine idea, but not necessarily the fastest route to success. And you may run into time-consuming roadblocks trying to raise money on your own for your own projects, even if they *are* low budget.

That leads us up to the choice that is the main subject of this chapter: packaging your own project.

WHAT CONSTITUTES A PACKAGE?

A movie package can be comprised of some or all of the following elements:

- Treatment
- Screenplay
- Production budget
- Production schedule
- Producer

- Director
- Key production personnel
- Actors
- Deals with labs, suppliers, etc.
- Promotional material
- Tie-in deals
- Financing commitments
- Distribution commitments

The more of these elements that you can pull together, the stronger your package will be. And the strength of the individual elements will determine how strongly your package can compete with packages that other filmmakers are trying to push. For example, if you live in a city that doesn't have a major film studio, you may be able to put together a package that includes the services of a production company that hitherto has produced only TV commercials or industrial films; this is fine as far as it goes, and it may be a step up from where you were before; it may even help you get your project financed on some level. But it pales next to a package that includes a production commitment from the De Laurentiis studio in North Carolina.

Notice that your package already contains the first two elements on the list, and they didn't even cost you much money. Your treatment and screenplay should be as polished as you can make them. If you have to rewrite while you're putting together your package, by all means do so. Make sure that before you try to pull key people into the package you're going to be able to show them the strongest possible story material.

You should also have already worked out your production budget and schedule. That way, people can see what they may be committing themselves to financially, and in terms of the time that you are asking them to invest. If you have the expertise, you will of course draw up your budget and schedule yourself; but otherwise, this expertise is part of what you will be after in lining up the services of others to become part of your package.

PULLING TOGETHER A PRODUCTION STAFF

If you intend to produce or direct your own movie, you already have another of the key elements of your package in place. But if you're going after a producer or director, you want to try to land the best one, not only for the job but to improve the marketability of your package. If you personally know someone who fills the bill and is willing to work with you, then you're in fine shape. If not, you've got to go out and find somebody. Hopefully, by this point you've done a good job of making contacts, as described in my previous chapter, so that you're not starting entirely from scratch.

If you're a relative unknown, naturally you're going to have an easier time obtaining commitments from people who are near your own professional level. But don't be afraid to "shoot for the moon." If your script is terrific, you may stand a chance of landing a commitment from a bigger name who just happens to love the concept and the way you handled it in your screenplay. And if you get lucky that way, all the other elements of your package may fall together much more easily.

I'll tell you why I say "may." I know a filmmaker from Pittsburgh, George Demick, who put together a package for the production of *Graveyard Shift,* a horror hit from Paramount. A few years before that, George was working as a movie projectionist and shooting his own little movies on video, when he wangled an invitation to the set of *Creepshow,* and met Stephen King. Somehow he talked King into letting him adapt King's story "Graveyard Shift" into a movie script. Demick then got John Esposito, a writer who was beginning to make some sales in Hollywood, to write the script on spec. Smooth sailing, right? Wrong. They had to fight and struggle for seven more years before the movie got made. But it *did* get made. And although he did not get to direct, George Demick did get a screen credit on a lesser level, along with the satisfaction of having implemented a big, successful project, and the possibility of using it as a springboard into other projects.

Sometimes it may behoove you to think beyond the producer or director positions when you're putting together your package. For instance, certain special effects specialists, such as Tom Savini or Rick Baker, have become such "stars," in the chiller/thriller genre that their presence on a project can encourage other key personnel to sign on, can lend clout with financing and distributing companies, and can help garner publicity and attract fans.

Here I am with some horror/film celebrities and Kirk Hammet from Metallica at the Orion Festival in Michigan.

At times it is advisable to make a deal with an entire production company to become part of your package. As an example, when George Romero, Russ Streiner, and I had our own film companies, we used to be interested in talking with anyone who had a good project that might come to us with full or partial financing. We could bring not only our expertise but also our company's resources to the project: shooting, lighting and editing gear, as well as studio space. These resources could be assigned a dollar value and made a part of the budget structure. And the company would receive an overhead payment *if* and when the project went into production.

OBTAINING COMMITMENTS FROM KEY ACTORS

Pretty much the same principles apply when you're going after casting commitments as when you're going after a producer, director, or other key production personnel. If you land a producer or director with substantial credits and experience, of course it becomes much easier to attract name or even star actors.

However, there are times when having part of your financing in place or, better yet, a commitment from a distributor, can swing some weight in enabling you to land a decent cast. It is up to you to wheel and deal with the packaging elements. If, for instance, the first time you approach a potential lead actor, you have only a tentative commitment from a name director, you can tell the actor about it honestly, hoping that the mere possibility of working with the name director will whet the actor's appetite. You can then tell the director that the key actor will probably come aboard once the director signs. By using one to interest the other, you might get both of them signed.

The reason that a commitment, even a tentative one, from a distributor is important is that actors are always fearful that their efforts will end up sitting on a shelf. Even if they believe strongly in a project and love the script, the movie may never be sold. Therefore, the presence of a distributor in the package maximizes the chance that the movie will be released and will act as a springboard for the actor's career.

109

If your package does not contain big production credentials, you will of course stand a small chance of landing name or semi-name actors. But this does not mean you should not try. The shoot-for-the-moon approach still applies. Also, remember that if you are doing a low-budget movie there are some actors whose careers have passed their zenith—and others whose careers may be about to take off—who might be available and just right to make an important contribution to your package. When I made *Midnight,* Independent-International Pictures helped me sign Lawrence Tierney to a major role. He had once been a big star and his name still meant a great deal in certain markets, and after my movie was released he landed roles in major productions, including *Arthur, Tough Guys Don't Dance* and *Reservoir Dogs* so his name still helps *Midnight* perform well domestically and abroad on home video.

Lawrence Tierney in *Midnight. Photo by John Russo.*

Even if you can't possibly obtain commitments from name actors, and you are resigned to using unknowns, it doesn't mean that they must be *complete* unknowns. What I mean is, they ought to at least have credentials, even if they're on a local or regional level. Look for actors who have won local awards and are well known in local theater. This can help you if you must resort to local, independent financing for your picture. But it also can help in your effort to land a distribution commitment of some type; any little nugget that bolsters the distributor's confidence in you is desirable, and one way of doing this is by showing him you are not going to work with total amateurs.

DEALS WITH LABS AND SUPPLIERS

Sometimes deferment deals with motion picture laboratories, art houses, animation houses, and other suppliers can be an important part of a production package. For example, a lab may commit to doing your film processing for you on a payment schedule that doesn't begin till six months after your first day of shooting. In order to do this, the lab has to believe strongly in the marketability of your project—that it will eventually get sold and reap returns sufficient to pay the deferred lab bill. Therefore, if you obtain such a deferment, it is an incentive for investors and other potential supporters on two grounds: one, it demonstrates that someone else has substantial faith in you; and, two, it lessens the initial capital outlay for your project and thus reduces the interest load that an investor may have to carry.

It also is sometimes possible to bring suppliers into a package as partners. In other words, they may contribute material and services in return for a profit participation. For instance, if your budget is $500,000 and you have figured on spending $100,000 on animation, perhaps the animation house will do the job you require in return for a 20 percent interest in your project. Again, it is up to you to wheel and deal with the appropriate suppliers in this way, always making shrewd decisions as to whether or not it behooves you to give up pieces of the pie. Remember, if you have $100,000 cash in the bank, and you happen to save *$20,000* on animation, you then have that cash to spend elsewhere. But if the $100,000 is in services, your $20,000 saving benefits only the animation company.

PROMOTIONAL MATERIAL

To make your pitch to those you would wish to become part of your movie package, it often helps very much to develop promotional material of various sorts, including brochures, posters, sample print ads, and TV and theatrical trailers.

To illustrate forcefully just how important this can be, George Romero told me that United Film Distributing came into the deal on his movie *Knightriders* on the strength of a *painting.* That's right. There was no script at the time, just a concept that George had about modern knights battling each other on motorcycles. The executives at United thought the idea was silly—till they saw the painting, which was done by one of George's friends, showing a knight wielding a mace, astride a souped-up motorcycle. This was so impressive that it landed a financing and distribution deal for the picture, and became the key art when it went into national release.

You should strive to develop similar material that can help you pitch your package. Often it can be done at low cost or even no cost, by you or any of your talented friends and associates.

With the easy and inexpensive availability of videotape gear nowadays, it is more feasible than ever to go so far as to produce a trailer for your proposed movie, which might involve getting some actors together and taping some sample scenes. This idea, carried a bit further, can turn into a twenty- or thirty-minute "short" of the movie itself. Sam Raimi, director of the hit movie *Darkman,* for Universal, got his start by making an 8-millimeter sample of his first horror movie, *The Evil Dead,* and using it to pitch investors.

Of course it is much easier to raise enough money to make a sample film of this type than it is to finance a full-scale production. Then the sample acts as a springboard to help you toward your larger goal.

TIE-IN DEALS

There are various kinds of tie-in deals that can contribute forcefully to a movie package, including novelization, sound track album, and merchandise licensing or manufacturing deals. With *Midnight,* for example, I wrote the screenplay first, but I was having trouble raising money to do the picture. So I novelized the screenplay, sold the novel to Pocket Books, and it became a best seller. The cover art was excellent, so now I had that to show when I pitched the screenplay. It helped me land a financing and distribution deal with Independent-International Pictures, and once I had the distributor lined up, I was able to get Traque Records to commit to releasing a sound track album.

Of course high-concept mega-budget movies like *Batman* are laughably easy to merchandise. But low-budget movies can often achieve considerable success in this area, too.

Articles that can be merchandised as movie tie-ins include tee shirts, bumper stickers, character masks, trading cards, buttons, comic books, toys, etc., etc. They are limited only by the imagination of the would-be merchandiser and the scope and style of the movie in question.

FINANCING AND DISTRIBUTION COMMITMENTS

Commitments for the financing and distribution of your picture are some of the most persuasive elements of your package, and often the hardest to achieve. To make it easier, bear in mind that you don't necessarily need to have a commitment for *all* the money, and you don't need to have an iron-clad distribution commitment either. Any little "plus" in these areas can help boost your project off the ground.

For instance, there are arrangements that are based on "contingent" financing: you might try to get one party to commit to putting up half the money, provided another party puts up the other half. The *Midnight* deal was worked that way between Independent-International Pictures and a private investor lined up by my producer. Often similar arrangements are made between foreign and domestic distributors, or between theatrical and video distributors, etc., etc. The percentages of ownership in the picture or the distribution rights in the various territories are parceled out between the financing parties in proportion to their respective contributions.

Sometimes a distributor will make a full or partial "negative pickup" deal. This means that, if he thinks your project has potential, he may agree to distribution terms in advance, including an amount of cash he will pay you upon delivery of a satisfactory finished movie. You can sometimes borrow money against the distributor's contract or letter of credit, and use this money to go into production. When I first wrote *The Majorettes,* I landed a negative pickup deal from Group One Films, in which Group One agreed to pay half of the cost of the production upon delivery of the negative. This enabled me to land private investment for all of the production budget, since the investors knew they'd be at risk only for half of the money they were putting up. (Unfortunately, as I mentioned earlier, one of the investors had to pull out for personal reasons, and the project didn't go forward till much later.)

Certain wheeler-dealers in the biz will sometimes go to a foreign distributor and tell him half the money is already lined up in the United States, and go to a U.S. distributor and tell him half

114

the money is lined up overseas, when none of the money is actually lined up anywhere. But if one of these parties makes a commitment based on this false information, then part of the lie turns "true" and the other party might tumble. Or some new party might come into the game. And the wheeler-dealer keeps on playing both ends against the middle.

However, most experienced producers and distributors are highly familiar with this scam, and so they're not such easy marks. I'd advise you not to try it. Instead, work hard and play all the legitimate angles to give your package an honest glitter that can help bring it to the silver screen.

12
Staying Power

ONCE YOU SUCCEED in packaging and producing a string of movies, you've got it made, right? Now you can make any movie you want to, right?

Wrong on both counts.

Even though you may have some substantial credits under your belt, you'll still be fighting some of the same battles that you fought before. And one basic fact will still be the same: you can make any movie you can *pay* for—or can talk somebody else into paying for. Superstars like Steven Spielberg and Oliver Stone still have to pitch the studios to land the megabuck financing and distribution deals they require for their projects, and your situation won't be much different from theirs, even if *you* become a superstar.

Once you've had a taste of success, you want more. You want to keep on being able to work in the biz. And you should be able to. However, although pitching people and landing their support becomes easier once you have a bit of a track record, it still requires persistence and hard work. In this chapter I want to discuss some specific ways of building upon your accomplishments and giving yourself staying power.

MANUFACTURING AND UTILIZING PUBLICITY

When you have a movie in any stage of production, it's a golden opportunity to reap publicity and make contacts. Get out publicity releases at every milestone. Announce the key stages in the progress of your project and turn them into hooks for news

116

articles. When you sew up your financing, hold your first casting call, sign your producer or director, finalize your cast, or land a star, it's a perfect time to send out a release. Also when you start the camera rolling, complete filming, ice a distribution deal, etc., etc.

Send the releases to newspapers, magazines, radio and TV stations. Once you stir things up, your production will become a hot item, and additional publicity will fall into your lap. You can do a lot of publicity work on your own just by devoting a bit of energy to it, but if you're too jammed, you will want to hire a publicist—particularly if there's money for a unit publicist in your production budget.

When we remade *Night of the Living Dead*, we had an excellent unit publicist, Joyce Wagner, who was hired by 21st Century Films and sent from Los Angeles to work for six weeks at our movie location, an abandoned farm in Pennsylvania. Joyce got *The Wall Street Journal* to run a front page article titled, "A Town Becomes Alive with Zombies Who Act a Little," and once we had gotten coverage in the *Journal*, everybody wanted to jump on the bandwagon. In short order, feature stories on us were run by the *Los Angeles Times, New York Times, Star, Premiere, Cinefantastique, First Edition, Entertainment Tonight*, and so on— a tremendous amount of national exposure. On my own, I wouldn't have imagined that *The Wall Street Journal* (with its prestigious reputation in business and finance) might run a front-page article on the production of a horror movie, or that once it did, the whole thing would snowball that way. Joyce Wagner's expertise is what made it happen.

Any time you have a movie released, a book published, a deal signed, you've got another occasion to reap publicity. When articles appear about me or my books or movies, I send copies to agents, editors, publishers, producers, and distributors that I am currently working with or hope to work with in the future. This encourages them to continue to see me as a marketable commodity, and gives them ammunition for persuading others to see me the same way.

I also frequently participate in enterprises mainly for their promotional rather than their money-earning value. For instance, some years ago I produced five forty-minute videos on various aspects of the horror movie business. I knew they wouldn't earn me as much as I could make by producing a feature film, but the time investment was minimal by comparison, and the tapes were to be widely advertised and distributed, so I did them for the publicity value. Since clips of five of my movies appeared in the videos, the movies got some great exposure, too, which I figured would boost their home video sales.

Anything you do that gets your name and your work in front of the public helps build your credentials and your marketability. If you write a book, appear as a guest speaker at a festival, or teach a seminar to young filmmakers still in college, you will meet fans and make contacts.

On a *Heartstopper* location.

Sometimes you can generate publicity even when you don't have a current project to use as a hook. In between my last two movie projects, I wrote an article on whether or not movie violence helps cause violence in real life, submitted it to *Newsweek,* and they printed it. Paid me for it, too. But I would have done it without pay, just for the chance of being read by the millions of people who buy *Newsweek.* The article generated such intense interest that I appeared on thirty radio and TV shows around the country to discuss movie violence versus real violence.

Although I enjoy meeting people, I am not overly fond of doing publicity. It's more fun to just go out and have a nice meal and some good conversation with close friends, in private. But publicity is an essential part of the biz. Our careers thrive on it. If you have two directors of equal ability and comparable credits, the one who's the most famous is more marketable—and packageable. In fact, even if a name director has a string of box-office flops, he can generally get hired again by somebody who will persuade himself that the director will generate substantial publicity and draw at least a fair number of fans—as opposed to some other director who will possibly do a good job but attract attention from nobody.

I know directors—some of them big names—who refuse to do publicity unless forced into it contractually. They say that their work speaks for itself, and that's all the publicity they need. But I believe they're doing a disservice not only to themselves but to the other people who work hard on their movies and have a huge stake in their success. They forget how they got there in the first place. And so they're likely to be just as easily forgotten when they fall.

So, even if you're basically a shy person, strive to be at least a little bit publicity conscious. Remember that you did not get to the top totally on your own. Be nice to the media people and the fans. And may your career continue to prosper.

STRIKING WHILE YOU'RE HOT

Many people make the mistake of putting on a big push to land a good agent, a big project, a top-notch contract just as they have a new picture coming out. They figure that's when they'll be hot because of the big publicity blitz. So that's when they'll have the best chance of staying in the limelight and capitalizing on it in a big way.

Sounds like a good strategy. So what's wrong with it?

Nothing. As long as the picture is a smash.

But what if it flops?

It sinks out of sight after two weeks in the theaters, and nobody associated with it is hot anymore.

The time to put on the big push is during the making of a movie, not when it's about to go into release. When you're already on a major gig—one that everybody feels is full of potential—you could be the hottest that you'll ever get. Because if the movie comes out and fails to fulfill its potential nobody will want to touch you with a ten-foot pole. It might not even be your fault that the thing flopped. But the sinking ship will carry you under with it, and it might be a while before you can fight your way back up to the surface.

Most (in fact, practically all) deals take months in the negotiating. So, make sure your agent has a project to sell while you're working on the current one. Then you may be able to go directly into another major production, even if the worst happens. And if the one you're working on now turns out to be a blockbuster, don't worry. Now you'll *really* be bankable.

Just as it's good timing to try to land new gigs while you already have a movie in production, it's also very often smart to try to sell the movie itself while it's being made, if it doesn't already have a distributor. Many movies seem to have "hit" written all over them—till they get into the theaters. When you offer a film to a distributor during the production period, he's buying the glitter, the potential. His imagination might make him more excited than the reality of the finished product ever could. So that's when you should go after your negative pickup deal. In fact, you might want to go after the negative pickup on *that* picture, plus a contract to produce a two- or three-picture package.

That way, you'll still be working, no matter what happens at the box office.

USING A SCATTERGUN APPROACH

Another mistake that many people make is to get a deal in the works and pursue that deal hot and heavy, to the exclusion of all others.

But a hundred deals collapse in this business for every one that ever amounts to anything.

So you always need to have lots of things on the fire and keep stoking those fires and starting new ones. That way, when somebody throws water on one of the fires, you still have some hope of staying warm.

Same thing with making contacts. If everyone who promised to do something actually did it, I'd have gotten to where I am now fifteen years sooner. The time that you waste in this business finding out who's honest and reliable and actually capable is often enough to kill you before you can get off the ground.

Therefore, when you have a deal that looks like it's going to come through, a movie that looks like it's just about to be given a green light, don't ever completely bank on it. Don't neglect it, but find a way to keep on pursuing all your other interests.

And when you're looking for new contacts, new people to agent or package or promote you or your projects, use a scattergun approach. Knock as many ducks as you can out of the sky. Then pull them in and examine them closely. Stay cheerful and open. But be careful till you find out who can be trusted to work hard and keep promises.

EMPLOYING UNORTHODOX STRATEGIES

There are times when your career might bog down and you can't figure a way to get it moving again. None of the conventional methods seem to be working for you. Your agent doesn't return your phone calls, your latest book outline didn't interest your editor, nobody wants to buy any of your screenplays or hire you to produce or direct a movie.

Now may be the time for unconventional warfare. Unorthodox strategies. Something that might light a bomb under your butt—or somebody else's.

One of the most exciting coups I ever heard of was pulled off by Michael Montgomery, who wrote *Eye of the Tiger,* starring Gary Busey. Before this project got made, Montgomery had been selling TV—movie scripts and had some minor credits on theatrical movies, but he felt his career was bogging down terribly. According to *Writer's Digest,* he fired his agent one day and sent out an "action package" —three of his screenplays, a sample video, and a poster—to one hundred independent producers. He ended up getting a production company to finance two of the projects, *Eye of the Tiger* and *Rolling Vengeance.*

The movie business is in many ways like the carny business. The glory belongs to the huckster, the pitchman, the entrepreneur. The guy who finds the best way to skin the cat—or at least a way that works. All the crazy success stories charm and delight us. We love hearing how Stallone held out till he got to play Rocky, how Spike Lee made *She's Gotta Have It* on crumpled dollar bills sent to him by his aunts and uncles and college alumni, how Robert Townsend paid for *The Hollywood Shuffle* on his credit cards.

Entertainment Weekly ran a titillating article about two young filmmakers, Tony Elwood and Tony Locklear, who shot a movie called *Killer!* on 8-millimeter film and transferred it to video cassette for release and made $40,000

So, there are all kinds of ways to skin the cat, whether you're trying to get your start or keep your career rolling. I already told you how the ticking black clocks were used to stir up a bidding war for *The Ticking Man.*

While was involved with a project called *Body Bags,* and my agent sent out the script, by Billy Brown and Dan Angel, in—what else?—little body bags.

Part IV
HEARTSTOPPER—
AN OBJECT LESSON

"Horror films have made a dramatic comeback at the U.S. box office over the past two years, and domestic production (spurred by home video) has reached record levels."

— Variety

"The resources are there as never before. The new companies are in place, the support groups aiding and abetting, the audience waiting. *Lights, camera, action . . .*"

— Newsweek

AUTHOR'S NOTE: The above quotes were used to convince people they should invest in Heartstopper, *which eventually got funded.*

13

Pitching a Hot Concept

NOW THAT THE groundwork has been laid, and our mutual understanding of the artistic and economic aspects of movie-making has been enhanced, I think we are ready for an "object lesson"—a step-by-step study, in illuminating detail, of a specific project, from concept to screen. Our object of study is my novel *The Awakening* and the movie that was made from it under a revised title, *Heartstopper.* I wrote the screenplay and directed the movie. Since this project went all the way from book proposal to novel to screenplay to finished motion picture, it dramatizes with firsthand impact all the lessons taught in this book.

THE LIGHT BULB LIGHTS UP

First let's set the scene. It was March of 1981, and I was in the throes of heavy negotiations with Fox Films over the purchase of *Return of the Living Dead.* We expected the deal to go through and produce a lot of cash, but as we all know by now, nothing in the biz is absolutely sure. My movie *Midnight* was just about to go into distribution through Independent-International, and I was trying to figure out what kind of movie I should try to do next. Meanwhile, I had just fulfilled a three-book contract with Pocket Books by delivering the manuscript of my novel *Bloodsisters,* and I was anxious to get another book contract going with Pocket. So it was natural for me to be trying to think of something that could be a book *and* a movie, and hopefully kill two birds with one stone.

The last five novels and three movies I had done did not have anything to do with the supernatural, and I was in the mood to try to do something in that vein, if I could find the right twist. At the same time, some seemingly conflicting images were swirling around in my brain. I was thinking a lot about the colonial period of American history because I had recently been to Philadelphia to see the Tall Ships come in—the eighteenth-century schooners and frigates that are maintained by the navies of various countries around the world—and I've always been enthralled by history anyway. I was also thinking quite a bit about the terrible rise in homicide statistics in America, and the inordinate number of mass murderers and serial killers making headlines. And I was thinking that I had never done a vampire movie, and maybe I could come up with a way of revitalizing the vampire myth, as we had done to the zombie myth when we made *Night of the Living Dead.* I thought perhaps one way of doing this would be to somehow create a *likable* vampire.

Suddenly, one day at my office, the light bulb lit up. It popped into my head that I could do a story about a reluctant vampire who follows a serial killer around to live off his victims, so that he won't have to kill anyone himself. Thus, we would have a symbiotic relationship. But one full of agony and conflict. The vampire, although he does not kill, must face the moral dilemma of doing nothing to stop the serial killer. While the serial killer, a psychopath to begin with, would be envious and desirous of the vampire's occult powers.

It then occurred to me that in colonial times bloodletting was practiced by surgeons to "cure" various ailments. What if my vampire was a surgeon, hanged as a sorcerer for experimenting with human blood, and buried with a stake in his heart, etc.—but somehow the mumbo-jumbo doesn't work, and he comes back to life in the twentieth century? And now he really *does* have a blood craving. And he doesn't want to lose his humanity. He doesn't want to have this second life if he has to live it as some kind of monster.

With all these thoughts swimming in my head and getting me excited, I phoned my editor, Liza Hatcher. At first she said, "Oh, no, don't do a vampire book. We're already doing a big vampire book! But then I explained my premise, and she said, "Oh, that's terrific—I love *that*. I'd probably buy it, but of course first I'd have to see an outline." Well, that's all I needed to hear to light a fire under me. I didn't dwell on the fact that Pocket Books was "already doing a big vampire book." Liza didn't say what the book *was* and I didn't ask—and later it turned out to cause me some unforeseen problems.

RESEARCHING MY MATERIAL

Before I could develop an outline that might ice the sale, I had tons of research to do. I wanted to completely familiarize myself with the colonial period and build an intricately believable personal history for my vampire character, Benjamin Latham. I must have read twenty or thirty books on the period, taking notes all the while. Included were books on colonial medicine, because Benjamin was going to be a doctor, and I had to know what *he* would know. I also read modern medical books to discover things about human blood that might provide good anecdotes or story angles.

Luckily, the area where I live—the Pittsburgh area—was a vital part of colonial and Revolutionary history, and nearby there were numerous historical sites that I could explore, including old inns, forts, courthouses, jails, etc., etc. In downtown Pittsburgh I revisited the Fort Pitt reconstruction and interviewed the curator of the Fort Pitt Museum. I happened to have a friend who was a member of the Royal American Regiment, the troop of enthusiasts who reenact the drills and maneuvers of the colonial soldiers who occupied Fort Pitt 250 years ago, and so I already knew quite a bit about the regiment and thought it could possibly fit into my story.

A group of modern people in authentic colonial garb acting out a scene from *Heartstopper*.

While researching at the Fort Pitt Museum, it struck me that perhaps there should be a lovely young woman who worked at the fort—and Benjamin should fall in love with her. He could be drawn to this site after his "resurrection" because it was such a strong connection with his past—in fact, it could be the place where he was hanged.

I continued to read books and articles about serial killers and mass murderers, too. I needed to know how this kind of person would think, plan, and act.

This was just the beginning of my research. As story and characterization points came into my mind, and as the material began to shape itself into a rough outline, there were still more books to read, places to visit and investigate, and people to interview.

DEVELOPING MY OUTLINE

I knew the outline had to be pretty good, or else Liza Hatcher might change her mind about buying it. After all, she had mentioned that other vampire book already in production.

Also, I wanted to impress my literary agent, Al Zuckerman of Writers House, Inc. I had gone ahead and made the pitch for this project without Al's help, which was fine at this stage, but he might be rubbed the wrong way in the end if the outline failed to strike him as the kind of raw material from which an excellent novel might spring. To observe protocol and fully enlist Al as part of my team, I intended to submit the finished outline to him first, and then let him fulfill his role as agent by submitting it to Liza and negotiating the deal.

I don't think we need to delve into the excruciating details of how I went about inventing my characters and story line. I used essentially the same methods as described in Part II, where *Voodoo Dawn* served to illustrate my techniques. Along the way, I came up with five principal characters who would hopefully interact powerfully through a complicated narrative that would carry the reader from colonial times to modern Pittsburgh, and then to Williamsburg, Philadelphia, and London. The five characters were:

Benjamin Latham. A surgeon. His neighbors hate him because he was a Tory during the Revolutionary War. They put him on trial for sorcery, accusing him of drinking human blood. An intelligent, charismatic man, he tries to defend himself by evoking the principles of free scientific inquiry. But they hang him, drive a stake in his heart, and bury him at a crossroad with a garlic necklace around his throat. However, he doesn't die. Somehow their mumbo-jumbo works backward, and he comes back to life two hundred years later. When he sees the mess we're in, he's sure the Tories were right—we should've remained part of the British Empire. Through his eyes we observe the ironic differences between what young America thought she could become and what

131

she actually has become. Benjamin is not only a vampire who must acclimate himself to the twentieth century—he is a vampire with a social conscience.

Matthew Latham. Benjamin's descendant, a vicious serial killer. Unlike Benjamin, he kills because he wants to, not because he *has* to. He is the personification of evil. He envies and wishes to acquire Benjamin's "special powers"—so he can continue to kill with impunity.

Lenora Clayton. A beautiful young woman who is working at Old Fort Pitt as an assistant curator while she earns her doctorate (in history) at the University of Pittsburgh. She falls in love with Benjamin and teaches him "the ropes." But, unbeknownst to both of them at first, his lovemaking is transforming her into a creature just like *him.*

When I brought my vampire novel to the screen, Benjamin Latham was played by young, handsome Kevin Kindlin. *Photo by Gary Di Bartolomeo, used by permission of Thinker Productions, Inc.*

Andy Bonner. A homeless derelict. The first friend Benjamin makes. Benjamin pretends to have amnesia to explain why he "can't remember" anything about modern life, and Andy takes him under his wing, showing him how to land hobo-like jobs, panhandle, get a room at the YMCA, etc.

Lieutenant Ronald Vargo. A state trooper, a homicide detective who gets on Benjamin's trail shortly after Benjamin comes back from the dead. This happens when a little girl named Stephanie Kamin is found dead in her sandbox—and the police lab proves that her death was caused by someone licking her cut finger. Amazingly, the killer had *poisonous saliva.* But Vargo does not really believe this at first—he thinks the lab must've made a mistake. His marriage a wreck ever since the murder of his own little girl a few years ago by an unknown assailant, he fanatically pursues the killer of little Stephanie Kamin, bent on making sure that the killer dies before he can be set free by some bleeding-heart judge or jury.

Note that at some point while I was developing my story, I had hit on the idea of *poisonous saliva* for my vampire. I had never heard of this being used before. It was a way for Benjamin to kill the little girl *by accident.* She cuts herself, he has an irresistible urge to taste the blood, and the little girl dies. A great shock for him and the reader! Now he knows that the same magic that brought him back to life has a hideous aspect. And he's not to blame. Even though he has done something horrible, we can still empathize with him as he tries to deal with his blood craving.

Now, the way he ends up dealing with it—just so you understand the story well enough to follow along with me at this point—is that he becomes a sort of vampire "Equalizer." He decides that if he must have this blood craving, he will only go after the evil ones in our society—of which there are plenty, by his lights. After her transformation is complete, Lenora takes her first blood—from Matthew. Then the novel ends with her and Benjamin vowing to be of service to all of mankind for the rest of their lives—which are possibly eternal.

133

MY AGENT'S REACTION TO THE OUTLINE

Well, I had a very complex story here (although the full force of its complexity wouldn't hit me till I actually started to write the novel). The outline was thirty pages long. I sent it to Al Zuckerman and hoped he would like it well enough to feel comfortable about submitting it to Liza Hatcher.

It took him four weeks to respond. Not knowing whether acceptance or rejection is to be your fate is always hard to take, and drives writers up the wall, but I knew better than to pester. Agents are generally overworked and have many clients to deal with. Finally I got a long letter. Just so you can see how a good agent works with a writer, here are some cogent excerpts:

". . . the story and materials here have lovely potential, and I think you could make them into a strong novel.

"My main suggestion has to do with focus and thrust . . . It's a horror novel after all; and I think that these work best when you have gradually mounting horror from one character's point of view .... The strongest candidate for that position . . . is Lenora. Benjamin runs a close second.

"Perhaps Matthew halfway through the book or so could kidnap her, torture her, etc. In the end she will be rescued by Benjamin, with the twist that she too becomes a vampire.

" . . . the story works best when the principals are involved with one another; and the principals which promise to be good continuing characters are Benjamin, Lenora, Matthew and Vargo.

"Andy Bonner takes up a lot of space in the story which might be better used with Lenora. And with Vargo. In fact, I would suggest that Vargo and Benjamin encounter each other in some way . . . Benjamin would have to get away . . . but I think that the face-to-face confrontation could build even greater tension and excitement than you have now.

"The beginning of the novel worries me somewhat. Usually an author has to establish some sort of very mundane reality before weird and occult elements can be introduced. Stephen King invariably has fifty or so pages before he introduces any fantasy element, and I think that's not a bad rule to follow . . .

"I'm a bit worried about all the confrontation between the man from another period who suddenly arrives at the present . . . it's fine as long as you use it within tight confines, strong scenes between the major characters; but it works a lot less well when you have a character wandering around and gaping at modern civilization.

"Still and all, John, I'm pleased, and I'm sending a copy over to Liza Hatcher for her reactions."

I received Al's letter in May of 1981. It took four months before I heard anything more from either him or Liza. Midway through this frustrating waiting period, I started making phone calls and sending inquiries—but I got little or no response, till finally Liza told me on the phone that she had turned my outline over to the editor-in-chief, and when he had read it she would get back to me and Al.

Finally, in late August, the word came down. I could stop worrying. My outline had not only landed me a deal on my proposed vampire novel, it had landed me another three-book contract with a handsome advance upon signing.

NOTE: You will find sample pages from the outline, the novel manuscript, and the *Heartstopper* screenplay in the Appendix.

14

Developing the Thirty-page Outline into a Five-hundred-page Novel

IN WRITING THE novel, I intended to keep in mind the comments that Al Zuckerman had made in his letter. Liza Hatcher liked the outline pretty much the way it was, and did not think she needed to give me any suggestions.

The outline had started with Benjamin Latham at age fifty-five in the years immediately following the Revolutionary War. Still harboring his Tory sentiments, he takes a sarcastic view of the thirteen new "United States." Because of his medical experiments, he is put on trial for witchcraft. After the trial, he's hanged and so on. His body molders for 200 years. In the words of the outline, "The cloves of garlic slowly turn to green, powdery mold and disintegrate to dust. The coffin becomes waterlogged and rots to pieces. The stake decays and falls through its cage of bone." Then new flesh grows onto Benjamin's skeleton, and he is reshaped into the image of himself as a young man. But as yet he is not alive, and cannot rise from his grave. The crossroad (in the shape of the Holy Cross) remains a guardian against the "vampire's" rebirth . . .

CHANGING THE BEGINNING

Often in making an outline that can *sell* a project, you have to be more "up front" with your story material than you ought to be in writing the novel or screenplay. The reason for this is that the editor (buyer) must be able to see right away what your premise is and what you intend to do with it. Slow, subtle development is not truly possible in the short space of an outline, and would not get the main and hopefully unique story points across forcefully enough to effect a sale.

This also has its downside, of course. The agent or editor might think that the material is too blatant and might not wholly believe in your ability to develop it properly. If you have proven yourself through your past work, and if you have a mutually respectful relationship with your editor and agent, the job of convincing them becomes much easier. And it is why established writers can sell from outlines, while unpublished writers cannot. The agent or editor requires much stronger proof from an unpublished writer.

I kept thinking about the fact that Al Zuckerman had suggested that I shouldn't get into anything supernatural till I was fifty or sixty pages into my story. I could comply by establishing Benjamin's life in the post-Revolutionary period at considerable length before having him get caught drinking blood. But this would be an awfully slow beginning. And besides, I wanted the focus of the novel to be in *modern* times, not colonial. Therefore, the minute details of Benjamin's past life weren't all that germane.

However, I still wanted those details to have as much impact as possible. So, I decided to change the time of Benjamin's trial and hanging from after the Revolution to right during the Revolutionary War—a much more dramatic time for these events to take place.

Then I made the more important decision to reveal Benjamin's past only through reminiscences later in the novel, rather than taking the chance of bogging the reader down in the early chapters. I jumped right into the scene of the crossroad being destroyed by a bulldozer (because of construction of a new shopping center), and right away Benjamin comes out of his grave. This violated Al's precept about not having anything supernatural happen till fifty pages into the story. But my way around this was to not let the reader know for sure that something supernatural really *had* occurred. And Benjamin didn't know either. He thinks the noose must not have broken his neck—somehow the shock must have put him in a trancelike state. He knows about the tricks of the Indian fakirs, and has read stories in his medical texts about people being buried alive, and he figures something like this must have happened to him. But then he spots the bulldozer—a huge metallic monster seemingly from another world—and he doesn't know if he's on earth or in hell. Before he can do much thinking about it, the men on the construction site spot him standing there nude, and they begin to yell and give chase. Benjamin runs for his life. Eventually he eludes them, and finds himself near a suburban housing development, where little Stephanie Kamin is playing in her sandbox.

But in writing the novel a new idea occurred to me, and instead of going directly into Stephanie's death scene, I gave Benjamin time, while he was hiding in the woods from the men who were chasing him, to examine his new body. He sees how taut and muscular he is, instead of old and flabby. He feels the back of his head, and finds no bald spot. But what really shocks him is—he has no navel. Why? He begins to accept that somehow he has been born into a new life, born of the earth itself and not born of woman—that's why he needed no navel, no umbilical cord connecting him to a mother of flesh and blood.

By this time, I was twenty pages or so into the manuscript—not the fifty pages that Al had suggested, but yet the pace of the supernatural revelations had a nice feel; I wasn't spilling them all at once; the bulk of them were still in store. Furthermore, the novel had opened quite powerfully, I felt, and the reader was being pulled along by a great deal of intrigue.

Benjamin, freshly resurrected from his grave, is stunned when he first glimpses modern Pittsburgh with its shiny steel bridges and skyscrapers. *Photo by Gary Di Bartolomeo/ used by permission of Thinker Productions, Inc.*

The fact that Benjamin had been discovered and was being chased—plus the fact that Lieutenant Vargo soon got on his trail after the death of the little girl in the sandbox—gave a heavy dose of suspense to the story in the early going, created deep interest in Benjamin as a protagonist, and made the reader ready to be entertained by his initial observations about modern life—which I intentionally tried to treat humorously and ironically—peppering them throughout the sequences where he is on the run from the police and manages to hitch a ride—his first car ride!—into downtown Pittsburgh.

REVAMPING THE CHARACTERS AND PLOT

I thought that Al Zuckerman's suggestion about cutting down the Andy Bonner character was a good one, and I wanted to do something about it. In the outline, Andy got killed three quarters of the way through the story by some street punks. Then Benjamin decided to hunt down the street punks one by one, so he could satisfy his blood craving while also meting out justice and taking his revenge.

Whereas the street punks were fairly generic in the outline, I now gave them strikingly distinct personalities. And I had them attack Benjamin on his first day in Pittsburgh—forcing Benjamin to kill one of them—Elijah Alford—in a parking garage. Thus, Elijah is Benjamin's first intentional kill. He drinks Elijah's blood, and the coroner's discovery that the same poisonous saliva that killed Stephanie Kamin is also present in Elijah's wounds causes Lieutenant Vargo to get hotter on Benjamin's trail.

Later, when the street punks kill Andy Bonner, they now have a motive—to get even with Benjamin for the murder of Elijah. These characters are therefore operating with more rhyme and reason and in closer relationship to Benjamin than I had originally conceived. I had them kill Andy Bonner much earlier in the novel, too. That solved the problem Al Zuckerman had pointed out, enabling me to focus sharper and sooner on the relationship between Benjamin and Lenora.

I continued doing research as I needed more information to flesh in story points, and I did more interviews, too. For instance, I interviewed a Pittsburgh coroner to gain insights into morgue procedures and blood analysis, and I interviewed a Pennsylvania state trooper to get accurate information on police procedures and fully develop the Vargo character.

With Vargo in close pursuit all the while, Benjamin and Lenora travel to Williamsburg, Virginia, and then to Philadelphia, so Benjamin can trace his family tree. He's trying to learn all he can about his descendants (he tells Lenora they're his "ancestors") in hopes of discovering whether any of them had a craving for blood, or if they learned how to cure it. So, I had to invent an entire lineage for Benjamin and the relatives he had during Revolutionary times; all of this had to be researched and made plausible, and it required a trip to Williamsburg, where the colonial part of the city has been reconstructed.

Eventually Benjamin and Lenora discover that he has a descendant, Matthew Latham, still alive in Philadelphia. In the outline, Benjamin was going to encounter Matthew in New York, but I changed it to Philadelphia to take advantage of my knowledge of the Tall Ships, and also because Philadelphia was the site of the signing of the Declaration of Independence, the First Continental Congress, the home of Benjamin Franklin, etc., etc.—a milieu echoing with reverberations of Benjamin Latham's past life. Here he begins to develop his occult powers even further, and makes some shocking discoveries about his descendant. In the words of the outline:

"In his attempt to locate Matthew, Benjamin is aided by a sort of ESP, a new power that has accrued to him in his supernatural development. He doesn't want to make a direct approach for fear of frightening Matthew . . . so he studies the man from a distance, following him, observing him, learning his habits and lifestyle.

"It surprises Benjamin to find out that Matthew is also following someone when he goes out at night—a beautiful young woman who works at an advertising agency. One night, while Benjamin is watching from a hiding place, Matthew rapes and kills the young woman, then flees the scene. Benjamin stays long enough to drink some of the woman's blood.

"It turns out that Matthew Latham is the killer-rapist who has been terrorizing the city. In the past year, he has claimed fourteen victims. Having made this shocking discovery, Benjamin wonders: Is Matthew a vampire? Was the curse passed on to all the Latham line? But no, this can't be so. Matthew didn't drink any of his victim's blood. If he is a beast, he is another sort of beast entirely: a human one; a product of this strange, dehumanizing twentieth-century culture."

Now, in writing the novel, I had a new idea—I did not let Matthew get away unpunished for this killing. Instead, the young woman, Janice Ridenour, sprays him with Mace and then shoots him twice with a purse pistol before she dies. This brings Benjamin and Matthew closer together right away—because, after drinking Janice's blood, Benjamin helps his badly wounded descendant to escape, and brings him back to his apartment. Here he operates on Matthew—a gruesomely ironic scene—where Benjamin extracts the bullets, using tools and methods similar to those he used in his first lifetime, when he was a colonial surgeon.

Lenora helps in this operation. And here we see for the first time her full acceptance of what Benjamin is. We also see that she is fascinated, even attracted, by the blood that she helps to swab from Matthew's wounds.

During his recuperation, Matthew discovers that Lenora is becoming like Benjamin, and he envies the transformation. This is the beginning of the serial killer's obsession with his ancestor's occult powers—an obsession that eventually is going to be his downfall.

THE NOVEL'S MIXED FATE

During the writing of this novel, the deal on *Return of the Living Dead* was finalized, and got me in really good financial shape. So I was able to take my time and put everything I had into the writing. I make this point because many people don't realize to what extent the momentum and direction of a writer's career depend on early financial success. James Michener once said that having a smash hit early in his career meant that he could afford to take six or seven years researching and writing his next book to make sure it could be considered "big and important"—a viable candidate for the best-seller lists. He went on to say that writers who never gain that kind of freedom always have to struggle, not only to sell projects but to be able to invest enough time and effort to maximize the projects' potential. Usually they can't pull it off, simply because they're always bogged down, working hard just to stay alive and pay the bills.

Well, in the case of my vampire novel, I had the time, thanks to the successful sale of another project. And I'm happier with this novel than with most of the many others I have had published. But even though I was satisfied with it, and it had entertained me while I was writing it, there was no guarantee that the finished product was going to entertain my editor. I had another agonizing wait for Liza Hatcher to read and report on the manuscript. Finally, I got a phone call from her that tremendously lifted my spirits. "John," she said, in bubbly, excited tones, "I just had to call and tell you that I really *love* your book! I'm reading it at home, and I'm forgetting to think critically. I'm just so caught up in enjoying it, I'm forgetting you're even one of my authors. I'm reading it like it's already a published book!"

She went on to make a slew of favorable comments. She didn't want anything changed. She loved it just the way it was. She said that the editor-in-chief at Pocket had wanted me to write a big

143

book, and this one was *it* as far as she was concerned—it more than justified the new three-book contract.

Her enthusiasm continued to run high all through the editorial and production stages of the novel, during which time we had to come up with a new title because nobody seemed to like my working title, *The Cross Road.* I didn't like it very much myself. I thought of *The Awakening,* but there was a movie with that same title, a movie about mummies and ancient curses, starring Charlton Heston. I submitted a few alternative title suggestions to Liza Hatcher. But about a month later she surprised me by announcing that the people at Pocket were sticking with *The Awakening,* even though I had said it might not be such a good idea. I was worried that the public would mistake it for a tie-in with the Charlton Heston movie, which had turned out to be a turkey. If you're going to appear to rip off somebody else's title, you might as well at least pick a winner.

Well, anyway, the publication date of *The Awakening* was set for April 1983, and I anxiously looked forward to seeing the novel on the stands. When I did finally see it, I was shocked. Suddenly I got hit with the full force of what Liza had meant when she mentioned that other "big vampire book." It was *The Hunger.* In every bookstore the racks were *loaded* with the paperback version of Whitley Streiber's hardcover best seller, its publication timed to tie in with the mammoth national release of the movie, starring David Bowie and Catherine Deneuve. My book was completely overpowered, lucky to occupy a mere slot or two next to these myriads of copies of *The Hunger.*

This made me puzzled and upset. I wondered how Pocket could be so stupid as to release my vampire book in the same month as this "other vampire book," forcing mine to compete with their own blockbuster. In retrospect, I suppose that instead of shelling out money to promote my book, the folks at Pocket were

144

going after whatever "rub-off" sales I could get based on *The Hunger's* supposed priming of the market for vampire novels.

Even though my editor believed strongly in *The Awakening,* it had apparently fallen victim to the in-house jockeying for promotional dollars, which is battle number two in the book-writing business. First you fight to get it published, then you fight to get it promoted. If I'd gotten the chance to have any input on this matter, I would've said, "All right, but even if you're not going to promote it, don't cut its head off. Hold up for five or six months on the publication of my book, instead of making it go head to head with your own major release."

The Awakening still sold pretty well, and it got excellent reviews. Although it did not become a best seller, I felt that it probably could have, if it had been properly distributed and promoted. I swallowed the disappointment, and continued working on other projects, hoping that someday I could make the book into a movie.

Turn the page and see how it eventually happened.

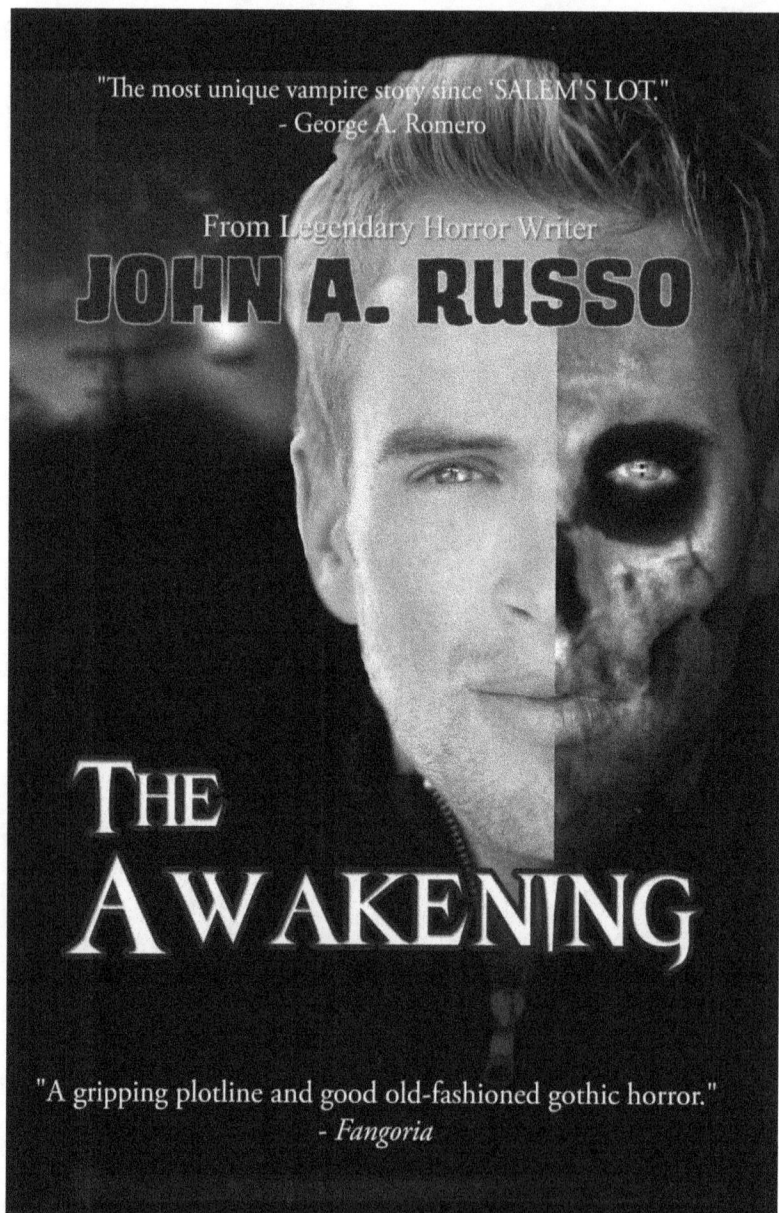

"The most unique vampire story since 'SALEM'S LOT."
- George A. Romero

From Legendary Horror Writer
JOHN A. RUSSO

THE
AWAKENING

"A gripping plotline and good old-fashioned gothic horror."
- *Fangoria*

The Awakening received new life when it was picked up for publication once again, this time by Burning Bulb Publishing in 2014. Pictured is the Burning Bulb cover, designed by Gary Lee Vincent.

146

15

Whittling the Novel Down to a Ninety-page Screenplay

BY 1988, five years after *The Awakening* was first published by Pocket Books, I had produced another movie, *The Majorettes,* and had published five more novels and a nonfiction book on the making of *Night of the Living Dead.* The biz was keeping me busy. Along the *way,* there had been sporadic talk from agents and distributors about turning my vampire novel into a movie, but nothing had firmly taken hold. I had just finished delivering the manuscript of *Making Movies* and was badly in need of a rest when I got a phone call from Charles Gelini, who with Charles King of Silver King Pictures had agented the foreign and domestic distribution deals on *The Majorettes.*

Gelini said he needed a finished screenplay of *The Awakening* within thirty days, in order to take it to the Cannes Film Festival. I told him I was exhausted from the other writing gig and couldn't possibly bring myself to crank out a script under that kind of deadline. He said he had half the money promised from private financing in Weirton, West Virginia, and he thought he could raise the other half at Cannes. I said that somebody would have to prove they were serious about money before asking me to kill myself on the word processor.

"What do you mean by serious?" he asked.

"Well, they have to agree to option the script, at the very least."

"How much?"

"Ten thousand dollars for a six-month option."

"I'll check and get back to you."

The net result was that the investor signed an option agreement, and now I had to knock out a screenplay.

ADAPTION PITFALLS

The rule of thumb in using a screenplay to estimate the screen time of a movie is: one minute on average per page. So in order to have a movie that will come in at about ninety minutes, the screenplay should be around ninety pages.

But the manuscript of my vampire novel was over five hundred pages. Not only that, but the stuff that so many people, including Charles Gelini, found so absorbing mostly went on in Benjamin Latham's *mind.* Although there was considerable action in the novel, its impact depended in large measure on how deeply intrigued readers were by the force of Benjamin's personality and his ironic outlook on our modern society. Caring about the vampire and *liking* him made them care about the physical danger he was facing from Vargo and from Matthew; and it made them root for him in his carrying out of revenge against the street punks. It also made it possible for them to continue to like Benjamin when Lenora fell in love with him, instead of despairing over what was happening to her and hating him for it.

In the novel, I had been able to play with the old vampire myths any way I wanted to, without any financial constraints, and now I was going to have to accomplish the same thing in a motion picture—for only $700,000—because that was the amount that Gelini had said he could raise.

There was a point early on when I asked him, "Charles, are you sure this is what you want to do for our first movie together?" I was referring to the fact that he was going to produce this one, not just agent it, and it would be his first venture as a producer, too. Was he willing to put everything on the line?

He said, "There is no question in my mind, this is what I want to do. It's a terrific novel, and I think it'll make a great movie—one that people will notice. It'll be a big boost for both our careers."

I pointed out that we could choose to do something much more exploitative for our first time as a production team—something that would probably carry much less of a financial risk. "This isn't like *The Majorettes*, where if the rough cut is playing a little slow, you go out and shoot an extra murder. This one has to work on an intellectual level *and* a visceral level. If the audience doesn't buy into Benjamin Latham as a character, there's no movie—it can't be saved."

"I understand," he said. "But this is the movie I want us to make."

Well, I still wasn't sure he fully realized the ramifications of trying to make a low-budget movie from a high-concept novel. In writing the screenplay, I would certainly have to strip away some of the location changes—the meandering of the story from Pittsburgh to Williamsburg to Philadelphia, and so on. I would also have to condense key events and characters. I might have to eliminate old characters and invent new ones to voice some of the sentiments and convey some of the information that had previously been conveyed by Benjamin's intro-spections. The only other choice would be to have him speaking as a narrator throughout much of the movie—a choice that I felt would be wrong both aesthetically and commercially.

Whereas I had explored Benjamin's first life only in flashbacks in the novel, now I wanted to actually dramatize some of the period stuff, because if I could make use of the Fort Pitt reconstruction, the Royal American Regiment, and other local historical resources for a relatively low cost in the movie, the production values would be heightened and the fact that it was low budget would be disguised.

With all these considerations in mind, I began the writing task by rereading the novel and listing each scene according to page number. If a scene struck me as a particularly good one to keep for the movie, I put a star beside it. Here is an excerpt from my list:

206—Making love with Lenora
208—In the Williamsburg cemetery, going to library
* 213—Benjamin's musing on how to take blood without making an innocent person die
222—The gang kills Andy Bonner
* 233—Vargo breaks into Benjamin's pad
237—Vargo and his wife, he lifts barbells

Perhaps you've already realized that listing the scenes directly from the novel in this way took the place of having to invent possible scenes from scratch, as I had needed to do in order to develop the *Voodoo Dawn* screenplay. This time I already had material that had been carefully thought out and crafted. I also already had backup research and notes that I could draw on to expand aspects of the screenplay or to give certain scenes or characters a new slant.

REVAMPING THE CHARACTERS

Note that in my scene list, above, I did not put a star next to the scene of the gang killing Andy Bonner even though this is obviously an important scene. I was already thinking that the Andy Bonner character would have to be changed or replaced. In the novel, Andy did not learn anything about Benjamin's past. Until the day of his death, he labored under the misconception that Benjamin was a "regular person" with amnesia. Andy was not a sounding board, because in the novel no sounding board was needed—the reader knew Benjamin's thoughts.

The screenplay was a different story (pardon the pun). I was going to need a character who could hear about Benjamin's past, so that the audience could hear about it, too. So I decided to make Benjamin's friend a priest instead of a hobo. I would tie this in with colonial times by showing Benjamin asking to make his confession, and being refused, before being hanged. So, when he first comes back to life, confession is on his mind—especially after he has killed Stephanie by accident and Elijah on purpose. He seeks out a priest, Father Ed, to make his confession. Therefore, Father Ed would replace Andy Bonner in my story and would become the one that the gang would kill.

Benjamin enters the church to ask Father Ed to hear his confession.
Used by permission of Thinker Productions, Inc.

I didn't think the Andy Bonner character would have had sufficient intellectual depth to cope with the weirdness of Benjamin's story. The priest would have difficulty coping with it, too. But at least in the confessional he would be forced to listen and give comfort, even if he thought he was listening to a crazy man. How would I make Father Ed into a believer and a friend? How about the missing navel? When Benjamin lifts his shirt and reveals this, the priest begins to be convinced. In subsequent dialogue, I would let the audience see that the priest *wanted* to be convinced. He was beginning to secretly doubt his own calling, to think that there might not really be a supernatural domain and a God to rule it. In appearing before Father Ed, Benjamin has revived the priest's faith in God by proving the existence of the supernatural.

The invention of colonial characters for the period scenes caused me to revamp the Matthew Latham character. Whereas the style of the novel flashbacks hadn't required me to describe any of Benjamin's persecutors in detail, now I actually had to portray them in a striking way, so that these scenes wouldn't bore a theater audience likely to be comprised largely of teenagers whose favorite subject would probably not be American history.

I had Benjamin's main accusers be his own brother and sister-in-law. And I gave them each a strong motive. Jacob Latham has a stump arm, and he hates Benjamin for performing the amputation (during an Indian battle), even though it saved Jacob's life. And Patience Latham hates Benjamin for turning aside her attempt to seduce him.

Around this time, I started toying with the idea of having the same actor who played Jacob also play Matthew Latham. Thus, the physical resemblance, made suitably subtle by changes in costume and hairstyle (and by the absence of the stump arm in the modem character), would lend force to the idea that Matthew really is Benjamin's descendant. And the dual role might be meaty and intriguing enough to interest a name or semi-name actor, if I had to go after one.

The Vargo character got some revamping, too. In the novel he was a state trooper, brought into the story when little Stephanie Kamin was found dead in her sandbox, near the site of a reconstructed colonial fort at Hanna's Town, Pennsylvania. When Benjamin kills Elijah Alford in a Pittsburgh parking garage, Vargo follows the trail to Pittsburgh, and begins working hand in hand with a Pittsburgh detective, Jack Harpster. But for the screenplay, I wanted to centralize the story and condense the characters. So I made Vargo a Pittsburgh detective, had Stephanie's death occur near Fort Pitt, and eliminated the Jack Harpster character. I still needed a sounding board for Vargo's thoughts, however, just as I had needed one for Benjamin's—so I expanded the role of the coroner, Ed Stanford, to give Vargo somebody to talk to in place of Harpster; that way, I only needed to cast one actor instead of two.

REVAMPING THE PLOT

In revamping the characters, the plot was already being revamped, and *vice versa* changes in the one invariably produce changes in the other. But some of the plot changes needed a bigger push. For instance, in the novel, Benjamin and Lenora didn't track down Matthew until they got to Philadelphia, more than halfway through the story. I needed to bring all the main characters in proximity to each other much sooner than that, in order for the screenplay to move at a brisk enough pace—and also to keep production costs down. It made sense to have everything happen in and around Pittsburgh, where suitable historical settings as well as modern locations were readily available. So, I brought Matthew Latham to Pittsburgh, too. I made him an antique dealer, specializing in artifacts of the colonial period, and secretly obsessed with the myth of his great-great-great-uncle Benjamin, who was hanged as a vampire. In fact, it is this obsession that had helped turn Matthew into a sociopath.

In the screenplay, Matthew already knew Lenora Clayton, as he purchased his antiques store from her when her father died. And he continued to give her advice and provide antiques for her to

153

photograph for the book she is writing about colonial Pittsburgh. Benjamin met them both in the same afternoon when, after killing Elijah, he went to Old Fort Pitt because he was drawn to this site, which had such powerful connections with his first life.

I made the Fort Pitt reconstruction a "mystical place" for Benjamin, and a key location in the screenplay. Whereas in the novel, he was tried and hanged in Hanna's Town (sixty miles away), in the screenplay I had him tried and hanged at Fort Pitt. So, in returning to the fort, he is revisiting the site of his own hanging. And, in the modern park that is part of the Fort Pitt reconstruction, he is set upon by the gang of street punks who figure so importantly in the rest of the story.

In the screenplay, I had Vargo kill Benjamin on a bridge overlooking the fort, whereas in the novel this had happened in Philadelphia. Thus, all the elements of the story were getting tighter and tighter, and easier to handle within the scope of a low-budget movie. But I didn't think I was losing any of the impact of the novel, either. All the basic ingredients were still there, but now they were being employed cinematically instead of just verbally.

I wanted to inject an element of magic—something visual—into the movie, too. So, I decided that when Benjamin came out of his grave and ran from the bulldozer, he would clutch at something to cover his nakedness—and find his own doctor's kit. All his clothing, plus the stake in his heart, the iron shackles, and the cloves of garlic had rotted and rusted away, and yet his colonial doctor's kit was perfectly preserved. And inside of it was his fleam—the very implement that he used to let blood from his patients during his first lifetime, and which had been used as evidence to condemn and hang him.

The fleam had not figured prominently in the novel, but it became, as I said, a "magical item" in the screenplay. Note also that by having Benjamin reach out and find his doctor's kit to cover himself, I had solved two problems: one, the introduction of the fleam; and, two, he now could be photographed from the front without showing his sex organs and making it tough to get an R rating.

Later, when Matthew Latham spies the doctor's kit at the Fort Pitt reconstruction, he offers to buy it from Benjamin, and during their ensuing conversations, at the fort and at Matthew's antique shop, we find out that Matthew is Benjamin's descendant. Thus, I eliminated all the complicated tracing of the family tree, which worked fine as a "fun and adventure and falling in love" period for Benjamin and Lenora in the novel, but would have irreparably bogged down the screenplay.

Benjamin using his doctor's kit to cover his nakedness. *Photo by Gary Di Bartolomeo, used by permission of Thinker Productions, Inc.*

MIXING EXPOSITION WITH ACTION

In taking the steps I've already described, you can see that I was working toward replacing much of the novel's exposition with scenes that could be handled visually. Where dialogue was still required, it could be cut back drastically. However, this is not to say that my goal was to totally eliminate exposition. Since my investors seemed to believe that I had made a vampire story that was more clever and witty than most, I wanted to preserve and enhance its distinctive qualities, not destroy them and end up with pap.

Successfully adapting a novel to the screen is largely a matter of finding effective ways to mix and blend action and dialogue sequences, employing action to move dialogue along whenever possible. For instance, you can have two characters sitting down talking to one another in an office, or you can have them talking while they're out jogging—the scenery always changing around them, and perhaps casting variations of mood or meaning upon the things they're discussing. Unembellished dialogue has a tendency to die on the screen—just like "dead air" on the radio.

As an example of how to add meaning and interest to dialogue, I'm reminded of the scene in *Night of the Living Dead* where the leading male character, Ben, had to tell the leading female character, Barbara, the things he had observed about the flesh-eaters and how he had gotten away from them. We could've had them sitting at the table across from one another while he told his story. But instead we had him tell it while he was ripping apart the dining room table and using its parts to make torches and board up the windows. Thus, a lengthy speech that could have made the audience fidget from boredom became part of an action flow that kept them fidgeting from nerve-wracking suspense.

In adapting my vampire novel, the biggest problem I faced was how to tell the story of Benjamin's trial and hanging and rebirth in a way that would keep the story moving fast enough so that the audience wouldn't lose interest before they were hooked. As I said before, I wanted to exploit colonial sets and costumes because they would give the movie a big-budget feeling. But if I stayed in colonial times from the trial to the hanging and the burial at the crossroads, I'd use up about ten minutes of screen time before I got Benjamin back from the dead and into modern times, and I didn't think a contemporary audience would sit still for it. And I *knew* that distributors wouldn't. I could just hear them saying, "All right, so *can* the history lesson!" Like it or not, I was dealing with the short attention span and craving for constant sensory stimulation which was one of the many demoralizing aspects of life in the twentieth century that Benjamin Latham had criticized in my novel. In his words:

"They had video games to bombard them with clangs and bangs and colored lights representing every kind of earthly and unearthly adventure, but they scarcely knew what anything *real* looked or sounded like. The only time they saw forest animals was when they went to the zoo . . .they zipped along in air-conditioned cars and didn't have to smell horse manure or new-mowed grass or blossoming flowers. Maybe they had to take drugs or murder each other in order to *feel* anything. Maybe the only time they felt intensely alive was when they were killing or being killed."

Introspective passages like that one were some of my favorite parts of the novel, but they would have to be ruthlessly edited down or eliminated from the screenplay. Yet, there had to be key places where Benjamin would express himself intelligently and eloquently, in order to establish him as a character of depth and substance. In fact, he had to come across this way right from the beginning. The audience had to care about him when he was hanged, be glad when he was reborn, and empathize with him despite the inadvertent death of the little girl.

That meant that I had to show him being persecuted by the ignorant mob right at the beginning of the film. However, it did not mean that I had to continue to tell the story in a linear way. In other words, I could use *parallel development* to simultaneously establish what was going on in colonial and in modern times. And that's what I decided to do. I laid out my opening scenes as follows:

1. The colonial mob drags Benjamin out of his house in chains, a huge bonfire blazing, his books and medical supplies being

tossed on the fire. Jacob Latham wants to burn Benjamin at the stake. But Constable Farley shouts down the mob and insists on "giving him a fair trial before hanging him by the neck till he's dead."

2. CUT TO Lieutenant Vargo arriving in the Kamins' backyard, where little Stephanie lies dead in her sandbox. Coroner Ed Stanford tells Vargo it looks as if the little girl might have been killed by poison. We also find out that somebody was seen talking to Stephanie. But we don't know who. Or do we?

3. CUT TO Benjamin in chains in the colonial courthouse, surrounded by a jeering, heckling mob. Jacob and Patience tell their lies about drinking blood, etc.

4. CUT TO sandbox scene, Stephanie's body being zipped into a bag. Vargo says he can feel in his bones that the little girl was murdered because he felt the same way the day his own daughter was killed.

5. CUT TO the courthouse where Benjamin makes an eloquent speech defending his quest for scientific truth.

6. CUT TO Stephanie's body in the morgue, being examined by Vargo and Stanford. There is definitely poison in her wound.

7. CUT TO Benjamin being hanged, the colonial priest saying his prayers, the stake in the heart, etc.

8. CUT TO Vargo and Stanford talking to the serologist, who tells them that the poison that killed Stephanie was poisonous *saliva.* Human saliva in most respects, except it contains certain enzymes normally found only in snake venom.

9. CUT TO a scene of the Royal American Regiment drilling in front of the blockhouse at Fort Pitt, where Benjamin was hanged. PULLBACK to reveal that this is modern Pittsburgh now, the reconstructed fort is surrounded by gleaming skyscrapers—and the Royal Americans are a reenactment troop. The other shock is that somebody who looks like (and is) Benjamin Latham is one of the

spectators, sitting in the grass with a group of modern people. Can he somehow be still alive?

Well, of course he *is* alive. And by using this kind of parallel development, I had brought him back to life and into our century in about ten minutes of screen time. I thought the pace was good, and the story was unfolding in an intriguing enough way that the audience would stick with me.

Filming one of the sandbox scenes. *Photo by Gary Di Bartolomeo, used by permission of Thinker Productions, Inc.*

What about Benjamin's coming out of his grave? It was such a potentially spectacular scene that I didn't want to lose it, and didn't figure I'd have to. We would see it in flashback before long, when Benjamin told his story to Father Ed.

Meantime, I already had him in the park—ready to be attacked and chased by the street punks—which would set off a flurry of action that would perk the audience up. I intended to have Benjamin hit by a car, but not killed—thus giving us one of the early indications of the supernatural powers he was reborn with.

And I intended to have Benjamin kill Elijah by throwing him twenty or thirty feet through the air so that he would smash head first through the window of a car in a parking garage. Then he would use his fleam to take Elijah's blood.

All of this would establish within fifteen minutes that there was going to be big action in this movie, even if some of the material was more intellectual than usual. If I could entertain with action *and* ideas, the movie might get some good reviews and attract a large following among those who were fed up with slasher flicks and run-of-the-mill horror films.

SYNOPSIS

Once I got through the confessional scene and a follow-up scene between Benjamin and Father Ed in the priest's study, my worries about being able to sustain a brisk pace were drastically reduced. By that time, the key facts about Benjamin's plight were already divulged. And these expository scenes came right after the killing of Elijah. So my hope was that the audience would be ready to slow down a bit at this point, and would hold still for the exposition. But I still tried to spice it up as much as possible. I mixed in flashbacks to colonial times—the jeering mob, the hanging, the stake in the heart (all the most graphic stuff)—and flashbacks to Benjamin's resurrection, his flight from the bulldozer, and his unintentional killing of Stephanie. I also intercut scenes of Vargo and Stanford back in the morgue, examining the body of Elijah Alford and making the discovery that his death was caused by poisonous saliva matching the saliva found on the little girl.

Therefore, the story kept advancing on many fronts, even while background information was being filled in. The scenes kept changing and intercutting, constantly giving the audience something new to look at, instead of requiring them to stay in one setting to absorb and digest a long stream of expository dialogue.

I kept this technique going throughout the writing of the screenplay. Even after I had worked my way past the flashback segments, I kept intercutting action and dialogue scenes, always driving toward a slam-bang wrap-up between Vargo, Matthew, Lenora, and Benjamin. I don't think it's necessary for me to keep on explaining the writing process step by step. But at this point, it might be helpful for you to read the synopsis that I wrote from the finished screenplay, so that the story continuity will be locked firmly in your mind during subsequent discussions.

NOTE: This synopsis is the same one that was used to help land production financing and to interest distributors when we were selling the movie. Therefore it starts out with an attention-grabbing quote from one of the novel's good reviews.

Heartstopper Synopsis

"Modern technology versus ancient evil . . . state-of-the-art forensic facilities and investigative techniques do battle with a soulless menace that has struck fear into hearts and teeth into necks since the Dark Ages. Russo peppers HEARTSTOPPER with police procedural elements worthy of a mystery novel, and juxtaposes them against a gripping plotline and good old-fashioned Gothic horror."

– DAVID SHERMAN, *Fangoria*

Heartstopper is the wryly funny and terribly frightening story of Benjamin Latham, reluctant vampire. Benjamin is a Pennsylvania physician, living during the time of the American Revolution. Out to get him for being a *Tory,* his neighbors accuse him of vampirism. During his trial, he makes the mistake of admitting he has been conducting experiments with human blood. This plays into the hands of his enemies, who not only string him up but also give him the traditional vampire burial to prevent him from arising—garlic necklace, stake in the heart, burial at a crossroads.

But, 200 years later, the crossroads are plowed under to make room for a shopping mall, and Benjamin is unearthed. He doesn't realize he's been dead, or *is* dead. He thinks the noose must not have done its proper job. But a series of rude shocks makes him realize he has somehow landed in the twentieth century. And this time around there's a major hitch: he really *is* a vampire. His tormentors managed to do their work backwards. Instead of preventing him from arising, they've conveyed a weird, horrible, undesirable immortality. Benjamin is consumed with an insatiable desire to drink blood, and he doesn't want to. He hates the idea of insuring his own survival by taking the lives of innocent people.

He finds a compromise solution to his dreadful plight when he makes a friend, a priest named Father Ed. When Father Ed is killed by a gang of reprehensible goons, Benjamin goes after them. Now he becomes an avenger—a blood seeker who has decided to feast only on the evil ones in our society.

Meanwhile, the reluctant vampire has fallen in love with Lenora Clayton, a lovely young lady who happens to be a historian specializing in the study of Revolutionary times, so she has much in common with Benjamin. But he knows that his loving her and having sex with her is changing her, slowly making her into a creature like himself. Eventually she becomes not only his lover but his accomplice. At the same time that he meets Lenora, he also meets his arch enemy:

Matthew Latham is Benjamin's descendant. He has read and reread all the stories about how his ancestor was hanged as a vampire. His fixation has contributed to his psychosis. He believes that he is a vampire and *wants* to be one, but he really is not. He is merely a deranged serial killer, drinking the blood of his victims, deluding himself that there is something magical in his behavior.

Meanwhile, the police, headed by Detective Ronald Vargo, are tracking down both Matthew and Benjamin, often confusing one with the other and blaming one of them for the other's crimes. When Vargo finally corners them, they are locked in a fight to the death. Matthew appears to be killed by Benjamin—then Benjamin and Vargo fight till Benjamin jumps out a high window and takes off running, with Vargo in hot pursuit. Vargo shoots Benjamin in the arm, blowing his arm off. He shoots Benjamin in the chest—a lethal shot, but the vampire does not die. Then Vargo shoots Benjamin in the head, and Benjamin plummets from a high bridge into a river.

But Benjamin's body is not found by police dredging crews. Later we see his bullet-riddled corpse under the water, and he is being reborn for a second time. His wounds are healing themselves, his body is being regenerated, made whole.

Lenora leads Matthew into a cemetery, ostensibly to perform a ritual that will cause Matthew's coveted transformation into a supernatural creature. There she kills Matthew, shooting him in the back of the head. Then Benjamin steps out of the shadows and congratulates her on a job well done. And, with deep love he watches her take blood for the first time from Matthew, her very own victim, who deserved to die to sustain her.

Together Benjamin and Lenora vow to continue to take blood only from the evil ones in modern society, so that the society will be cleansed and their special craving will be of great benefit to all of mankind.

NOTE: As you already know, the novel was published under the title *The Awakening* and the first draft of the screenplay was also written under that "working title." But we knew for sure that we did not want to give our movie the same title as the Charlton

Heston movie. So, during production, because Benjamin Latham's poisonous saliva stopped people's hearts, I came up with the title *Heartstopper,* which is how we will refer to our movie from now on.

Turn the page to begin following the process of translating the script to the screen—in other words the producing and directing process—which will be explored at length in the next two chapters.

16

The Production Gets a Green Light

AS SOON AS the screenplay was written, I delivered it to Charles Gelini, he gave me the investor's check for the option money, and then he left for the Cannes Film Festival. Even with staying at the word processor ten to fifteen hours a day for thirty days, I had barely made the deadline.

The investor had put up enough money at this point not only to cover the option but also to send Charles Gelini to Cannes to pitch the project to various distributors and sources of foreign investment. When he came back, in June, his report was positive. It looked as if we could land the rest of the money by preselling foreign distribution or by making a negative pickup deal with any one of several distribution companies that expressed strong interest.

However, we were running out of time. Financing and distributing deals usually take months to negotiate and sign, and we needed to be into preproduction in less than a month so we could be shooting no later than September. If we waited any longer than that, we'd have continuity problems—leaves on trees changing color and falling off in the middle of the shooting schedule—so that we wouldn't be able to count on making the look of the locations match when shooting out of script sequence. Also, the weather would be turning cold—a great discomfort and handicap for actors and crew—inevitably slowing down production and causing costs to escalate.

To our great relief, the investor decided to not only put up the first $350,000 of the production budget but also to put up the second $350,000 (more on how this happened in Chapter 18). So, by July of 1988 the movie had a green light, and we were officially ready to go into preproduction.

This chapter will explore the preproduction process. I'm not going to cover each and every detail, because that would require a book in itself. Instead I'm going to focus on the highlights, zeroing in on facets of this particular production that can cast the most light on the movie-making process in general. The areas that I intend to cover are:

- A budget overview, so you can see how creative decisions were affected by budget.
- How we established our preproduction staff and headquarters.
- How the movie was cast using local as well as name actors.
- How the film crew was hired.
- How special logistical factors were handled, including animation, stunts, special effects, and historical costumes, sets and locations.

BUDGE OVERVIEW

I didn't wait till we had a green light to start putting together budget figures. I did this right after I made the screenwriting deadline, even though I would rather have relaxed and breathed a great sigh of relief. I couldn't relax just yet because Charles Gelini was on his way to Cannes, trying to raise the rest of the $700,000 budget—and what if it wasn't enough?

I wanted to immediately do a budget breakdown, because I was anxious to have some verification as to whether I had in fact succeeded in writing a script that actually could be produced for only $700,000. I will summarize the results of my budget breakdown instead of going through the process step by step.

Budget—Heartstopper

Lab Costs	$90,000
Supplementary Equipment Rental	$25,000
Production Staff	
Executive Producer	$60,000
Director	$60,000
Production Manager	$20,000
Assistant Director	$10,000
Production Assistant/Publicist	$10,000
Crew	
Cinematographer	$15,000
Assistant Cameraman	$8,000
Sound Engineer	$10,000
Lighting Supervisor	$12,000
Grips	$10,000
Editor	$15,000
Assistant Editor	$7,000
Still Photographer	$5,000
Casting Expense	$6,000
Cast	$95,000
Locations, Sets, Historical Sites & Personnel	$15,000
Props	$10,000
Costumes	$5,000
Animation	$50,000
Special Effects	$40,000
Stunts	$5,000
Music	$20,000
Financial Fees	$15000
Publicity	$7,000
Insurance & Legal Fees	$15,000
Overhead	$20,000
Contingency	$40,000
	$700,000

I was satisfied at this point that it was within reason for the movie to be produced for $700,000. However, to understand how I could figure on producing a motion picture of this complexity on such a low budget, you again must bear in mind that I have much experience in employing skeleton crews made up of extremely talented and competent people whom I've already worked with on previous projects; in utilizing equipment and studio facilities that I already own; and in making maximum use of certain resources that I know are available at low cost within the Pittsburgh area. Also, as I have said, I tailor my scripts from the outset to take advantage of those resources.

Now despite all this, I must point out that the movie did end up costing considerably more than I originally figured. Oops. Was I off in my budget estimates? No, I was estimating the budget based on making the movie in a style similar to what we had used in making *The Majorettes.* But later we decided to upgrade certain production values, thus incurring additional costs (which the investor agreed to in advance). We ended up bringing the movie in for just under $800,000. But my original budget will be a good one for you to refer to as we go along, because as a learning exercise I intend to delineate the areas where we decided it would be to our advantage to incur the additional costs.

THE PREPRODUCTION SETUP

As I said, by July of 1988 we had secured our financing for *Heartstopper,* and we had to move into preproduction posthaste because the summer weather was running out on us. With eight weeks of preproduction anticipated, the camera was slated to roll on September 12. We got a kick out of the fact that the end of the world was also being predicted for that date, and pinned the newspaper article announcing it on our bulletin board even as we went about setting up our production headquarters and organizing a preproduction staff.

Moving into the headquarters was relatively painless, since I maintained offices and a small studio in downtown Pittsburgh, under an arrangement with my friend and landlord, Lou Grippo, that allowed me to expand the space according to the needs of any particular film production that I was embarking upon. We agreed on a rent figure and a space requirement for *Heartstopper,* giving us enough room to carry out everything from preproduction through shooting and editing, and moved into the building under the name of Thinker Productions, Inc., the corporation we had formed to make the movie.

Lauren Wyse, whose normal job was to head her own international corporate development firm in New York, had been our financial consultant in the effort to raise production financing, and now it was decided that she would join the production staff as an associate producer. Charles Gelini of course was to be the executive producer—a credit he later shared with Robert Donell, of the investor company, who originally joined us during preproduction as an assistant director. I was to be the director. Gelini brought in a friend of his, Marcus Dodell, who had worked on a number of Hollywood movies, to be our unit publicist and a production assistant; and he also brought in his cousin, Gary Di Bartolomeo, to be a production assistant and still photographer. I hired Raymond Laine to be our production manager, as I had worked with him successfully on several previous productions; his regular job was producing, directing, and acting in live theater and teaching at the Pittsburgh Playhouse, and he hired a former student, Sean Redmond, as an additional production assistant.

So, counting myself, we had a preproduction staff comprised of seven people, many of whom had never before worked on a feature motion picture. I accepted the challenge because the group seemed so highly motivated. Similar situations had worked in the past, and

I was hopeful that it would work this time. But it works only when you have people who are able to admit their inexperience and accept leadership. Unfortunately, the group that we had on *Heartstopper* suffered through many self-induced problems, doing much excellent work that was at times jeopardized by terrible mistakes. Although the mistakes were overcome and the movie turned out well, we could have gotten there with considerably less grief.

LANDING A GOOD CAST

One of the commonest mistakes made by novices (and even by many professionals) is to lose sight of monetary reality while fantasizing about things that would be "just great" to have in the movie. Number one in the pipe-dream category is the wishful thinking and pie-in-the-sky patter that invariably goes on concerning name actors:

"Wouldn't it be great if we could get David Soul to play Benjamin Latham?"

"He' d never do it for less than a hundred grand, and anyway why would he want to be in a low-budget movie?"

"Maybe he'll just love the part."

"Even if he did, how would we pay him? It isn't in the budget."

"Maybe the investor will cough up the extra bread just so we can have David Soul in the cast."

"If that happens, fine with me, as long as it happens quickly, because we only have eight weeks of preproduction, and until the leads are cast we can't make their costumes, and can't make body molds for special effects and so on. The whole production will be jeopardized if we keep putting everything off till we sign a name actor."

"Come on, how could it be that ominous?"

"Believe me, it is. I've been through this many times before, and you haven't. The only way to put a low-budget movie or any kind of movie together in eight weeks is to get cracking on the logistics and *keep* cracking."

"Man, I didn't think making a movie was supposed to be so hard."

"Making a movie is one of the hardest things anyone could ever try to do."

"Well, I still want to have a name actor."

"We have Tom Savini—he's got tons of fans in the horror genre."

"I'd still like to have one or two mainstream stars."

"Two? How much money do you think we have to work with, $3,000,000?"

"There must be a way to pull it off"

"Like I said, you better pull it off in a hurry."

One of the first things I had done 1 even before we went into preproduction, was to talk to Tom Savini about acting in the movie and creating the special effects. I had been impressed with Tom's role as the Black Knight in George Romero's *Knightriders,* and wanted him to play Lieutenant Vargo in *Heartstopper.* He had given a tentative consent and had given me cost figures that I had incorporated into my preliminary budget. As soon as we were officially into preproduction, we finalized the acting and special effects deals with Tom, so we'd be sure to have one of the top names in the horror business working on our movie in two important capacities.

The part that we thought would be the most difficult to cast was that of Benjamin Latham. I read actors in New York, some of whom were very good, but my hope was to cast a Pittsburgh-based actor so we would avoid the travel and per diem money that SAG would require for an out-of-town actor. I even had someone in particular in mind: Kevin Kindlin, who had played a high school quarterback in *The Majorettes* a few years ago, and during the making of that movie I thought I had glimpsed a terrific amount of untapped talent in Kevin. He was only twenty-two, a little young to play Benjamin Latham the way I had originally conceived him1 but I wanted very much to find out if Kevin could pull it off anyway. The upshot was that he came in and read with such power that his youthfulness didn't matter, and his exceptional good looks and photogenic qualities made him a shoo-in for the lead role.

Tom Savini (left) played Lieutenant Vargo and was also responsible for the special makeup effects in *Heartstopper*. Photo by Gary Di Bartolomeo, used by permission of Thinker Productions, Inc.

Up to this point there had been one other Pittsburgh actor that I was considering strongly for the part of Benjamin: John Hall, who eight years earlier, when he was still a drama student, had played a key role in *Midnight* and had done a very good job. Now he was more mature not only physically but professionally; he had been living in New York and working in off-Broadway productions. Since he still retained a Pittsburgh residence, he could work as a local under SAG rules. He had dark good looks, like Kevin, so an audience would have little trouble believing they were related, and I cast John Hall to play the dual role of Jacob/Matthew Latham.

While these decisions were being made, Raymond Laine and Sean Redmond were helping me fill in the rest of the cast with local actors—a job that was not too difficult, since there is an excellent pool of talent in the Pittsburgh area. (For those who may not be aware of it, Pittsburgh is now the third leading film production city in America, and many features are shot here, in addition to a huge slate of commercial, industrial, and educational films.) We could have cast *all* the roles very well here, but in an attempt to improve the marketing potential still further, our first-time producer, Charles Gelini, kept pushing to try to land a couple of name or semi-name actors.

By this time I had convinced him that the roles of Benjamin and Matthew had to be filled by locals because we had a thirty-day shooting schedule, and Benjamin was on camera about twenty-eight of those days, and Matthew about fourteen. It'd be far too expensive to bring in anybody from Hollywood or New York for that length of time. And what if something went wrong and we had to reshoot? The costs would go through the roof.

The two supporting roles that seemed to lend themselves to at least the *possibility* of being filled by names were the Lenora Clayton and Father Ed characters. They both had a lot of screen time. But screen time means shooting time. Perhaps I'd be able to shoot all their stuff in six days if the crew and I damn near killed ourselves and if we got tremendously lucky with weather—in other words, if none of the exteriors got rained out.

But this isn't the only hurdle when you build your schedule around actors who have to be brought in from out of town. Naturally you try to knock off all the shooting with them in a block—in our case, six days. That way you don't have to fly them back and forth more than once, hopefully, and you get the SAG weekly rate, which is a money-saver. However—and this is often the killer—you must finagle your entire shooting schedule around the availability of those out-of-town actors. This costs you time and money in almost every area: cast time, crew time, setup and breakdown time, etc. Instead of getting to one location and staying there till everything that needs to be shot there *is* shot, you shoot only the stuff that involves the out-of-town actors. Then you move to the next location, and so on, knowing you must come back to these locations later to wrap up with the locals.

I wasn't convinced that having a couple of name or semi-name actors in our movie was worth blowing the budget, but I tried to go along with the pipe-dream for the sake of harmony. To this end, I contacted my agency, Triad Artists, and obtained a sheaf of resumes and photos of people they hoped would be in our budget range. We figured we might be able to afford $5,000 to $10,000 apiece for Lenora and Father Ed. Over and above that, we would have to cover travel, lodging, and meals. Well, on Triad's list was one person that I would've loved to have had playing Lenora, Tawny Kitaen, who had recently impressed me in her lead role in *Witchboard.* But we couldn't get her for less than $25,000 a week. End of story. All the other actors Triad submitted were either not well known enough for our purposes or were well out of our budget range.

The next step was to phone a Los Angeles casting agency, McSharry/Collins, where I made a deal to pay them $5,000 to land two suitable actors for us. They worked hard and produced a long list of people who would've been great—like Phoebe Cates, Jennifer Jason Leigh, Jack Warden, Jerry Orbach—but they wanted from $30,000 to $100,000 to do a week's work for us. And the ones that McSharry/Collins came up with who would work for less didn't have enough of a name to do us much good.

Meanwhile, time was flying by, many things hanging on these casting decisions, so that our preproduction period was not serving its proper function. But the inexperienced ones on our staff didn't fully understand this.

By this time, I had made up my mind that there was no way we could afford a name actor to play Father Ed and no way was I going to jeopardize the shooting schedule by casting one. I decided that it would behoove us instead to put the male semi-name (if we could find one) into the role of Dr. Harrison Lubbock, a self-styled "vampire expert." The character had considerable screen time, but his stuff could be shot in only one day—he appeared on various television screens at different *times* throughout the movie, which meant we would crank out all the footage in a TV studio, speeding the process up by using a teleprompter, and then matte it into the movie in the right places during the editing process, after the actor was gone. If we could find a name actor to play Dr. Lubbock, we'd only have to pay him for one day on camera.

At around this time, Marcus Dodell came up with an idea that cracked us all up and got us pulling together. He suggested Moon Unit Zappa for Lenora Clayton and Michael J. Pollard for Dr. Lubbock, the vampire expert.

It was nutty, offbeat casting. Everybody knew Moon because of the song "Valley Girls," and her iconoclastic musician father, Frank Zappa. Everybody remembered Michael J. Pollard for his Academy Award nomination for *Bonnie and Clyde* and his zany appearances in numerous other Hollywood movies.

Charles Gelini did quite a bit of heavy wheeling and dealing, and we ended up landing Moon Zappa and Michael J. Pollard at the right price. This got our adrenaline flowing because we figured that Tom Savini would sew up the horror fans for us, while Michael and Moon would strike the fancies of the mainstream and the offbeat audience. This actually worked pretty well because by the time our movie was finished, Moon had done a TV series with her brother Dweezil, called *Normal Life,* and Michael had appeared in *Roxanne, Scrooged, Dick Tracy, Tango and Cash,* and several other hit movies.

Also, we were able to get Michael for two days instead of one, so I hurried up and wrote an additional scene for him that did *not* have him on television, augmenting his screen time still more, and varying it, thereby making it seem like we had him working for us much longer. (I'll tell you how this was done later, in the section on the actual directing of the movie.)

I directed **Michael J. Pollard (left) in several scenes that we shot at a local TV studio.** *Photo by Gary Di Bartolomeo, used by permission of Tinker Productions, Inc.*

HIRING THE FILM CREW

Well, one thing leads to another. If you upgrade one aspect of the production, you've got to upgrade others, and the costs keep going up, too. We decided not to shoot the movie "out of the back of a van"—in other words, with the kind of bare-bones equipment package and skeleton crew that *The Majorettes* was shot with—

because, for one thing, people like Moon Zappa and Michael J. Pollard, accustomed to the look and feel of bigtime production, might walk off the set if ours didn't appear to measure up. For another thing, many elements of the project that were falling into place during preproduction were making us feel that it truly could be a rather classy movie, and therefore we shouldn't sell it short in any area if we weren't forced to. However, I should interject here that having a big crew and a lot of fancy equipment doesn't necessarily make a good movie. Sometimes a smaller crew and equipment package is more than adequate—but we're getting into a question of *belief* and *appearances* here—in other words, part of the reason we upgraded these areas was to improve our credibility with certain people, including some members of our own staff.

I had heard from other producers that John Rice, who had worked on *Midnight* eight years ago as a lighting assistant, had now developed into the best director of photography in Pittsburgh. I also was told that Eric Baca, who used to be a sound engineer, was now one of the best lighting directors, and that he and John Rice usually worked as a team. I met with them, looked at their latest sample reel, and was highly impressed. Triad had sent me sample reels from people with fine Hollywood credits, but I liked John and Eric's reel better. And of course they had the advantage of being local—which would save travel and lodging costs.

Besides, John and Eric were totally familiar with local crew people, and I wanted to let them recommend the best ones to hire, as I had made my last picture three years ago and was not acquainted with some of the new faces on the scene. Also, since John and Eric were involved with much commercial production—with its stringent time and budgetary restraints—they would know the crew people who worked hard and fast at an affordable rate.

In addition, John and Eric could put together a list of equipment that would suit their cinematic style; and could help me negotiate a good rental deal on the equipment.

In seeing to all of the above, we upgraded the equipment package from what was intended when I made my preliminary budget, and of course we hired an expanded crew. This cost us an additional $40,000.

SPECIAL LOGISTICAL FACTORS

As I mentioned, one of the special logistical factors was covered when we hired Tom Savini to play a lead role and also do our special effects.

Two key members of Tom's crew were to be Jerry Gergely, who had done an excellent job on the special effects for *The Majorettes,* and Greg Funk, who in addition to being an excellent special effects technician is also a fine actor and stunt man. Greg was going to do the stunt where Benjamin throws Elijah Alford through the car window in the parking garage, the one where Benjamin gets hit by a car, and the one where Benjamin hurtles through a window, jumping onto a street from two stories up.

At around the time I had talked with Tom Savini about all this (right after I had written the screenplay and was putting my preliminary figures together), I had also talked with Rick Catizone, of Anivision, Inc., about doing the effects for Benjamin's regeneration. Rick is an animator, and had done a beautiful job on the animated effects for *Creepshow* and *The Evil Dead II.* I wanted Benjamin's regeneration to be first class. This was the climactic supernatural moment in our movie, and if it wasn1t fully believable we'd lose the audience just when we hopefully had them in our pocket.

I had written this scene to take place underwater, after Vargo blows Benjamin's arm off, blasts him in the chest, and then delivers the killing shot to the head, sending Benjamin over the bridge railing and into the river. Here's the way I described it in the screenplay:

EXT UNDERWATER MONTAGE—DAY

CAMERA ZOOMS through rippling water till it finds Benjamin Latham's corpse turning over and over, the limbs buckling and unbuckling, fingers clenching and unclenching, agitated by the river currents, turning and turning, like an unborn baby in its cradle of amniotic fluid.

The corpse emits an aura, a Kirlian glow.

CAMERA focuses on the gaping head wound. Magically, it begins to heal. Flesh slowly grows, covering the bullet hole ...

Bullet *hole?* What about the other wounds? Well, when I first wrote this scene I figured that seeing the head wound heal would be sufficient to carry the regeneration idea. But then Rick Catizone told me that we couldn't really afford to do these effects underwater on the $50,000 that we had in our budget. What I had had in mind was making a series of models of Benjamin Latham and using those models to animate the effects, as Rick had done with the Henrietta character in *Evil Dead II*—seemingly the live actor transforms into a demon, her head growing fifteen feet from her body on an elongating neck, right before the audience's eyes.

But Rick pointed out that the transformation of the Henrietta character had not taken place *underwater.* If Benjamin were turning and turning underwater, as I had written it, Rick would have to animate the subtle shifting and floating of his clothing, his limbs, even his hair—and this would be impossible to do on $50,000 and would probably never look right, even if we had the money to spend.

"Well," I said, "what if we have Benjamin coming *out* of the river, in a kind of supernatural trance, with eerie music and so on. It could be really spooky. You *know* he should be logically dead, but somehow he's not. Instead he finds a place in the woods, not far from the riverbank, to lie down and go into a much deeper trance, for his regeneration."

"Works for me," Rick replied, grinning. "But how can he still be walking with a hole blown through his head?"

"Don't forget, we've already set the audience up for it. They've already seen him keep going with his arm blown off—and with his chest blown apart when Vargo shoots him right through the heart. After seeing all that, they might almost *expect* that the head shot didn't really kill him either. Besides, earlier in the script, when he's talking to Father Ed, he says he'd almost rather commit suicide than live as some kind of monster, but somehow he knows he wouldn't even stay dead."

Rick agreed that it would work, and we made arrangements for him to be on location with us when we shot the live-action scene of Benjamin coming out of the river and lying down to begin the regeneration. Rick would help us pick the spot that would present the fewest problems for his animation techniques, and we would provide him with the live-action footage so he could duplicate the look of the scenery—and the actor—in fine detail. This would involve working with Savini's people to make molds and sculptures of the parts of the actor's body that would have to take bullet hits and then regenerate.

Besides the areas of special effects, stunts, and animation, there was another key area where the movie could fall on its face financially and creatively if I didn't get plenty of cooperation for a low cost. I'm referring to the need for historical sites, costumes, and personnel. Because this was so critical, I tried to take care of it right away, in the very first days of preproduction.

The problem was complicated by the fact that I needed *two* historical sites to double for one. I wanted Benjamin to be tried and hanged at Fort Pitt, and to make his first reappearance in the movie at the Fort Pitt reconstruction, so we could have that dramatic camera pullback, revealing that now Fort Pitt is in the middle of the gleaming skyscrapers of downtown Pittsburgh. Except, how could I make the Fort Pitt reconstruction look as it did in colonial times with skyscrapers, telephone wires, highways, and bridges looming all around it? Furthermore, although inside the Fort Pitt Museum there are various rooms reconstructed and refurbished as they would have looked 250 years ago, none of these rooms was large enough to give us freedom to work with lots of actors and extras surrounded by bulky camera, lighting, and sound gear.

Thus, the need for the second historical site, which I wanted to be the colonial stockade, courthouse, and jail reconstruction at Hanna's Town, Pennsylvania. I figured that Benjamin Latham could be tried at the courthouse there and hanged at Fort Pitt in front of the reconstructed blockhouse, which is a key tourist attraction—and the audience would accept that both buildings were a part of eighteenth-century Fort Pitt. The blockhouse was located in such a way that I thought we could film it and it alone without revealing skyscrapers, etc., in the background—but this took considerable doing, as I will explain later. At Hanna's Town there is also a colonial cabin, which would serve as Benjamin Latham's house, if we were permitted to build a bonfire there for the scene where he is arrested and his books and medical supplies are burned.

To gain all these permissions, Raymond Laine and I met with Robert Trombetta and his staff at the Fort Pitt Museum and with Ned Booher and his staff at Hanna's Town. The results were better than we had hoped for.

We ended up getting full permission to use both these sites, plus we made arrangements to use as featured extras the members of the Royal American Regiment and members of the Hanna's Town Historical Society, who would in authentic colonial costume portray the mob and jury that condemned Benjamin Latham. We also arranged to use horses, wagons, and livestock to populate the scenes that we would film there, adding a considerable flavor of authenticity.

One of the crucial things that Mr. Trombetta gave us permission to do was to build our own gallows in front of the Fort Pitt blockhouse. We scouted the location several times with John Rice and Eric Baca, in order to determine how the camera could be placed so as not to show any aspects of modern Pittsburgh when Benjamin Latham was being hanged. At first this looked to be nearly an impossible task. Finally we solved it, but the time and expense were considerable. We had to make fifty feet of artificial stockade to match the stockade at Hanna's Town and to block from the camera's view some of the city buildings in the background. Also, part of a hillside in the background had been stripped away by a construction project, leaving it looking decidedly non-rustic. We had to buy hundreds of yards of camouflage material to cover the hillside and make it appear wooded.

By carefully choosing our camera angles, we were able to film the colonial scenes and make them genuinely look as if they were taking place at Old Fort Pitt. We got all the historical elements we needed for the unbelievably low price of $15,000. This included about fifty extras in authentic costumes, with muskets, swords, cannons, and other appropriate accoutrements which would have cost us a fortune if we were working in Hollywood.

We still had to have period costumes made for Benjamin and Jacob Latham and our other key actors for these scenes. To this end, Raymond Laine and I met with Don Di Fonso, costume designer for the Pittsburgh Playhouse. Don had made the witches' robes for *Midnight,* and had done an excellent job at an affordable price. This time the demands were far more complicated, but Don once again came through for us in fine style. We also met with Tracy Truax, from the playhouse, and hired her to make Benjamin Latham's colonial doctor's kit, including the fleam. All of this was accomplished within our budget.

Another major asset was obtaining the cooperation of the city of Pittsburgh. For a low-budget movie, *Heartstopper* required an exceptional number of locations. In fact, there were twenty-four locations in all, spread over only a thirty-day shooting schedule—which was all the time we could afford to pay for actors, crew, and equipment.

Benjamin being hanged at Old Fort Pitt. *Photo by Gary Di Bartolomeo, used by permission of Thinker Productions, Inc.*

Most of the people involved with the production, including John Rice, Eric Baca, and the rest of the film crew, said that I'd never shoot this movie in only thirty days. But I replied that I *had* to, and so I'd just have to make sure I got it done. There would've been no way of doing this—in fact no way of making the movie at all—if the city of Pittsburgh had not already had in place a mechanism for handling film productions and encouraging film producers to come to the city.

When Raymond Laine, Charles Gelini, and I had our first meeting with city officials, about twenty-five of them showed up. Every possible area of support was represented—blocking off of city streets, parks, and bridges, furnishing of security officers, furnishing of power and parking for mobile dressing rooms, camera and grip vehicles, etc. Everyone there clearly knew his job and had done it many times before. There was absolutely no bureaucratic resistance; the city's cooperation was extremely generous and virtually total. Intelligent, well-thought-out guidelines were laid down for us to follow to make sure everything went smoothly and that we disrupted the affairs of the city as little as possible.

Although shooting on all these urban locations was going to require stringent control of motor and pedestrian traffic, and was going to present many problems for our sound recordist, we were thankful that the locations were accessible and we'd be allowed to go ahead and make our movie. None of the city's requirements prevented us from doing anything that we really needed to do. All of this was very refreshing, to say the least.

17

Using the Screenplay as a Recipe to Direct the Movie

A SCREENPLAY is a recipe for making a movie. A finished movie is as different from its script as a loaf of bread is different from its list of ingredients. It's up to the baker to make sure the loaf doesn't fall flat. A good recipe doesn't guarantee a good loaf of bread, and a good script doesn't guarantee a good movie.

In this chapter I'm going to show you how I handled key ingredients in *Heartstopper*. Just as in the previous chapter, I'm not going to cover each and every detail, but instead I will highlight the areas that can be most illuminating for you when you set out to direct your own movie. The areas that I've selected are:

- How I directed with a view toward being able to change and improve the movie all the way through the editing process.
- How thorough location scouting paid big dividends.
- How I made maximum use of our name actors within our time and budget constraints.
- How I used the shooting schedule to best advantage.
- How I kept changing and adding to the script even as the shooting schedule progressed in order to best use various resources and hype up the action.
- How key stunt sequences and difficult logistical sequences were set up, directed, and filmed.

A DIRECTING AND EDITING OVERVIEW

It is fitting and proper that directing and editing should come under a single heading because, when you direct a movie, every single thing you do is geared toward the editing of it—the enabling of it all to come together in a technically and creatively successful way. The director needs to know editing and to always be thinking in terms of editing in order to direct. If he doesn't, no matter how wonderful the bits and pieces of the movie might look when the dailies are being screened, the end product is doomed to fall flat on its face.

In directing *Heartstopper,* I was not only trying to execute the script as it was written, I was simultaneously trying to shoot each scene to give me a great amount of editing freedom—in case the script as written didn't play as well as I hoped, or in case better ideas occurred to me or more effective juxtapositions might become possible later on. Also, one must bear in mind that the eventual distributor may request editorial changes; and, perhaps more importantly, the MPAA may ask for certain changes before it will grant an R rating or whatever other rating is being sought.

Trying to direct for maximum editing freedom and still bring *Heartstopper* in on a thirty-day shooting schedule was a complex and difficult task. This was not basically a one-location picture like *Friday the 13th* or *Night of the Living Dead.* If you are working in a single location for the entire shooting schedule, you don't have to set up and break down and be somewhere else each day. Your camera gear stays put. So do your actors, dressing rooms, etc. If you would like to spend more time on a particular segment of the movie, you can do it knowing you're going to be on that location tomorrow and tomorrow and tomorrow to play catch-up.

But on *Heartstopper* we had twenty-four locations to cover in thirty days. If I didn't get everything I needed on a particular location, I had to figure that there would be no way of coming back. On the other hand, if I did get everything I needed in, say, half a day instead of the full day that may have been allotted, I generally couldn't use the other half day to shoot the next scene on the schedule—because the next scene almost invariably needed to take place on some other location. We'd *have* to wrap, break down, and set up again somewhere else the following morning.

All of this tells you why low-budget films generally are single-location films. *Friday the 13th* had the same budget as *Heartstopper,* but was way easier to do because everything took place at a summer camp. The filmmakers on that picture didn't have to contend with complicated urban logistics including traffic noise screwing up their sound takes. And of course they didn't have to deal with period sets, costumes, and locations.

We accepted these complications in the making of our movie because if we pulled it off, it would have a more sophisticated, higher-budget look than many other horror films.

The intercutting of colonial and modern scenes called for in the opening of the screenplay (and described in fair detail in Chapter 15) was a device that in and of itself was going to give me a great amount of editing freedom. I wrote the colonial scenes *long* on purpose, figuring that if I got great performances out of the actors and/or the visual spectacle of the period pieces turned out to be rather impressive, then I might want to let these segments play for greater screen time. On the other hand, if the pace started to flag, I could break the scenes up into shorter, punchier fragments by cutting back and forth more abruptly between colonial and modern times.

However—and this is extremely important—in employing this style of direction, it is not simply a matter of shooting a long colonial scene and a long modern scene and then cutting them wherever you want to later. The cut-ins and cutaways should ideally happen at very *pointed moments*—imparting a flavor of style and pace to your editing flow. Therefore, these kinds of sequences should be planned with editing choices carefully thought-out beforehand, striving for several pointed moments within each sequence, any of which could be used to edit in and out with proper dramatic emphasis. And the choices don't have to be finalized till after you've had a chance to work and rework your rough cut.

Now, these pointed moments can be comprised of or enhanced by a key phrase of dialogue, a specific sound effect, or a bar or two of music. For instance, if you would refer to the opening pages of the *Heartstopper* screenplay (in the Appendix), I had Farley firing his flintlock to stop the mob in their tracks. This would have been a potential cutaway point, if I had needed it. In actually shooting this scene, I wanted to heighten the moment still further, so I had Isaac Morse, instead of Farley, trying to use *his* pistol to shoot Benjamin—but Benjamin knocks it aside before launching into his big speech. Thus, I could have cut away from the scene *before* the speech, leaving the audience shocked and waiting for more revelations.

But, on the actual night of shooting, I ended up being deprived of the moment entirely. What happened was that we filmed everything right up to the firing of the pistol, and then someone lost the bolt to the hammer of the pistol, and it was pitch black out, and we couldn't find it. In a big-budget movie, perhaps this particular prop would have existed in duplicate.

But we couldn't make our pistol fire, and I had to edit out that entire moment in the scene. However, I had gotten enough cutaways of mob action, etc., that I could do it successfully. And Kevin Kindlin did such a good job with the big speech that the bonfire scene was very effective.

While we're on this subject, notice how I used the chanting of the mob and the rapping of the colonial judge's gavel to punctuate my cuts back and forth from colonial to modern times. This set the audience up for the scene changes, generally leaving them in suspense over one thing or another, and making the scene changes play well aesthetically.

However, in the actual movie, the cutting of the first dozen scenes varies considerably from what was indicated in the screenplay. In general, the scenes are much shorter. My carefully designed pointed moments are always used for cutting, but the scenes are shortened internally. The scenes were blocked and directed to give me the freedom to keep the best moments and discard others which either didn't play quite as well or would have weakened the internal pace of the scenes.

The first fifteen minutes of the movie being the most critical in terms of capturing and hanging onto the audience, editor Paul McCollough and I must have cut this section ten or twelve different ways before we picked the best way and stuck with it. We even experimented with ways of cutting the movie that we were sure wouldn't work, just to make ourselves doubly sure. The ability to experiment to such a great extent is not usually one of the luxuries of a low-budget movie and is a product of the way that the movie was directed and shot. I am not holding this movie up as a perfect specimen. But I believe that it did come close to being the best that it could be, considering its extremely low budget and high aspirations.

MAKING MAXIMUM USE OF NAME ACTORS

In Chapter 16 I promised to explain exactly how I expanded Michael J. Pollard's part to fully utilize the scant two days for which we could afford to pay him. Originally, Dr. Lubbock was to appear in three different scenes scattered throughout the movie, and always we would see him on different television sets being watched by the main characters. This was a device to impart necessary information and build in some comic relief.

Well, it occurred to me that since Lieutenant Vargo was one of the main characters who sees Dr. Lubbock on TV, a logical thing for Vargo to do would be to call Lubbock in and question him as to why he seems—or pretends—to know so much about vampires. Vargo figures that perhaps this nut has some idea who the vampire is. So I wrote a scene where they parry with each other in an ironic way, Vargo ends up being disgusted by the sanctimonious twerp, and tells him (and the audience) some poignant details about how his own daughter fell victim to a homicidal maniac a few years ago.

Again, I wrote this scene long, knowing we wouldn't be able to afford to bring Pollard back, and wanting to maximize the chance of cutting a good scene out of it. The confrontational scene ended up working well, shedding important light on both Vargo and Lubbock. It also lent much more weight to the presence of Michael J. Pollard in the movie, because now he didn't appear just on a tiny TV screen.

I also scheduled the shooting of his scenes in a way that was *extremely important* to our particular production. Our shooting schedule wasn't slated to begin till September 12, but I arranged to film the Pollard scenes on August 29 and 30. I did this for several key reasons:

1. To galvanize our staff into action, because its general inexperience and lack of cohesiveness was a threat to the entire production. I wanted to force us as a group to do some meaningful catching up with the areas in which we had fallen short during preproduction.

2. If I could finish with Pollard early, at a relatively low cost, I would hopefully gain some shooting time—because I might be able to still shoot for the anticipated thirty days of the regular shooting schedule that the main crew had already committed to, and for which our main camera, lighting, and sound equipment had been rented.

190

3. By finishing with Pollard now, I would have only one out-of-town actor (Moon Zappa) to contend with during the main part of the shooting schedule, and it would thus be much easier to block in her time and work around it.

In the first draft of the screenplay, Dr. Lubbock was being interviewed by a news reporter in his office. But now, because of the quirkiness that Michael J. Pollard is noted for, I wanted to stage his scenes with considerably more zaniness. So, I had him being interviewed on the set of *Freaky Features,* a TV station's set for their Saturday run of spook flicks. I got Bob Michelucci, an artist and publisher of horror books, to build the set in one of the studios of Channel 13 Television in Pittsburgh, a first-class facility. For roughly $5,000 I was able to hire the station's crew, studio, and video editing facilities to tape and put together all of Michael J. Pollard's TV sequences.

Now, for the scene with Lieutenant Vargo, we turned my small shooting studio into a set of a police station. This took considerable doing, but the alternative—shooting at a real police station—would have cost us setup and breakdown time that we couldn't afford if we were to finish with Pollard in only two days. By doing it in my own studio, I was able to bring in a skeleton crew to have all the gear set up and the scene blocked out beforehand. I wanted to make sure that Michael J. Pollard was going to come into town and find some well-prepared professionals waiting for him instead of a passel of disorganized amateurs.

In the case of Moon Zappa, I blocked her into the third week of the main shooting schedule. This gave us two weeks to get used to working with a large crew and handling complicated logistics. Going into this, we didn't know Moon and she didn't know us. Any time an actor comes into town and you've never worked with him or her before, you don't know what kind of cooperation or lack of cooperation you're going to get. And from the actor's standpoint, he or she doesn't know if the production company will turn out to be made up of professionals or hacks. If an actor walks off the set of a big-budget movie, they hire another actor. But a low-budget movie might not be able to recover from such a disaster.

I give Moon Zappa a lot of credit. She found herself among a bunch of strangers, not knowing exactly what to expect or what implications the project was going to have for her career, and she performed professionally. Filming all her scenes in only six days was grueling for her and us. She helped us overcome problems as they arose, and contributed to the process creatively, particularly when we needed to come up with a way of filming Lenora and Benjamin's bedroom scenes with taste and restraint but still with enough pizzazz for a contemporary audience.

Moon Zappa and Kevin Kindlin as Lenora Clayton and Benjamin Latham.
Photo by Gary Di Bartolomeo, used by permission of Thinker Productions, Inc.

Now is a good time for a discussion of "cover sets." A cover set is one that you can go to in case of bad weather or any other problem that would make the primary set choice unworkable. We didn't need to worry about cover sets for Michael J. Pollard because his two days of shooting were to take place inside the two studios that I described. But, in Moon's case, we had her for only six days, and four and a half of those days were to be exteriors. The odds of getting rained out were frighteningly high. Therefore we had to try to come up with cover sets, where possible, and allow for as much freedom as we could give ourselves to juggle the indoor and outdoor shooting days according to weather. Here is the way the schedule was originally laid out:

Sept. 18—Ext. Modem Ft. Pitt and Point State Park
Sept. 19—Same as above
Sept. 20—Int. Lenora's apartment
Sept. 21—Int. Lenora's apartment (morning)
Sept. 21—Ext. city montage (afternoon)
Sept. 22—Ext. city alley at night
Sept. 23—Ext. cemetery at night

I wanted to start with the absolutely critical exteriors at Fort Pitt and in the park, because if these days got rained out up front, we could hopefully shoot the interiors at Lenora's apartment instead, picking up the exteriors when the weather got better. One of these exteriors was a scene of Matthew and Lenora having a lunchtime discussion about Benjamin, so the cover set could be inside the foyer of the museum. There could be no possible cover for the other exteriors needed on these two days.

There was no possible cover for the city montage, either, but I felt that this was not absolutely critical to the movie and could be scrapped if it came down to it. It did, and we scrapped it.

Notice that both the night shootings are scheduled in succession on the last two days of Moon's stay in Pittsburgh. One must always make an attempt to schedule day shootings in a block and night shootings in a block. That way the actors and crew get sufficient "turn-around time"—to give them proper rest, and to comply with union regulations.

There was no possible cover for the alley location, which was where Benjamin was going to kill one of the gang members after the gang killed Father Ed. I wanted the rest of the gang to peel out in their car, firing a machine gun at Ben, and we could not afford to do the bullet-squib effects in an indoor location, and besides I did not want to lose the impact of the dramatic events in this scene. So we decided to risk that we either wouldn't get rained out or that the "cover" of being able to switch around Lenora's apartment scenes would give us sufficient leeway.

There was no cover for the cemetery either. It had to be a cemetery for our big final scene where Matthew is killed and Lenora takes blood for the first time.

As it turned out, we did get rain on some of these days, but were able to work around it by juggling the schedule and, as I said, by scrapping the city montage. Any further bad luck would've jeopardized our entire project financially. It is why I have pointed out that the cost of paying the wages of a name or semi-name actor isn't the only hurdle. If a local actress had been playing Lenora, rain in that particular week would not have been potentially devastating—she'd still be in town the next week and the next week. We wouldn't be paying her hotel bills, and we'd only be paying her SAG rate when she was actually on camera.

USING THE SHOOTING SCHEDULE TO BEST ADVANTAGE

Scheduling time with name actors isn't the only factor that should guide the establishment of a shooting schedule. I already mentioned, for instance, that the schedule should be set up according to location; that is, you should attempt to work from location to location in a logical fashion, finishing all the shooting on a given location before moving on to the next one. This saves on crew and equipment travel, breakdown and setup time.

There are certain locations that have to be blocked into specific time slots because they won't be available any other time. For instance, we were originally told that we could film at Fort Pitt anytime we wanted to, but further investigation showed us that there were various festivals slated to take place in the surrounding park that would have made crowd control and decent sound recording impossible; and by the time we ironed all these things out, we were left with only one certain week that we could shoot there. We were also told that we could shoot in the morgue only on a certain day. So those locations were blocked in where they had to go, and that left the rest of the locations to be juggled.

Weather considerations were very important, too. It could be pretty darned cold in mid-September, and we had to film Benjamin coming out of his grave naked and coming out of the river after he was shot by Vargo. I didn't want Kevin Kindlin to die of pneumonia. So I scheduled the resurrection for the very first day of shooting. But, unfortunately, the body molds and sculptures that Savini's crew had to make would not be ready for several weeks, and so I couldn't schedule the regeneration till the first week in October. Luckily, we got a burst of unseasonably warm weather right about then, and the filming of that scene went quite well.

I wanted to leave the entire last week of the schedule for the action-packed wrap-up—the fight between Matthew and Benjamin, the fight between Vargo and Benjamin, and the pursuit and shooting of Benjamin on the bridge. This is where we would invest all that was left of our resources—all the time and money that had not been expended on the rest of the filming. Tom Savini and I had discussed at length how to make these climactic scenes pay off in a big way, and Tom and his people had storyboarded our ideas, and I kept promising Tom that this wouldn't be one of those movies where some of the best stuff never gets shot because the production runs out of time and money. So, all through the shooting, I had in mind not only to do the best job I could of getting each day's scene in the can, but to work expeditiously enough to leave that all-important week free for the big fireworks at the end.

Since the fights between Matthew and Benjamin and Vargo and Benjamin took place in Lenora's apartment, we didn't need a cover location for those scenes. And there was no possible cover for the shooting on the bridge. Benjamin's body had to plummet into the river in order for the body not to be recovered and to later come out of the river to regenerate. We just had to hope we didn't get rain on those particular days. And if we did get rain, maybe it would come at the end, where it wouldn't necessarily present a continuity problem. As long as we were shooting these scenes in script sequence, if it rained and continued to rain—so that we wouldn't have a wet look mixed with a dry look—we'd be okay. Drenched maybe. But okay.

NOTE: That's exactly what happened. We spent the last sixteen hours of our shooting schedule up on the Fort Duquesne Bridge in freezing rain, and got our last take of the movie—Benjamin being shot in the forehead—in the can just as the sun was coming up. Savini later said it was the most exciting wrap of any movie he had ever worked on. I had bought a case of champagne to celebrate with, and coincidentally it was somebody's birthday, and so there we were, eating cake with our fingers and drinking champagne straight from the bottle on the banks of the Monongahela River at dawn.

IMPROVING THE MOVIE AS WE WENT ALONG

When I'm making an action film, if a cop ever stopped me and looked in my car trunk, I'd probably get arrested. He'd think he must've stumbled onto a hit man or a serial killer. I have a bag in there full of guns, knives, ropes, handcuffs, etc.—anything I can think of that might come in handy in an emergency to spice up the action.

Sometimes I'll be driving to the location, and an idea pops into my mind. For instance, on the day we were to film Benjamin's first run-in with the gang that eventually kills Father Ed, it occurred to me that I could put some fireworks into the chase. I had a pistol and some blank ammunition in my trunk, and I asked the policeman who was working security for us that day if it would be okay, as far as city regulations were concerned, for us to fire off some blank ammo in the park. "Sure," he said. "They know you're making a movie. So as long as you don't upset any people in the park, I guess you can fire some blanks."

Vargo kills Benjamin on the bridge.

This gave me the opportunity to block out a nice piece of business for Mountain, the gang member who would later stab Father Ed to death, and who would be the one that Benjamin kills in the alley. I gave Mountain the pistol. So, instead of the chase being just a chase, there was now some gunplay involved. And I

197

figured that the audience would be wondering whether or not Benjamin, being a vampire, could actually be killed by gunfire. But I wouldn't let them know right away—because all of Mountain's shots would go wild.

Benjamin wouldn't get hit by the machine-gun bullets in the alley either—which was also an ingredient I added after the screenplay had already been written. Garth, the gang leader, fires wildly that time because the car lurches as it peels out, spoiling Garth's aim. So the audience doesn't find out that Benjamin can actually be damaged by bullets till Vargo shoots him on the bridge.

Highly conscious that I was making a low-budget movie that we did not want to *appear* low-budget, I kept adding as much production value as I could all through the shooting schedule, instead of sticking strictly to the screenplay. Tom Savini, Jerry Gergely, and Greg Funk were cheerful and willing accomplices in all this. Together we had a field day improvising the murder of a baby-sitter by Matthew Latham (in a scene that shows him trying to copy crimes attributed to Benjamin). As it was written, Matthew was supposed to choke the baby-sitter, Sally Minton, to death and then slit her wrist and drink her blood. But we hyped it by having Matthew lay her unconscious body down on a pool table. Then he tapes his knife to a cue stick and uses it to torture her, as if he's "playing pool." This sounds more lurid than it actually was in the finished movie, because we indicated what was happening instead of dwelling on it, and we intercut the scene with a conversation in a bar between Vargo and the coroner, Ed Stanford, where they are making salient points about the maniacs on the loose in our society.

During the making of *Heartstopper,* I was trying to put to good use some lessons I had learned in making other movies, like *Midnight* and *The Majorettes.* I had seen areas in those movies where, even though they were low budget, I could have taken the time to inject more action, more snap, more pizzazz. With today's

198

audience, there is almost no such thing as "too much." You have to pull out all the stops in an effort to give them the thrills and chills that they crave.

Shoot as much of it as you can. And make sure you can tone it down, if you have to, during the editing of the movie.

DIRECTING COMPLEX ACTION AND STUNT SEQUENCES

Our biggest scenes in terms of logistics were the ones at Old Fort Pitt and Hanna's Town—the historical enactments. We had to make sure everything looked authentic and came across with sufficient dramatic power while working with livestock and dozens of extras who (in the case of the livestock) would not take direction or (in the case of the extras) were quite willing to take direction but were not as skilled as professional actors would have been.

In the colonial courthouse in Hanna's Town, the mob just would not loosen up enough to heckle and jeer convincingly and shout rabidly for Benjamin Latham to be hanged. So I resorted to a trick. I asked Raymond Laine and several others of our production staff, whom I knew to be good, uninhibited actors, to stand in a group just off-camera and add their voices to those of the mob.

There had been a scene in *The Majorettes* where a crowd of non-actors could have been "seeded" in this way, and we had failed to do it. The scene, instead of being as powerful as it should have been, had come off entirely too limp. I didn't want to make the same mistake in *Heartstopper*.

The courthouse mob responded to our little trick. The shouting, vehement off-camera voices inspired them to new heights. And they became, for the camera, the kind of fanatics they were supposed to be.

It is important never to take adversity lying down. Almost always there is something you can do—some trick of ingenuity or imagination that will prevent a scene from falling flat on its face.

When you are working with huge crowds, particularly when there are crowds of non-actors, you must be well prepared and you must have your scene blocked out carefully and logically. And you should explain to the people exactly what is going to happen. Tell them what is going to be required of them, how their piece of business fits into the overall scene or story, and what steps will have to be gone through to put it on film. They will have more confidence in you if you don't let them stay in the dark. And if you proceed with confidence and dispatch.

It is important also to remember that most people *love* the chance to be in a movie. For many, it is one of the highlights of their life. Because they feel this way, they are perfectly willing to give their all, so long as you treat them with dignity and respect. In fact, they often feel hurt if you don't ask them to do enough. So don't be afraid to let people help you make a good movie. Everyone will have a better time that way.

Usually, the special effects crew on a movie is one of the most enthusiastic groups. They're in the biz because it's fun for them. They get off on making tricks, stunts, and effects work. They like to scare, shock, and fool with the audience. While making *Heartstopper,* if John Rice and I were busy setting up a shot or rehearsing a scene, I'd often ask Tom Savini and Greg Funk if they would like to choreograph some action for an upcoming scene. They were always delighted. By the time we were ready to shoot the scene in question, they'd already have a good fight, stabbing, or shooting all choreographed and rehearsed.

Greg Funk, as I mentioned, performed some elaborate stunts in the movie, during which time he had to double for Kevin Kindlin. He and Savini and Gergely made a cast of Kevin's face and from that made a latex mask that looked exactly like Kevin. In some scenes Greg wore the mask, so that if we caught a glimpse of the stuntman's face it would look like Kevin to the audience and the

200

shot wouldn't be blown. He wore this mask when he got hit by a car and when he jumped out of a second-story window.

One of the cleverest and best-looking stunts was when Benjamin tossed Elijah Alford through the window of a parked car. Greg did this stunt, doubling for Elijah, and hurtling thirty feet through the air. To pull it off, he used a trampoline. Wearing a latex mask of Elijah's face and duplicates of the clothes that Elijah had been wearing, Greg took a run and sprung from the trampoline, which was placed off-camera. As he came into the air, Kevin made as if he had Greg by the trousers and throat and followed through on his movements as if he were doing the throwing. Greg kept on flying and landed with a crash on the hood of the car. He was wearing pads under his clothing, so he had some protection, but it was still a terrifically daring stunt. And it worked perfectly. The next shot was a cut to Elijah's face crashing through the windshield—we used breakaway glass. With Elijah's loud scream and the sounds of crashing and shattering glass, the effect is utterly believable.

Stuntman Greg Funk doubles for Elijah to take a spectacular dive through a car window.

Greg didn't dive off the Fort Duquesne Bridge into the freezing waters of the Monongahela River after Benjamin was shot in the head by Lieutenant Vargo. We used a dummy for that. It would have been too risky for a stuntman to attempt in the freezing rain.

Making a movie ceases to be fun when anyone gets hurt. The idea is to use your ingenuity and imagination wisely—maybe a bit daringly and innovatively—but always within the bounds of good sense. The safety of cast and crew must be paramount. Remember we're out to produce vicarious chills and thrills. Not the real thing.

18

An Overview of Movie Distribution

IT IS ESSENTIAL for you to understand the marketplace before you set out to make any kind of movie. That is what enables you to tailor the movie's concept and style of production toward the goal of making something that the distributors and the public will be eager to buy. In today's world, the digital revolution has opened enormous opportunities for aspiring filmmakers. It is not nearly so tough as it used to be, to not only make a movie but get it distributed on at least a minimal level.

Once upon a time, the drive-in movie screens offered opportunities to small independent producers and distributors. Movies produced for less than $100,000, as opposed to the millions of dollars spent by major Hollywood studios, could succeed in attracting millions of customers—if they were carefully tailored to exploit the special interests or desires of those customers. *Night of the Living Dead* is a good example of this kind of success. Produced on a budget of $114,000, it went on to gross millions and to spawn numerous sequels and spinoffs.

Today the drive-in screens are virtually gone, and have been replaced by home video. It is possible to make product for the home video market much cheaper than for the drive-in market—and to have the same shot at millions of customers. That's how companies such as Vidmark and Vestron, starting with little cash in their bank accounts, were able to fairly rapidly become multi-million-dollar enterprises. Just as *Night of the Living Dead* is a good example of a low-budget movie becoming a hit in the days of the drive-ins, my movie *Midnight*, made for $71,000, is a good example of a movie that became a hit on home video. *Midnight* netted about $160,000 in theaters, during the period when most drive-ins were going out of business and few screens were available. But, released with an excellent publicity campaign by Vidmark, it sold over a million dollars' worth of videocassettes.

When you make a low-budget movie, even if it is shot and edited on video, the domestic home video market is not the only place where it can be sold. There are also free television, cable television, pay-per-view television, Internet-based video on demand (VOD) and other ancillary markets, both domestic and foreign, where your movie can be sold. Therefore, it is vital to understand these markets, how they operate, and what their special needs are, if you are going to maximize your movies' chances of breaking even and turning a profit.

THE MOTION PICTURE INDUSTRY

The entire motion picture industry has been undergoing a cycle of dramatic change. These changes are being felt at every level of the movie business, from the most major of the "majors" to the smallest of the independents. The proliferation of DVDs, VOD options and of cable TV channels has offered people many ways of seeing movies besides going out to a theater. So the major studios have been producing mega-budget pictures in an attempt to lure people away from their TV screens. We've all heard about the hundred-million dollar budgets of pictures like *Batman* and *Terminator*. But even the negative cost of the "average" Hollywood picture has gone way up—to more than $30,000,000.

NOTE: The term "negative cost" refers to all the various costs (including financing charges) involved in producing a completed "negative" of the movie: script charges, producer, writer and director fees, talent costs, studios, crews, camera and lighting equipment, film stock, processing, etc. etc.

The economic law of supply and demand is currently working in favor of the independent, "leaner" producer. The negative cost of the average independent production is about $8,000,000—one-fourth of the average cost of a major studio production. That's why it is often said that the old "major studio system" is dead. The majors don't make movies anymore. They commission movies or they buy movies so they can distribute them. And they usually buy from huge, powerful independent producers, like Largo Entertainment or Castle Rock Entertainment.

In a way, calling large companies like Castle Rock "independents" is a misnomer, for they would be lost without their ties to the major studios who guarantee that their pictures will get released nationally in thousands of theaters, with millions of dollars spent on prints and publicity. Even for an "average" major release, prints and publicity will usually cost around seven to ten million dollars. Therefore, the true "independents" are the smaller production companies who have to scramble to get distribution for their pictures, and the smaller distributors who have to scramble to get their pictures onto theater and television screens.

There are eight majors and so-called mini-majors. There are many independents. Whether made by a major or an independent, the real question is not what a picture costs to produce, but what the probabilities are of that picture making back its negative and marketing (prints and advertising, or "P&A") costs, plus earning a suitable profit. Only one out of every ten pictures produced by the majors is a hit, despite the mega-budgets and the use of star actors and directors. Vast resources are no guarantee of success. And, conversely, modest resources do not doom a picture to financial failure.

HOW MOTION PICTURE INCOME IS FIGURED

"Box office gross" means just that; it is the total amount of money that customers pay, at the box office, for tickets to see a particular movie. The amount of box office income is important, but the amount returned in film rental to the distributor is more crucial, because it is the figure which is used to calculate all subsequent percentage participations.

"Film rental" is the amount of money that a movie theater (exhibitor) returns to a film distributor as the distributor's portion of the box office gross.

"Producer's share of film rentals" is the percentage of film rentals that the distributor pays to the producer.

"Domestic film rentals" refers to rentals from both the United States and Canada. All other countries are considered part of the foreign market, which is one of the several "ancillary markets."

Sometimes the majors insist on film rental guarantees from the theater chains before they will allow the chains to book their mega-budget—and presumably blockbuster hit—pictures. In some cases, the majors can command up to 90% of the box-office take. The average big-budget picture needs to take in at the box office about three times its negative cost in order to break even.

The independent distributor's share of film rental usually is determined on a sliding scale, ranging from 25% to 50% of the "net" that remains after "cooperative advertising" costs are deducted from the box office gross. When the picture is booked, the exhibitor and the distributor meet to discuss how much will be spent on radio, TV and print advertising to open the picture. The exhibitor then places the advertising, using press books, ads and trailers provided by the distributor, and deducts the cost of the advertising after the picture has had its run. The exhibitor also may deduct certain other agreed upon costs, such as his "nut"—the money he says he must lay out for light, heat, projectionists, ushers, ticket-takers, etc. After the advertising costs and the exhibitor's nut have been covered, what remains is the "net rental." If the picture has done quite well, the distributor's share may hit the aforementioned 50% on the sliding scale which has been set in advance of the picture's opening. On the other hand, if the picture has not performed well, the distributor may not be entitled to any more than a lowly 25% of the net. As you may guess, it is rare for an independent picture, with a shallow P&A budget, to hit the high end of the sliding scale.

However, it is nice to know that, as a rule of thumb, a picture will usually earn, in the ancillary markets, a sum of money equal to or greater than whatever amount it earns in domestic theatrical rentals. Once a picture has played theatrically, it still has foreign rights, network and cable television rights, pay-per-view rights, home video rights, and many other ancillary rights left to sell.

Because of the virtual monopolizing of theater screens by the majors nowadays, it is wise for the small independents to cut production costs as much as possible and to produce highly exploitable pictures, in order to give themselves a reasonable chance of making a profit out of the ancillary markets alone. By doing so, any theatrical revenue becomes "icing on the cake," the main goal of the theatrical release being to gain valuable exposure for the picture that will enhance its salability to foreign, network and cable television, pay-per-view television, home video, college circuit, armed forces, and other markets.

A CLOSER LOOK AT THE ANCILLARY MARKETS

The "foreign market" refers to all countries outside the United States and Canada, and the term usually is used to encompass all foreign outlets and rights within those outlets. In other words, when a picture is sold, for instance, to the United Kingdom, all rights including theatrical, television, home video, etc., are sold to a British distributor for a lump sum, or else an advance plus a percentage.

Either the independent producer or distributor can negotiate his own foreign deals, country by country, or he can make an overall deal with a distributor who specializes in foreign rights to represent his picture.

The foreign market generally is worth about 50% of the total world market. Some of the key territories, with an approximate percentage of their value in the world market, are: Italy, 10.5%; Germany, 8%; United Kingdom, 8%; France, 7,5%; Australia, 7%. These figures can be deceptive to an independent producer since the relative worth of each territory will vary widely from picture to picture. The "television market" refers to domestic network TV, cable TV, pay-per-view TV and home video. Usually a distributor wants his picture to be offered to hone video before it plays on free or cable television, so that people won't make their own dubs of it off the air and then not rent or purchase any units. Home video is a facet of the television market that has become all-important. Many pictures that are box office flops turn huge profits in home video. And of course, home video is the playing ground and the mainstay if many independent productions.

The "video sell-through market" encompasses the low-priced high-volume releases of DVDs to the huge department store chains like Walmart and K-Mart. This is a "mop-up" market; it is where old movies that have enjoyed their run in theaters and on TV and in the video stores will finally end up. By this time, they will have been discounted down to the lowest possible price, usually $9.95 or lower. Also, this is where exercise tapes, specialty tapes with small audiences, and movies that have been totally unsuccessful elsewhere, might see their only exposure to a potential buyer.

Remember, however, that no market should be treated as if it is "beneath you." Lots of money is made each and every day in the "lowly" sell-through market. And if you are going to make your own movie for little cost, you might very well earn back that sort of production investment in the sell-through market alone, if all the other outlets fail to come through for you.

MARKETING AND DISTRIBUTION HIGHLIGHTS

Distribution is where money is made in the movie business. It makes no sense to produce good movies—or even bad movies—if you cannot get them distributed successfully.

The best distribution situation is when the distributor is enthusiastic about the film and is willing to make a substantial commitment to its marketing. Under these circumstances, the producer may receive a large advance and strong minimum guarantees in the various markets. You may wonder how there can be "minimum guarantees" in a business where ticket sales are so unpredictable. Well, what it means is that the distributor will commit, for instance, to reaching certain dollar figures in each foreign territory, and if he fails to achieve those amounts within a specified time period, then those rights revert to the producer.

When a distributor makes a strong financial commitment to a picture, the producer of course benefits in many ways, not the least of which is that the movie gets tremendous exposure to the public and to people within the industry; thus becoming a meaningful credit on the producer's resume, even if the grosses turn out in the end to be disappointing. But, when the distributor gets strongly behind a picture, the financial prospects rise accordingly, and the chances of failure are greatly reduced.

A distributor who makes this sort of commitment has a lot at stake if the picture dies. He must push the picture by developing a high-impact campaign, testing the campaign, and opening the picture with a large enough advertising budget to draw people to the theaters. Then, if the picture clicks with the public, the distributor will cut back on advertising (to maximize profits) and let word-of-mouth carry the film during subsequent weeks.

The kind of distribution deal a picture will get depends, first, on the picture itself and how it is perceived and, second, on the stage of its development. If the producer began production without a distribution deal, he will be offering the distributor a finished, or partially finished, film. Regardless of the stage of completion, it is important to the distributor to at least have a look at just about any picture. His business is distributing films, and he needs to always be on the lookout for marketable product.

A basic distribution deal may involve the following:

- An advance paid to the producer by the distributor in exchange for the right to distribute the film. This advance will usually be deducted from the producer's profit participation in the film. However, there are also distribution agreements in which the producer receives no advance.

- A commitment by the distributor to spend a specified minimum amount of money on prints and advertising. Also, the amount the distributor can spend on prints and advertising may be limited by the producer, or the producer may have the right to approve or disapprove certain expenditures, so that the distributor is prevented from becoming too enthusiastic and spending the picture into a hole that it cannot climb out of.

- A definition of the territories covered by the agreement and certain minimum guarantees for those territories.

- Coverage of who will get what percentage of income from merchandising and other ancillary rights not directly attributable to exploitation of the movie per se. Games, toys, books, trading cards, sound track albums, and many other types of goods can become movie tie-in merchandise. They not only help to publicize a movie and give it high visibility; they also produce substantial additional revenue. T-shirts, posters and other "giveaways" become valuable incentives for theatrical exhibitors and video dealers. It is therefore advisable for the producer and distributor to enthusiastically seek out merchandising deals and ally themselves with companies that can bring the tie-in possibilities to fruition.

Knowing that a winning picture can be a "gold mine," a producer may be inclined to hang onto all rights till he's ready to display his "treasure" and rake in the juiciest offer. But it's a strategy that can easily backfire. If the picture is so good and so sought after that it stimulates a "bidding war," then it may be lucky enough to claim top dollar in the marketplace. But if the reception is lukewarm, the distributors then know that the producer is "sick" to the full extent of his production investment and might be forced to make desperate concessions in order to try to "get well."

That is why the safest sort of situation for a producer is either a negative pickup deal or a co-venture arrangement with a distributor before the picture is even made. With a negative pickup deal, the producer knows that all, or at least a fair portion, of his investment will be recouped from the distributor as soon as the picture is delivered. With a co-venture deal, distribution of the picture is guaranteed, and an advance to the producer upon delivery may or may not be part of the arrangement.

BECOMING A PRODUCER AND DISTRIBUTOR

Anyone can distribute movies on at least a small level. "Anyone," that is, who has enough money to buy a few prints, make deals with theaters, and advertise. That is how the smaller independents like Independent-International, American-International and New World Pictures survived and even thrived in the business for many, many years. They did not open their pictures nationally all at once on 1,500 screens. Instead, they pulled twenty or thirty prints of a film, opened on a few screens in a few territories, then moved the prints across the country region by region, until the entire exhibition possibilities were played out. In the meantime, they sold foreign rights, television rights, and so on.

Today, with home video distribution being such an enormous potential revenue provider, it is even easier in many ways for a cash-poor producer to distribute his own movie. It costs about $2,000 to pull a 35mm print for a theater, and only about ten dollars to pull a dub for a video store. The cost per dub goes down even further if hundreds of dubs are pulled at once. Sometimes they can even be made for as low as three dollars apiece, including packaging. Furthermore, the dubs don't have to be made until the producer has orders for them. Therefore, he needn't make a heavy investment until he is pretty sure it will pay off. The large home video distributors spend hundreds of thousands of dollars promoting each release. But a small producer may be able to get his picture launched by spending only few thousand dollars on packaging and promotion.

How can this possibly work? Well, let's suppose the producer has made his picture for $100,000. He would like to recoup all of that money, or at least a meaningful portion of it, out of domestic home video sales. But, no large distributor wants to take on his picture, and the smaller ones won't pay him any advance or give him any guarantees.

It begins to occur to him that if he can distribute the picture himself, he can keep all of the proceeds, instead of merely the ten percent share of the jacket price that is the standard royalty. He figures his picture is good enough that it can go out with a jacket price of $19.95. When he sells to the public or to video stores by direct mail, he receives the full $19.95. And when he wholesales to sub-distributors, he keeps half, or roughly $10. His cost-per-unit for dubbing and packaging is no more than $5.

Therefore, if he averages taking in $10 per unit, by combining direct-mall and discounted sales he only needs to sell 1,000 units to make $10,000. This begins to look pretty good to him, because he knows that to make that much money on the 10% royalty the established distributors are willing to pay him, his picture would have to sell about 5,000 units.

Since his picture is a horror picture, he designs some ads and places them in the leading magazines for horror fans, such as *Fangoria, Film Threat*, etc. He also gets a list of video stores in his area, and begins sending out press kits and fliers. Then he waits for the orders to start coming in.

Although this type of self-distribution is by no means easy, and success is by no means guaranteed, there are many instances where young filmmakers have done it with wonderful results. Of course, the lower the production budget, the greater the chance of recouping through self-distribution.

Maybe you are doing a film on a "shoestring budget" (like $10,000) and you know that it won't be able to command a $19.95 jacket price. Maybe you'll only be able to ask $12.95. But, even at that low price you should be able to clear an average of about $10 per unit (if you make them for $3). Therefore, you would only need to sell 1,500 units to recover the production cost. And home video will not necessarily be your only outlet. If you are going to distribute your own picture, you will not have just the domestic home video market in which to operate. All the other rights, both domestic and foreign, will be yours to negotiate, yours to wheel and deal.

At this point, I think you can clearly see that the goal of making your own movie and getting it into the marketplace is within your grasp. Now I'm going to take you step by step through the process, filling in key details as we go along.

Part V
DIRT CHEAP PRODUCTION

"I don't think you can bury the B-movie for good. Even if people become so affluent that they can eat steak and lobster every day, there will always be days when they want hot dogs and hamburgers."

— Bill Links, Producer

AUTHOR'S NOTE: In the years since Part V of this book was written, digital production has become the cheapest, easiest and most preferred method of video production. Most filmmakers already know this, and will readily apply the lessons herein to accommodate the type of equipment that they are already using— or ever more advanced equipment that may become "state-of-the art" in the near future.

19
El Cheapo Shooting, Editing and Finishing

IT MAY SEEM to you that I've put the cart before the horse by going into a discussion of shooting, editing and finishing before we've had any discussion at all about what kind of movie we're going to make. Doesn't the script come first? Yes, but in order to write a good script for a dirt-cheap movie, you must first have a shrewd overview of the kinds of production limitations that the movie is going to be saddled with.

People writing for the major studios don't have this problem to the same degree that you do. If they write something that requires blowing up a building or "morphing" a man into a monster, so what. The extravagance will be absorbed somewhere in the $30,000,000 that it costs to make the average Hollywood release.

When you aim to make an ultra-low-budget movie, the shooting, editing and finishing costs can gobble up the lion's share of the budget, leaving almost no elbow room for anything else. Therefore, if you don't understand how to cut those costs, you may be doomed to make either a ridiculously simplistic movie or an overly ambitious one that ends up falling flat on its face.

The purpose of this book is to help you cope with those problems, by pointing out avenues and strategies that can lead to success.

Let me reiterate right here and now that this is not intended to be a "nuts and bolts" kind of book. I am not going to teach you how to set a light, focus a lens, or make an edit or a splice. I assume that you already possess those skills or are in the process of learning them. In other words you pretty much know how to make a movie. Even though there might be some gaps or rough edges to your knowledge, you feel ready to polish your skills by moving on to the next level. But the financial part of it has you stymied.

Can a movie made for $10,000 or less actually end up looking like a real movie? Will the result be worth the effort? Or will it look like a piece of crap?

Let me assure you that, within your particular budget limitations, how your movie will turn out is still largely up to you. It depends on your level of expertise, your creative and business judgments, and the amount of hard work and sacrifice you are willing to expend. A good, entertaining movie can be made for a ridiculously small amount of money.

In this chapter we will begin to see how to "make a big bang with a few bucks," how to "put the dollars up on the screen." When you don't have cash, you must make up for it with "sweat equity." But in the end there is no reason why your movie should not look and sound professional, no matter which format it was shot in.

THE ISSUE OF FILM VERSUS DIGITAL

"What to shoot on" is invariably the first major dilemma that every low-budget filmmaker must face. Of course the advantage of shooting on film is that audiences have a much greater aesthetic appreciation for that format and has been the only format truly suitable for theatrical release. Buyers for television, home video and foreign markets also prefer movies that are shot on film.

On the other hand, shooting digitally is less expensive, and so one might be willing to sacrifice sales in certain markets in order to maximize profits in other markets by lowering the amount of production capital that must be put at risk.

Often I do budget breakdowns for several different formats so I can more easily make up my mind or more graphically demonstrate the pluses and minuses for a potential investor.

Below are multi-format budget figures for a movie project I had in development some years ago when 16mm production was still worth considering:

THE PLEDGE
- Budgets -

ITEM	VIDEO	16MM (Low)	16MM (High)	35MM
Film, Processing, W/P	———	$5,400	$7,200	$80,000
1/4" & 16mm mag film	———	1,000	1,500	10,000
Editing Gear/Editor	$2,000	5,000	15,000	30,000
Camera & Sound Equip.	2,000	2,500	5,000	30,000
Crew/Staff	8,000	15,000	20,000	50,000
FX/Makeup	1,000	1,000	2,000	5,000
Stunts	1,000	1,000	2,000	5,000
Costumes	2,000	2,000	5,000	5,000
Locations/Sets	5,000	5,000	10,000	20,000
Props	1,000	2,000	5,000	20,000
Catering/Craft Svc.	3,500	5,000	10,000	20,000
Music	500	2,000	5,000	15,000
Insurance & Legal	1,000	5,000	5,000	15,000
Office/Overhead	2,000	2,000	5,000	5,000
Postproduction	2,000	10,000	10,000	30,000
Contingency	2,000	5,000	10,000	20,000
Actors	10,000	20,000	30,000	100,000
Producer	10,000	10,000	20,000	40,000
Assoc. Producer	5,000	5,000	10,000	20,000
Director	15,000	15,000	25,000	50,000
	$75,000	$114,000	$202,000	$570,000

Don't let the above figures scare you. They were for a project that was extremely complicated logistically, requiring a five- to seven-week shooting schedule, and including substantial salaries for a staff of professional production personnel and a large cast of actors and extras. The high "bottom lines" do not mean that it will be impossible to do your own movie for a lot less.

What these figures do point out, though, is that it is generally much more expensive to shoot and edit on film than digitally.

However, it is possible, with precise and clever planning, based around a well-designed script, to make a feature movie shot on digitally for $10,000 or less. To accomplish this, you must:

1. Either own a lot of your equipment or be able to rent it cheaply or borrow it for free.
2. Shoot your movie in just a few days.
3. Shoot it on a very low footage ratio.
4. Pay crew and actors very little or nothing at all.
5. Spend next to nothing on costumes, sets, locations, props and music.
6. Do almost all of the work yourself.

SHOOTING DIGITALLY

Suppose you have written a script for a feature-length movie about two college friends who are trying to keep a third friend from committing suicide. He's bound and determined to kill himself and keeps trying various ways of doing so, even while eluding and outwitting his buddies, and that's what gives the story drama, continuity and conflict.

Note that you have a small cast here in a suspenseful and potentially ironic or even humorous situation. There is room for sex scenes, chase scenes, etc., all revolving around the central theme and shedding light on or adding dimension to it. Yet, it is a contemporary story that does not require costly props, costumes or sets, and it should be of high interest to the 18-25 year olds who buy 80% of the movie tickets sold in America.

You're going to shoot on your own college campus, which will give you free use of suitable locations. Three of your friends are excellent actors with much experience due to their enrollment in the college drama program. Some of your fraternity brothers will

220

jump at the chance to appear as extras and to help out in many other ways. All of these people will work for free.

You can use the college film department's equipment without charge, but you must pay for filmstock, processing and printing. You will "wear many hats." In other words you will take on a multitude of tasks, including writing, producing, directing and being your own cameraman and editor. You are willing and even anxious to do this because you have your beady "eye on the prize" of coming out of it with your very first feature movie. Luckily you have a few zealous helpers. fellow film-school student will be your sound man, and another will do grip work, clap the slate, and run errands.

The score for your movie will be provided by a music student who can compose and perform electronic music. And for a party sequence in the script, a local rock group has agreed to appear live and play some original tunes that you won't have to pay for, as long as you give them a mention in the closing credits.

Let's assume that, by busting hump and working night and day, our movie can be shot in one week and edited in two weeks. Let's also assume that we have to pay our actors, crew and composer a little bit, but that we can cut back on expenditures for costumes, props, special effects and miscellaneous.

Costly props, costumes or special effects would blow the budget. Not only that, but having to shoot too many scenes at too many locations would prove prohibitive. So would complex editing and soundtrack work, since it would require the renting of editing gear for much longer than a week or two.

Shooting on Film and Finishing on Tape

You could cut the budget by aiming for an 80-minute movie. You could even conceivably cut it to 72 minutes. This is generally okay if you intend to release only to home video. But for television sales and theatrical sales, a running time way below 90 minutes will turn buyers off.

In the past, we filmmakers faced issues that were similar but perhaps even trickier than the digital production of today.

When I wrote and produced *The Majorettes*, which was shot in 35mm for a low budget of $200,000, the editing was done by director Bill Hinzman and cinematographer Paul McCollough utilizing a 16mm reduction workprint. Then they conformed the workprint to the 35mm camera original, and that original was then transferred to one-inch tape, accompanied by the sync sound mix. Titles were added during this process, so that we ended up with a very nice product to sell, and we did not go to the expense of pulling a 35mm print until after deals were made with Vestron Pictures and Manson International Pictures, and we had obtained advance payments of $165,000 for our movie, which made our investor and executive producer, Joe Ross, a little more willing to front the money for the answer print.

With the money that you can save today by editing and finishing digitally, you can afford to pay more for the special effects, props, costumes, etc., that your movie may require. Making a low-budget movie is a constant juggling act between the elements that you desire to have and what you can actually afford. It is up to you to decide how best to scrape, scrimp and juggle to end up with the best possible production values overall.

Today's Preferred Low-Budget Format: High-Definition Video

The quality, ease and comparatively low cost of shooting and finishing on hi-def equipment has become such a strong factor in contemporary movie making that it deserves its own special section in this chapter.

This is the preferred format of young filmmakers working in video because the camera and editing equipment that is available on the supposedly non-professional or semiprofessional level is relatively inexpensive and yields professional looking results. You can buy a good to excellent hi-definition camera for $1,000 to $5,000.

Today, in the throes of the Digital Revolution, many filmmakers all over the world are making their own feature movies and selling them to distributors or finding ways to market them outside the normal distribution channels.

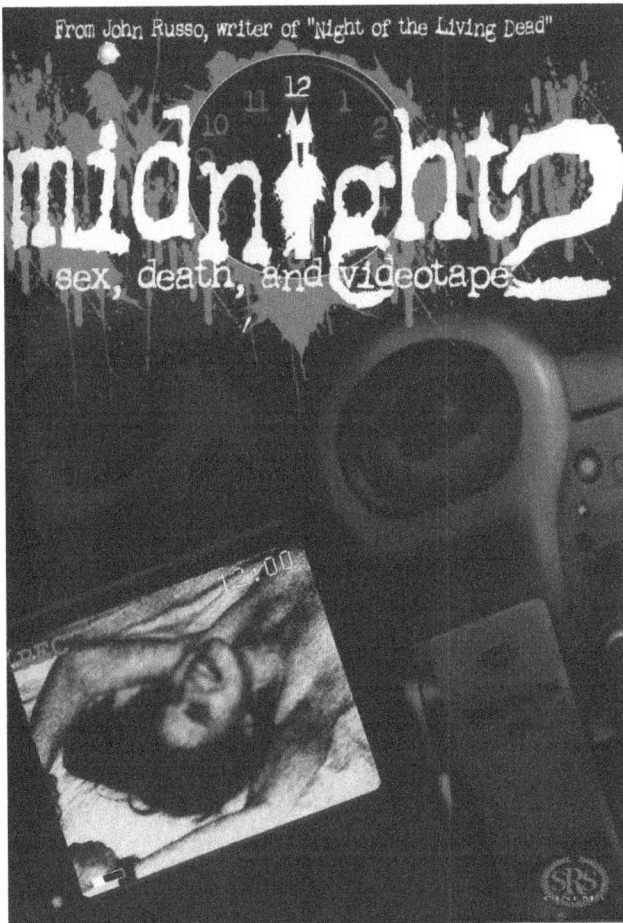

Cover of *Midnight 2*, distributed by SRS Cinema.

Always be Cost Conscious

I hope this chapter has given you a sobering overview of what you are about to undertake. I urge you to keep the cost factors in mind even before and during the time that you are conceiving the ideas for the movie that you want to make. It is the best way to tailor your ideas to reality.

Someone once said that the best two things that a parent can give his children are: roots and wings. That same caveat might well be adhered to by aspiring artists, especially those whose aspirations must be exercised in the tough but exciting world of low-budget movie making. Let your dreams soar. But anchor them in reality.

Further doses of reality await you in the upcoming chapters.

20
How to Write a Good
Dirt Cheap Script

IF YOU ARE going to make a good low-budget movie, whether you intend to shoot on film or on video, you will need to begin with a tight, enthralling script. To achieve this, you must:

- Find a hook.
- Build an intriguing plot around the hook.
- Let a few key characters carry the plot.
- Incorporate impressive but cost-effective production values into your story.

FINDING A HOOK

It is not just "schlock" or so-called "exploitation" movies that need a strong "hook." The hook is the "theme"—what the movie is about. Every movie needs a strong theme if it is going to be of sufficient interest to attract a wide audience or even any audience at all. To prove this, let's examine a list of movies that at first glance may appear to have little in common:

Porky's
Revenge of the Cheerleaders
The Pom Pom Girls
She's Gotta Have It
Working Girls

225

The first three movies were light, fluffy (some might even say crass and coarse) pieces of entertainment. Teenage escapism. What could they possibly have in common with Spike Lee's *She's Gotta Have It* and Lizzie Borden's *Working Girls*, which were considered serious yet entertaining works of art?

The answer, of course, is sex. The hook for all of these movies was sex. The first three movies exploited sex frivolously. The last two dealt with it in a more incisive, thought provoking way.

Sex is a big box office draw. Spike Lee and Lizzie Borden wanted to make movies about sex, but they didn't want to make something as inane as a *Porky's* or a *Pom Pom Girls*. *She's Gotta Have It* is about the Sex Revolution and how it affected the relationships between men and women. *Working Girls* is an examination of the lives of several women working in an urban brothel. Both films deal with important aspects of our society in considerable depth. Both films launched their directors' careers in a big way. Both films prove that you don't have to make a horror flick, an action flick, or a vulgar sex flick just because you're working with a low budget.

However, no matter what genre you choose to work in, you need to strive to make a movie with a strong, involving theme. A movie without a strong theme is a piece of pap.

Because I have made my reputation in horror, many young filmmakers send me copies of the horror movies they've shot on video. Most of these movies are pretty bad, for the simple reason that they lack a strong theme. The movies are often well shot and well directed; they often contain excellent makeup and special effects; and often the acting is pretty decent. But usually the "plot" is just scene after scene of a monster or a deranged person going around killing one person after another.

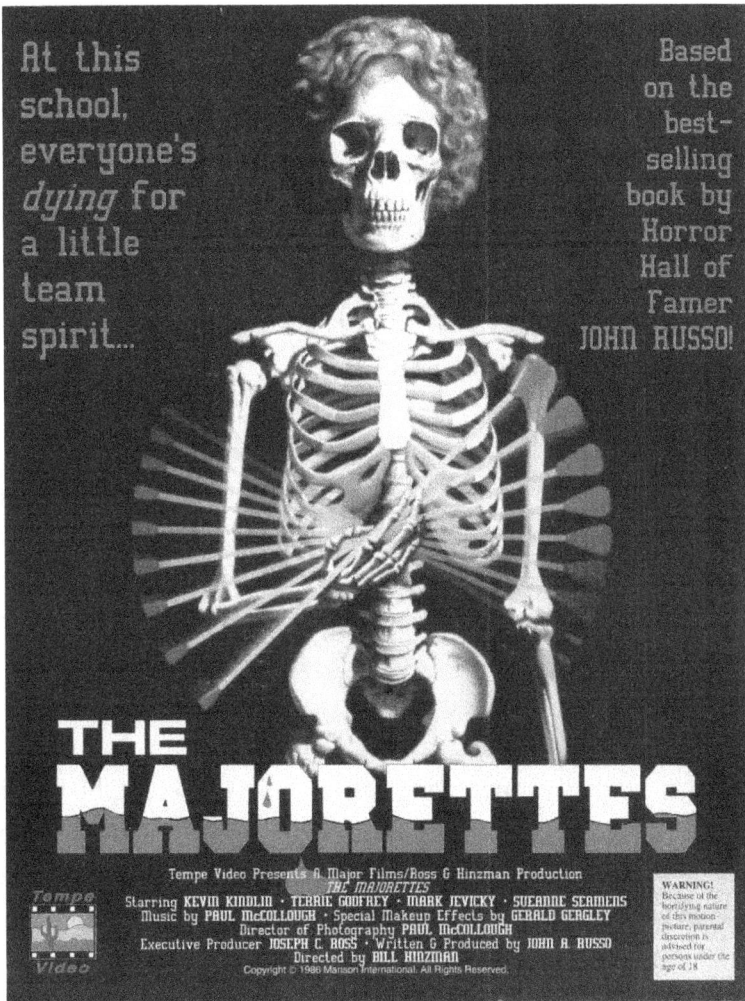

Tempe's slick for *The Majorettes*.

Sometimes the monster is well designed and well executed, but you don't fear him because there's no depth to his persona and no mystery about what he's going to do next. And you don't care much about the victims either because they're cardboard characters, interchangeable. No interesting questions are explored. You don't ask yourself how the monster got that way. Who's responsible? Are we all responsible? Are there aspects of the monster in all of us?

Your ability to come up with a good hook for your own movie depends on your own particular personality, your own intellect. If you have an intelligent, perceptive, unique view of the world, that uniqueness must be expressed in your movie making. Don't flinch or shy away from it. Strive hard to bring it out.

In the previous chapter I brought forward an idea for a movie with a pretty strong hook. Let's go back and retrieve that idea and show how we might develop it into a good script for a low-budget movie. The hook was teenage suicide, a subject of powerful concern these days, so topical and so scary that it has been covered on just about every prime-time news magazine, including *20/20* and *Sixty Minutes*. Most of the coverage focuses on how parents might be more aware when their children are considering suicide and how they might intervene and prevent it. But you will recall that our idea comes at the problem from a different angle: not from the parents' viewpoint, but from the viewpoint of several young people. It is the kid's college friends who are trying to save him.

Since the story focuses on young people rather than adults, it takes on a uniquely interesting slant, and it also might be more commercial because it features the age group that buys most movie tickets. We can choose to go a number of ways with the concept: we can play it as a tragedy, a comedy, or a wry social commentary. But we must firmly decide which way to go with it in order to know how to build our plot and develop our characters.

BUILDING AN INTRIGUING PLOT

A plot basically answers the question: What is going to happen? From the few ideas I jotted down in the previous chapter, we already have a skeleton plot for our story:

Our lead character, let's call him Jeremy, is thinking about committing suicide. Three of his best friends become aware of this and try to talk him out of it. When that fails, they try to stop him. He gets more and more clever and determined in his efforts to elude them and carry off his suicide, till he finally succeeds or else they change his mind in some way.

This plot is very sketchy. Not much of it is "nailed down." In fact, a lot of it might change as we start jotting down notes for possible scenes.

Since this is to be an ultra-low-budget movie, one thing that occurs to us right off the bat is to make Jeremy and his friends brothers in the same fraternity. This enables us to film a whole lot of scenes at one location—the fraternity house. It also gives us an opportunity to make good use of all the fraternity members who are anxious to work as extras and will give our little movie the added production value of a large cast with a great built-in camaraderie that is bound to make itself felt on screen.

Before we can go much further with our plot, we need to answer the key question: Will Jeremy be saved or won't he? And if so, by whom? And how? Writing a story is a lot like driving a car; you can't know exactly which turns to take along the way unless you have a pretty good idea where you would like to end up.

I think I would like to see Jeremy saved. I'd prefer an upbeat ending rather than a bummer. So, who is going to save him? Better yet, *what* is going to save him? Is he going to do it by himself? No. I don't think so. I think love is going to save him. I think he is going to fall in love.

With whom? One of his fraternity brothers?

Nope. Let's make one of the brothers a she. In other words, let's change the list of central characters from Jeremy and three fraternity brothers to Jeremy, two fraternity brothers, and a fraternity brother's girlfriend. The girlfriend falls out of love with her boyfriend, who never really cared for her anyway, and falls in love with Jeremy, whose real motive for wanting to commit suicide was that he was secretly, hopelessly, in love with *her*. This is an ironic, amusing, and potentially uplifting plot twist. And it can give the movie the upbeat ending that we desire.

Okay. With this plot skeleton in mind, we can begin to come up with ideas for specific scenes, which we will jot down at first, and later arrange in their logical and proper order. The result will be a plot outline, or synopsis. But before building in the details of the synopsis, we'll have to know a little more about our characters. And that obliges us to begin developing them, fleshing them out.

LETTING A FEW KEY CHARACTERS CARRY THE PLOT

We don't want any of our key characters to be cardboard; we want them to be real flesh and blood. We want their different and conflicting attitudes, styles and personalities to strongly and logically affect what happens in our story every step of the way.

Let's begin with Jeremy. What's he like? What makes him tick? What makes us care deeply about him? What is there in his past or what kind of traumatic experience has he recently undergone that has caused him to lean toward suicide? Well, what if he was sexually abused when he was a child? Perhaps the abuser was his uncle. Sexual abuse of children is a powerful issue nowadays, which also makes it a strong story element. When people are abused as children, they often carry feelings of worthlessness and self-denigration into adulthood. Perhaps this is what is really wrong with Jeremy, and there can be a cathartic scene in our story where he faces up to his past and reveals it to one of the other characters.

What else is there about Jeremy that makes us empathize with him? We don't want him to be just any college student. He's in a fraternity, but probably too shy to have been elected an officer. That's not to say that he doesn't have special abilities or talent.

Let's make him a fine arts major who paints hauntingly beautiful canvases that reflect his torment and the dark side of his nature.

Perhaps one of his buddies, let's call him Frank, is the president of the fraternity. The other fraters wonder why the president, a BMOC, hangs around with a "semi-dweeb" like Jeremy. But straight-up-and-down Frank sort of envies Jeremy's eccentricities and knows that Jeremy's quirkiness masks the light that he's hiding under a bushel.

Jeremy's other buddy, Jason, is a semi-dweeb like Jeremy, yet another "art school nerd" who was lucky to be rushed and pledged. Jason's sensitivity causes him to catch on first to the fact that Jeremy might be depressed enough to do himself in.

Everybody, including Jeremy, has Frank the BMOC on a pedestal. He's "pinned" to the fraternity sweetheart, a knockout named Lisa. Unfortunately, Lisa is the girl that Jeremy has a crush on, a hopeless crush that can never be satisfied because in his mind she's too fine and gorgeous for a nobody like him.

Lisa is not just a beautiful airhead, though. She's a music major, an accomplished violinist, who often performs solos in college concerts.

INCORPORATING IMPRESSIVE BUT COST-EFFECTIVE PRODUCTION VALUES

Making Lisa a solo violinist gives us a chance to introduce her at one of the aforementioned college concerts—a setting that will add production value to our movie even while it establishes Lisa in a striking way that causes the audience to like and admire her.

We should strive to use these sorts of settings to the hilt. Since we will have the full cooperation of the fraternity, we can center our story around normal fraternity activities that will give our movie a "big look" while costing little or nothing. Perhaps we'll open at a big Halloween party at the frat house, and close with the fraternity Christmas party. By doing this, we can use our free rock band in two key scenes—and we'll have plenty of goodlooking extras.

The campus itself might provide lots of striking locations—the student union, the dorms, the class buildings. Perhaps one of our major scenes can be shot at the stadium during a big football game—giving us the proverbial "cast of thousands" and infusing our movie with a realistic and exciting college atmosphere.

With all these ingredients in mind, let's write a partial synopsis of our story. I'm not going to give you a full synopsis here—just enough of a synopsis to show you how we can begin to flesh out the character and plot notes we've been making:

Synopsis
JEREMY'S SIDCIDE

Jeremy Walsh, the oddball of his college fraternity, is having worse problems than his two best buddies suspect. At the big annual Phi Psi Halloween party that opens our movie, Jeremy stays up in his room painting a dark, brooding nightmare on canvas while music blasts and happy young voices echo from downstairs.

Jeremy's pal, Jason Foster, barges drunkenly into Jeremy's room and tries to coax him into joining the party. But Jeremy just sits there in his skeleton suit, mask off, splashing oil on canvas.

The president of the Phi Psis, Frank Halcomb, even comes upstairs to talk with Jeremy. Frank has his luscious date, Phi Psi Sweetheart Lisa Barnes, on his arm. Jeremy stammers out a bunch of excuses for not joining the party. When they leave, he climbs out the window and up onto the fraternity house roof.

He creeps to the edge, looking down, working up the nerve to jump. Suddenly Jason's voice intrudes: Jeremy! Jeremy! What in the world are you doing up here?" Jason, who is quite tipsy, manages to haul himself onto the roof but then staggers, stumbles and almost falls three stories –Jeremy saves him in the nick of time, pulling him to safety.

Next day, after he sobers up, Jason realizes that although he almost *fell* off the roof, Jeremy was up there actually thinking about jumping. He tries to convince Frank of this, but to no avail. However, the next time Jeremy tries to kill himself—by jumping off a pier at an off-campus restaurant—both Frank and Jason are there and Frank dives in and saves Jeremy.

Jeremy laughs the whole thing off, claiming that he lost his balance and fell into the water. His buddies pretend to be fooled but later, in private, they discuss how they might try to save Jeremy from himself. This discussion takes place at the student union, and Frank's girlfriend Lisa is present. She is stunned and extremely worried and wants badly to help Jeremy.

At a concert, we learn not only that Lisa is the solo violinist for the music school's symphony orchestra, but that Jeremy is mesmerized by her. Jason notices this too, but Frank is oblivious to it.

In Jeremy's room at the fraternity house, Jason works up the nerve to "accuse" Jeremy of being in love with Lisa ... and after a bunch of awkward denials, Jeremy ends up admitting it. He says he can't let Lisa know how he feels because she belongs to Frank and all the guys would hate him if he tried to steal the president's girl.

A football game, the stands full of fun-loving students. The Psi Phi's are there in mass, most of them in matching blazers. A lot of the guys have dates. Frank is there with Lisa, of course, and Jeremy is fondly gazing at her from a distance. He ends up walking out on the big game and wandering by himself on the lonely, forsaken campus.

At Thanksgiving break, Jeremy goes home and we learn that there is great tension between him and his father, who wanted him not to be an "artsy fartsy art major" but to major in business administration. Jeremy's mother is a meek person who obviously loves her son but does little to protect him from his father's bombastic belittlement.

On the Saturday after Thanksgiving, Jeremy gets drunk and plays "chicken" by himself in the car, driving really fast and purposely coming dangerously close to guard rails. He even almost crashes head-on into a truck, averting the crash by swerving into his own lane at the last instant.

Shaking after the near crash, he pulls off the road by a pay phone. He dials Lisa's number long distance, and when her mother calls her to the phone he hangs up before Lisa can get on the line.

Back on campus, the art school is having an exhibition of students' work. Jeremy is there, stammeringly trying to explain his stuff to the few people who don't snicker at it.

Suddenly he looks up and sees Lisa. He starts to apologize for the moroseness of his paintings, but she makes it clear that she likes them and thinks he has real talent. Although he is painfully shy, on a strange level they communicate well with one another; it is a meeting of artistic minds. She finds she can say things to Jeremy that Frank wouldn't probably understand or appreciate. She makes Jeremy promise to come to her next concert...

For the purposes of this chapter, we have taken the synopsis far enough, illustrating how our basic story points can be fleshed out, building in suitable production values without overextending ourselves and making production too expensive.

21

How To Hire
Low-Cost Actors

AS WE HAVE already discussed, one way to economize on your cast is to write a script that can be shot in just a few days. Currently the minimum wage for Screen Actors Guild (SAG) principals is about $800 per day. Therefore, if you can shoot your movie in just three days and it has a cast of three principal actors, the fees for those actors will be 3x3x800 or $7,200. Your budget will be eaten up before you've even started into production.

I think you can clearly see by the above calculations that the hiring of actors is a crucial factor in determining whether or not you will actually be able to make a low-budget movie. Most scripts call for more than just three principal actors, and they usually require quite a few supporting actors and extras to boot. Furthermore, it is an extremely rare movie that can be shot in just three days. A more reasonable schedule would amount to perhaps eight or ten shooting days.

If you cannot afford to pay SAG rates, here are some of the alternatives available to you:

- Working with Avocational Actors.
- Hiring Student Actors.
- Finding People who have Star Power in a Non-acting Field.
- Paying in Screen Credits or Profit Participation.

WORKING WITH AVOCATIONAL ACTORS

Low-budget producers often make a habit of attending straw hat theater and community theater productions, looking for "discoveries." Many highly talented actors choose other kinds of careers because of the difficulty and the luck required to make it in acting. Then they give vent to their urge for expression by acting avocationally. Somebody who holds down a day job at a construction company may work in the theater in the evenings or on weekends, or may accept occasional roles in TV spots or industrial films.

The best of the avocational actors are every bit as good as working professionals in their level of skill. And they can be a terrific asset to your movie. Since they don't depend on acting for their livelihood, they can afford to work for low or no pay.

The main drawback is that they do have regular jobs to hold down, and it's where they owe their allegiance. Unless they're willing to take vacations or leaves of absence to act in your movie, you might have great difficulty working your shooting schedule around their jobs.

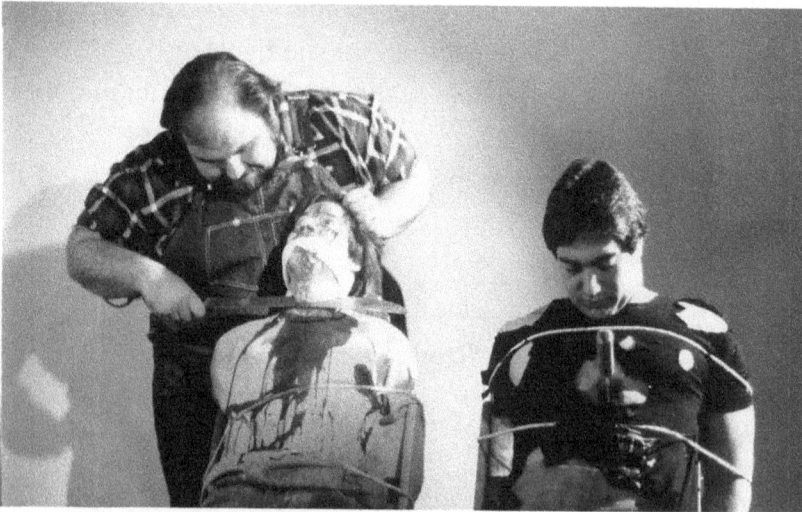

A scene from *Midnight,* which was cast mostly with student actors.

HIRING STUDENT ACTORS

Again, there are many exceptionally talented people in the nation's acting schools. You should make a habit of attending college productions, especially when you are developing a project and getting ready to cast.

The drawback with students is almost the same as with avocational actors. Getting a degree comes first; they must attend classes. Even during semester breaks and summer vacations they might not fit perfectly into your schedule because they often have to work odd jobs to earn their way through college.

When I made *Midnight*, I cast students from the Pittsburgh Playhouse in almost all the roles. I was assured at the outset that they would be allowed to cut classes and use the movie experience as a credit. But in practice this turned out not to be the case. They weren't allowed to be excused from any of their classes, and it played havoc with my shooting schedule. None of them had cars either. I lost critical shooting time chauffeuring them back and forth and waiting for them to show up at odd, disjointed hours. It was tough to get any two of them on set at the same time.

I don't think they intentionally tried to sabotage me by lying about their availability. I think they wanted to believe that the Playhouse instructors and administrators would cooperate. When you're interviewing actors you have to grill them thoroughly about everything involved. In their zeal to land a role they often say they can ride a horse when they barely can, or that they can get out of school or off work when the chances of doing so are remote.

FINDING PEOPLE WHO HAVE STAR POWER IN A NON-ACTING FIELD

If you can't have a big-name actor in your low-budget movie, sometimes it pays to consider casting somebody who has a big name in another field. A star baseball player, for example, may have a yen to try his hand at acting, and he might have a natural flair for it. You may be able to use him and capitalize on the publicity value, without having to pay him SAG rates, because he probably doesn't belong to the actors' union and doesn't need the money too much either.

Star models sometimes are fair or even excellent actors and actresses. They're used to lights, cameras, makeup, rehearsals and on-set hassles. They're comfortable in the glare of publicity. And they are of course extremely photogenic or else they wouldn't have made it as models.

You can watch locally produced TV spots to get an idea of which models you might like to use. Or you can check with local modeling agents, commercial film production companies and advertising agencies. Most of the models will belong to AFTRA (American Federation of Television and Radio Artists) but they probably won't belong to SAG unless they've landed a movie role somewhere along the line. That means they can work for you at a low salary if they so choose.

PAYING IN SCREEN CREDITS OR PROFIT PARTICIPATION

Movie credits and experience are important to most actors, and they like being able to put that kind of stuff on their resume. An appearance in a low-budget movie may get them noticed and lead to something bigger. It happens all the time.

Patricia Tallman, who worked for just a little above the SAG minimum when we made the 1990 remake of *Night of the Living Dead*, got seen by one of the producers of *Babylon 5* and got cast in that TV series.

Another way of affording a good cast is to offer some or all of them profit participation. When we made the original *Night of the Living Dead*, we offered stock and royalty percentages to the lead actors. Duane Jones declined and Judy O'Dea, Karl Hardman and

Marilyn Eastman accepted. As a result, Karl and Marilyn made twenty times as much money as Duane made, even though we were gracious enough to pay Duane a nice bonus once we knew that the picture was going to be successful.

In offering profit participation to anybody, you have to be careful not to "give away the store." You don't want to make a successful movie only to have all the money end up in other people's pockets. You need to make a profit in order to go on to your next venture and keep on building your career as a filmmaker.

22

How to Hire
Low-Cost Crew

HIRING A GOOD production crew for your movie can break the budget just about as easily as hiring the actors. If you can get by with three crew people (in addition to yourself and whoever else may be willing to work for free), and if you can get away with paying them as little as $200 per day apiece, the wages for those crew people will be 3x3x200 or $1,200.

That's not so bad, you may say. But it's pretty tough shooting a movie with just a three-man crew. And, as I said in the previous chapter, most movies cannot be shot in three days. In fact almost no movie can be shot in three days. I say "almost" because there are admittedly a few exceptions. *Nightmare Sisters*, starring past horror genre "scream queens" Linnea Quigley, Brinke Stevens and Michelle Bauer, was shot in only three days, and turned out to be quite a campy, financially successful little flick.

However, it would be safer for us at this point to allow for an eight or ten day shooting schedule rather than deluding ourselves into thinking we might pull off a fluke success. A good skeleton screw for our enterprise would include:

- Director
- Cameraman
- SoundMan
- Lighting Man
- Grip

Supplementary personnel on hand for all or part of the shooting schedule might include:

- Makeup Person
- Special Effects Person
- BoomMan
- Lighting Assistant
- Additional Grips

Support personnel during preproduction, shooting and post production might include:

- Producer
- Accountant
- Writer
- Editor
- Assistant Editor

Whoa! How in the world can a low-budget movie afford to pay all these people? Well, the good news is that they aren't "people." They are production slots. One person can fill many slots. You, for example, may be your movie's writer, producer, director, cameraman, lighting man and editor. You may also handle the accounting. And some of the special effects or stunts.

If you're good with a synthesizer, you may even produce your own music track.

And, as I said before, you may also have talented friends and partners willing to wear many hats.

You and your small group of dedicated pals will be the entire production staff, from preproduction all the way through editing and finishing and beyond into the marketing and distribution phase and the reaping (hopefully) of profits and disbursement thereof.

If you and/or your associates cannot fill all the production slots on your own, and you find yourself in the position of having to wheel and deal, here are some of the strategies you might resort to in order not to drive your movie into bankruptcy:

- Keeping the crew small but efficient.
- Working with talented novices.
- Making deals with established production companies.
- Paying in Screen Credits or Profit Participation.

KEEPING THE CREW SMALL BUT EFFICIENT

A small, efficient, highly motivated staff can sometimes be more effective than a large, bloated one. On the first day of shooting our 1990 remake of *Night of the Living Dead,* George Romero and I were wryly amused that this time around it was taking 110 people to shoot basically the same cemetery scene that we had shot with a six-man crew 23 years earlier.

Most scenes on most $30,000,000 Hollywood movies could be shot with a four to six person crew. I'm talking about just the *shooting* of the scenes, not the frills and the behind-the-scenes rigmarole. In a war, only ten percent of the personnel do the actual fighting; everybody else is part of the support troops, behind the lines handling all kinds of complicated logistics. A major movie production is a lot like that. Union regulations alone cause the staff, the problems, and the costs to multiply horrendously.

For instance, SAG requires that on location each principal actor must have his or her own dressing room, or else must share a dressing room with no more than one other actor. This means that trailers—so called "honey wagons"—must be brought onto the location in sufficient number to accommodate the cast. Teamster drivers must be hired to drive those trailers. And a contingent of people must be hired in order to keep the trailers supplied with heating oil and water, and hook them up to generators that furnish the electricity for the many creature comforts that they provide. And somebody has to drive and maintain the generator trucks (which, mind you, wouldn't have been there were it not for the trailers), and every time you hire somebody to take care of this kind of stuff (which has little to do with the actual shooting of the movie), he or she must be housed and fed and paid.

This is why you can end up with 110 people on location, with only ten of them actually needed to pull off a given scene. On the low-budget, non-SAG, original *Night of the Living Dead*, the actors and crew made do with the rudimentary facilities of the farmhouse that was the picture's primary setting. We had to carry our own bathing, cooking and toilet-flushing water from a cistern down a hill and through a patch of woods a hundred yards away.

But that picture got made and became a critical and commercial success, because it's what goes *into* the camera that counts, not the hoopla and rigmarole behind it. If you're willing to make similar sacrifices, your movie can be successful, too.

I actually prefer working with a small staff and camera crew. Too many people just get in the way. To stick with the military analogy, there are times when you need an entire division to take an objective, and there are times when too many troops stumble all over themselves while a lean, mean combat squad runs circles around them.

John A. Russo, a.k.a Tire Iron Ghoul from *Night of the Living Dead*, 1968.

WORKING WITH TALENTED NOVICES

If you and your friends can't fill all of the production slots on your own, one way of cutting the costs of the staff people you must hire is to work with talented and capable novices. Whereas years ago filmmakers were a small and select group, nowadays—because technological advancements have given you your break—there are lots of people heavily involved in shooting and editing their own home movies and learning everything they can about the movie making process. It's a fertile talent pool that you can draw on.

There are also many people with film school training who are itching to work on a feature movie but don't have the on-the-job experience that would enable them to get hired onto a major production. Your feature, even though it's ultra-low-budget, can

244

give them that experience. After all, why did they enroll in a film school in the first place? Because they have a burning desire to make movies. You can help them fulfill that desire, and they can show how much they appreciate your help by working cheap.

MAKING DEALS WITH ESTABLISHED PRODUCTION COMPANIES

Sometimes you can benefit enormously by what I call "one-stop hiring." There are companies out there shooting wedding videos or TV commercials who would love to be involved with a feature movie—something exciting for a change, something to get their creative juices flowing.

Many of these companies have a lot of "down time"—business isn't booming the way they'd like it to, and their equipment and staff are sitting around being a drain on the overhead and accomplishing little. Here's your chance to help them out by giving them something to do.

A production company may be willing to make a deal with you whereby they provide equipment and services in return for a small fee, or else for no fee and a percentage of your movie's profits. Such an arrangement is as good as cash. You would have had to pay the money out anyway. Therefore, if you can make a suitable deal with a production company, it will lessen the amount of capital you need to raise to make your movie, or else it will free capital you've already raised so it can be used in other important categories.

PAYING IN SCREEN CREDITS OR PROFIT PARTICIPATION

Just as actors are often anxious to work for screen credits and/or profit participation, production personnel may also be agreeable to those sorts of compensation. I'll remind you once again not to give away the store.

Another thing to guard against, in getting hooked up with production companies or bringing in help from outside your own circle, is the danger of losing creative and business control of your own movie. Ego freaks abound in the entertainment business. And greed abounds everywhere. Those who think they have more credits, experience and know-how than you do, might try pushing you into the background.

One of the most difficult aspects of building a career is finding out who you can work well with and who is going to be a drain on your time, energy and resources. Therefore in hiring or making working arrangements with anybody, try to be a shrewd judge of character, be fair, and strive to protect their interests as well as your own.

23

How to Obtain Cheap Props, Costumes and Locations

THE FIRST AND EASIEST way to keep down the costs of props, costumes and locations is to write a script that doesn't require very much in those areas. As a general rule, you will erase from your brain any thoughts about making a movie that takes place in some other time period, past or future, or on a fabulous estate or in a foreign country. You will also give up any notions of making a movie that requires exotic special effects, animation, weaponry or vehicles.

I said this was a general rule, not an ironclad one. Computer technology and highly sophisticated software are being made accessible and inexpensive so rapidly on the consumer level that some fantastic things can be afforded nowadays that previously could only be dreamt about.

Also, sometimes lavish and exotic props, costumes, sets or locations can become available in unorthodox ways. For instance, a while back I was talking on the phone with Sam Sherman of Independent-International Pictures, who produced a low-budget movie, *Beyond This Earth,* a study and investigation of the UFO phenomenon. Sam's partner Al Adamson insisted on flying to Australia at his own expense to film some interviews and reenactments, and while he was there he was able to borrow props and sets left over from a big-budget sci-fi movie produced by Warner Brothers, This stuff, at no cost, is going to add it measurably to the production values of Sam and Al's movie.

247

Often impressive logistical elements that normally would be denied you will become available because of people who may be excited about working with you on your movie or those who have chosen to become investors. When Joe Ross financed *The Majorettes*, he gave us the use of the Fox Chapel Yacht Club, which he owns, as a key location, and the chef of the club allowed us to film several scenes at his home, an elegant mansion of the exact sort that was called for in the script, but up till then we hadn't been sure we could find a place like that without paying a huge location fee.

Back when we made the original *Night of the Living Dead,* our biggest preproduction obstacle was finding a farmhouse that we could utterly destroy without having to pay to rebuild it. We hunted for months for an abandoned place that we might use, but all the ones we found were so decrepit that it would have cost a fortune to dress them up to make them look livable. Finally, though, a part-time worker we had hired told us about a farmhouse that was about to be torn down so the grounds could be used to grow sod. We were able to pay the owners $300 a month to postpone demolishing the building—and that's how we landed a perfect location for our movie.

You have to keep your eyes peeled and your ingenuity in high gear in order to maximize your chances of making a movie on a ridiculously low budget. Here are some of the major ways to cut costs on props, costumes and locations:

- Sticking to a Contemporary Story.
- Purchasing Stock Footage and Movie Clips
- Borrowing and Bartering.
- Making Instead of Buying.
- Utilizing Inexpensive but Talented People.
- Wearing many Hats.
- Trading Goods and Services for Screen Credits.

248

STICKING TO A CONTEMPORARY STORY

Even though *Night of the Living Dead* was set in the present, thereby relieving us of many logistical burdens, we did inject into the story several elements that—if we could pull them off—would give our picture a bigger-budget look. We've already discussed one of those elements, the need for a farmhouse that we could destroy. We also had molotov cocktail and fire effects, squib effects, a truck explosion, and a cast of hundreds—the posse and the horde of zombies.

The extras who played the zombies and the posse were our friends and associates who gladly and enthusiastically worked for free. We had a couple of big "zombie days" and "posse days" so we could keep down costs by shooting all that stuff in a couple of bursts.

If you have lots of friends willing to be extras you may not have to limit the size of your cast very much. But falling that, it is wise to stick to a small cast in a contemporary setting, as we did with our outline for *Jeremy's Suicide*. Even with that project, though, we built in certain logistical advantages, such as the use of a college campus and fraternity house at no cost, and the potential use of fraternity members and crowd at a football game.

Even though it's generally best to stick to a contemporary story, there are exceptions. For instance, I have some friends who produce and direct plays at the Pittsburgh Playhouse. Some of their productions are lavishly mounted. I could probably make arrangements to film one. In fact, one time I actually did tape a dress rehearsal for a student production of *Hamlet*, but since it was only for critique purposes, not for commercial distribution, I only used one camera and did a "rough" taping.

What if I wanted to produce and sell that production on tape? *Hamlet* is a classic, and it's public domain. The original music for the version we're talking about was done by my friend Paul McCollough, who has worked on many of my movies, and so I could probably buy the rights from him. Maybe he'd help me do the taping, too, for a percentage of the profits. I'd make a similar deal with the Playhouse and with the student actors, technicians and instructors. To do a good professional job taping the show we'd bring in a lighting and sound crew and use three or four cameras. We'd tape the entire two hour performance in one night, straight through, so I'd only be paying the crew people for a day's work. Paul and I would then go away and edit the stuff, and we'd end up with a beautiful film for a very small capital outlay. We'd probably start the money rolling in by selling a few hundred copies to Pittsburgh Playhouse students, alumni and faculty, but beyond that Shakespeare lovers all over the world would be potential buyers and we might even get some sales to cable and educational TV channels.

Similar opportunities may open up to you, in which you can take advantage of projects that are already a going concern. If you know someone whose contemporary play is being performed, go and see it. If you can't afford the cost of bringing in a large crew and many cameras to tape the play in performance, then you may be able to "lift it" from the stage and transport it onto real locations where you can film in the conventional way, over a short shooting schedule with one crew and camera. It's one-stop buying of the entire production! And you may be able to pull it off relatively cheaply by making a royalty deal with the copyright owners.

PURCHASING STOCK FOOTAGE AND MOVIE CLIPS

There is a way that you can get elements of your own movie already produced and on film. This is by buying material that someone else has already shot. For *Jeremy's Suicide*, we could buy football game action and crowd scenes from a stock footage library. If we wanted to show Jeremy flying home for Thanksgiving, we might buy shots of an airplane taking off and landing, then film the interior of the plane on a set we put together ourselves or inside an actual plane that we film while it's on the ground.

The possible applications of stock footage are virtually unlimited, but you have to keep an eye on the quality of the stuff. Sometimes it is dated, or else the prints may be full of scratches. Even when the prints or tapes are clean, they may be so many generations down from the original that they stick out like a sore thumb when cut into your movie.

There are times when it makes good sense to buy entire scenes from somebody else's movie. You could have dinosaurs, flying saucers, gladiators, atomic bombs, shipwrecks or plane crashes in your movie by obtaining the material in its entirety, already shot and edited.

You could have your movie take place in a foreign country or on an alien planet—all you have to do is buy the footage or scenes needed to establish these locales, and then skillfully construct your screenplay and movie around them.

Often this is badly done. But it needn't always be so. It depends on your own skill and ingenuity, coupled with the quality level of the scenes you are able to obtain.

In his book *B-Movies In The 90's And Beyond*, J.R. Bookwalter tells how he made *Galaxy Of The Dinosaurs* on a budget of $1,000 by building the story around one minute of clips purchased for $300 from a film which had been shot in 35mm. To take any possible onus off the use of clips from another movie, *Galaxy* was done as a sci-fi comedy. It was shot in only three and a half days and was commercially successful, thanks partially to the presence of the cheaply-acquired dinosaurs in the movie and on its video sleeve.

I happen to have an idea for a contemporary story about a woman whose brain is warped by an encounter with visitors from another planet. Because of the way my story unfolds, it is not strictly necessary to see a saucer landing or to see alien creatures coming out of it, and the story is designed that way so it can possibly be produced for under $10,000. But it would surely be nice to be able to open the movie with a striking dramatization of the woman's encounter, and I think I might be able to do so by acquiring UFO scenes from some other production.

BORROWING AND BARTERING

You might be able to borrow props, sets and costumes from theater groups, from film and video production companies, or from display houses. Sometimes extremely good looking stuff is made for a single, highly expensive TV spot and is stored or discarded afterwards. You may succeed in getting the use of it for free, even if you have to modify it for your own purposes.

Trade-offs are also sometimes possible. You may be able to barter your own goods or services in return for the use of somebody else's inventory. Still photographers, for instance, often keep a plethora of sets, flats, props, costumes, and assorted paraphernalia stored at their studios. They also frequently need an extra hand moving lights, stringing cables, working smoke-blowing machines, etc. You can be that extra hand, in return for the use of the studio or the wealth of materials that it contains. And while you're working there you might also meet a model or two who would be perfect additions to the cast of your movie. For that matter, the photographer himself might be interested in taking stills for you, in return for a credit on the sleeve of your video release.

MAKING INSTEAD OF BUYING

When I was in preproduction on *Midnight*, I was faced with the problem of building an elaborate Black Mass set and costuming four witches in hooded robes. In trying to figure out how to achieve all this as cheaply as possible, I remembered that quite a few yards of black velour material had been in storage in a back room of my studio ever since it had been used to make a limbo set for a steel company's product film five years earlier.

Why couldn't I use the black velour to drape the walls of the Black Mass set, which was supposed to be a room in a farmhouse inhabited by a crazy family? I could build the set in my own studio, cutting to it from shots taken at the actual farmhouse, enabling me to work under controlled sound and lighting conditions for a large portion of my shooting schedule. The black motif would suit the witches perfectly.

I could also have their hooded robes made from some of the black velour. I got in touch with Don DiFonso, who was the costume designer for the Pittsburgh Playhouse but also took on outside work in his spare time, and he made the four robes out of the material I supplied for only $100.

A few years before that, when I was making a sex satire called *The Booby Hatch*, I needed bondage paraphernalia for a couple humorous scenes, and the prices on the stuff that I got at a Pittsburgh "adult shop" would have broken my budget. So I went out and bought a bunch of cheap belts and chains at a military surplus store, and made my own bondage gear for one-tenth of what it would have cost to buy it.

You may have to become a jack-of-all-trades in order to bring your movie in on budget. If you will dig in and try, you may be pleasantly surprised at the extent of your own abilities in certain areas. In low-budget filmmaking, more than in most other endeavors, necessity is the mother of invention.

Sometimes, even if you are not especially skilled at a certain thing or if the items available to you are not particularly refined or elegant, even that can be turned to your advantage. For instance, for *The Booby Hatch*, I could have made the sex-product factory where the movie took place into a place where ultra-sophisticated, futuristic-type stuff was invented and tried out on the hapless workers. But instead, knowing my budget limitations, I wrote a story where the absolute funkiness of the products would be played for laughs.

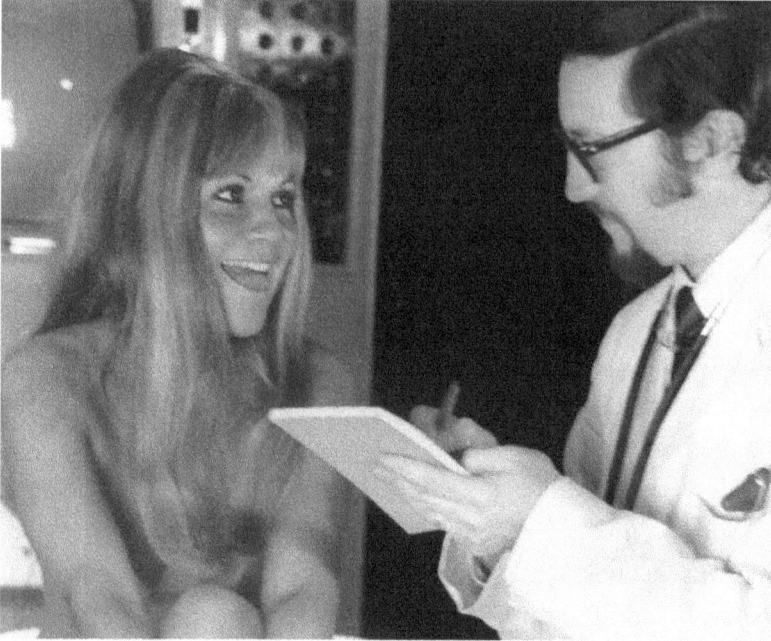

A sex lab scene from *The Booby Hatch*. Photo by Paul McCollough.

Similarly, in the case of *Midnight*, I could have had my crazy witches living in an old mansion, and the Black Mass room could have been elaborately and artistically conceived by a professional set designer. But I decided to portray the banality of evil, not the perverted glamour of it, and so it made sense to build a makeshift set that, while costing me little, would be an accurate portrayal of what the witches would have built on their own and would be a logical reflection of their character.

UTILIZING INEXPENSIVE BUT TALENTED PEOPLE

You may be surprised by the quality and quantity of work that will be done on your behalf by people who want to be involved with a movie.

I already mentioned Don DiFbnso, who made those hooded witches' robes for a hundred bucks and a screen credit. You may have a mother or an aunt who's an excellent seamstress and could do a similar job for you if and when it becomes necessary.

From my friends and relatives I've been able to borrow weapons, vehicles and locations and get highly specialized props made for my movies.

For *Heartstopper*, some factory workers made a set of arm and leg irons for a vampire who was being hanged in the year 1776. Some students from the Pittsburgh Playhouse made a huge scaffold for the hanging for a cost way below what might have been paid by a major production, and yet it gave my movie major production value in that particular scene.

When you absolutely must pay for something, be a bargain hunter. In these days of high unemployment and uncertain economic conditions, there are many suppliers who will do an excellent job at a more than reasonable price.

WEARING MANY HATS

The above phrase keeps cropping up in this book, for an excellent reason. To have the best chance of success, you and your partners are going to have to do most of the low-cost or no-cost work. That includes making props and costumes, building sets and finding and/or modifying locations. In the case of that Black Mass set for *Midnight*, I hung the black velour myself and built the alter and an executioner's chair for the witches' victims. I made a huge black cross that went above the alter, with a human skeleton crucified upon it.

I made just about all of the funky props for *The Booby Hatch*. This included not only the bondage stuff, but some pretty strange "experimental" sex apparatus and sticks of fake dynamite and a detonation box for blowing up the factory in one of the final scenes of the movie (don't look for it—it was later cut from the version released by Independent-International).

It's not easy taking all this incidental work on your shoulders and also writing, producing and directing a movie. But it's the price that must be paid, and you'll pay it as long as you keep your eye on the prize.

TRADING GOODS AND SERVICES FOR SCREEN CREDITS

Again, the purchasing power of screen credits has been mentioned several times, but I keep coming back to it for good reason. In the case of *Heartstopper*, we got soft drink companies, candy companies and sportswear companies to donate goods in return for a mention in the movie. The sportswear company wanted its clothing to be seen in the movie, which was no problem for us since we needed those kinds of costumes for our main characters. The soft drink and candy companies provided their stuff for the cast and crew to consume during the production.

When you're making a low-budget movie you may think that these kinds of companies won't be interested, but this is not necessarily the case. Often the people you will be dealing with hear the word "movie" and don't bother to question the budget. To them any movie has a certain aura of excitement. If they choose to help you in a modest way, they'll get their money's worth in all likelihood, because your little movie is probably going to be seen by thousands of people and can give their company and its products a fair amount of exposure.

Another advantage of going after these product tie-ins is that you will be meeting influential people. Some of them may later become supporters or investors. When we made *Night of the Living Dead*, many people who came out to be zombies or posse members ended up putting cash into our movies. The same thing can happen to you if you work at it.

24
How to Shoot on a Short Schedule

AS I POINTED OUT earlier, to make a movie on an ultra-low budget, your shooting schedule generally should run no longer than eight to ten days. I am talking here of productions that are shot in one burst in order to keep down the costs of actors, crew and equipment. If you and your friends own your equipment, are going to do the behind-the-camera work for free, and won't have to pay your actors very much, then you might choose to drag your shooting schedule out over a period of weeks or months, perhaps shooting mainly on weekends.

When the costs of equipment and services must come out of the budget, it becomes a necessity to stick to a short, efficient shooting schedule in order to keep those costs to a minimum. The main ways of doing this are:

- Preparing Thoroughly During Preproduction
- Sticking to Easily Lit Locations and Sets
- Picking Setups that are Easily Miked
- Rehearsing Well to Save Costly Time on Location
- Maintaining Esprit de Corps During Long Hours

PREPARING THOROUGHLY DURING PREPRODUCTION

Preproduction is the time to gather all the loose ends together, anticipate trouble, and correct potential mistakes. By the time the camera rolls, your staff and crew should be like a well-oiled

258

machine, used to working with each other and knowing exactly what is expected and how it is going to be accomplished. The hearts and minds of all the people involved should be solidly behind the project.

You should strive to have every single prop, costume, set and location lined up and ready prior to the day you begin shooting. The entire cast should be hired well in advance, too. That way they can iron out any scheduling difficulties or job conflicts, and will have time to rehearse and learn lines and be fitted for costumes. Costumes that might be damaged might need to be made or purchased in duplicate or triplicate. The same goes for props, especially those involved in special effects. They should be inspected and tested to insure they will work in the desired way when they are called upon; a prop that doesn't work can blow the effectiveness of an otherwise excellent scene.

If you begin shooting with some things left undone, you'll be playing catch-up and chances are good that you will never get up to speed. Poor planning and preparation will wreck your shooting schedule. The result will be a movie that either does not get finished or crosses the finish line a pale, dismal imitation of the winner it might have been.

STICKING TO EASILY LIT LOCATIONS AND SETS

From the moment you begin conceiving your story concept, considerations of the types of sets and locations it will require ought to be interwoven with your thought processes. I don't mean this simply in terms of the cost of building the sets and renting the locations, but in terms of lighting them.

As long as the weather cooperates, outdoor locations are in many ways the least demanding. If you have a film that can be shot largely outside, the expense and time involved with lighting will be minimized. If you are shooting on video, the image resolution will be excellent. Remember, video loves light: even though your digital camera may be able to record a picture under low light conditions, if you shoot scenes for your movie under those conditions, without lighting adequately, the results are likely going to be amateurish.

The disadvantage to trying to shoot most of your movie outdoors is that you may not have enough control over external factors, such as extraneous noise, unruly spectators and bad weather. You may lose hours of shooting time waiting for the sun to peep in and out from behind traveling clouds so that the look of your takes will match within a given scene.

When you do have an indoor location, you'll probably have more control over the situation, but even so, if you have too many indoor locations that require large, tedious lighting setups, your shooting schedule could be jeopardized. So you should probably strive for intimate, easily lit setups, conversations between two or three actors at a cozy restaurant, at a bar, or in an office, for example.

Sometimes, in order to give your movie greater production value, it helps to design the script so that much of the action takes place on one or two large, impressive sets. The Black Mass set for *Midnight* served that purpose. Paul McCollough and I were able to build and light it during preproduction, so that it was always there and ready to accommodate us for five or six major scenes in our movie. We also built a "dungeon" set in an adjoining room of my studio. And by bringing in gun racks and other props, we transformed my own office, right downstairs, into a sheriff's office that was required by the script. What it meant was that we were able to stay at the studio for ten or twelve days out of our 24 day shooting schedule. Without having to load up a van or travel anywhere with cast and crew, we had at our disposal plenty of studio lights and the cables and high-amp op outlets to power them without blowing fuses.

This is exactly why many of the movies made by the studios in Hollywood's so-called glory days were shot on sound stages instead of on location. The sound stages gave exquisite control to the movie makers. You can give yourself a measure of that same kind of control by shrewdly calculating exactly where you shoot the scenes in your movie and how you're going to light them.

PICKING SETUPS THAT ARE EASILY MIKED

Many low-budget movies that have good looking photography give themselves away by having lousy sound. Since you are not likely to have the money to post-dub extensively, the dialogue that you record on location is what you probably have to live with, and so it is imperative to do a top-notch job.

While outdoor locations can minimize the lighting hassle, they can maximize the difficulty of recording good sound. Just when you would like a wide, panoramic shot to show off the terrific scenery, wind noise or traffic noise is giving the sound man fits. He tells you that the beautiful wide and medium shots you had planned have to be sacrificed in favor of much tighter ones so he can boom the mike closer to the actors.

In situations like that, you can sometimes get away with using wireless mikes. I say "sometimes" because even the expensive ones often pick up lots of static or clothing rustle (when they're hidden under actors' shirts or blouses), and the cheaper ones are almost not worth considering. The alternative, of course, is to post-dub, which costs plenty of time and money unless you are the only doing it for a line or two here and there, in situations where imperfect sync won't be especially noticeable.

I have found that it is much better to go with close-ups that can be well-miked than to stubbornly insist on shots that will look good and sound bad. In blocking action for a scene where it is desirable to show off a wide vista, I try to plan the wide shots so they don't have to take much dialogue, so that the few lines that there are can be recorded wild and laid in during editing. Another way to do it is to shoot the scene *so* wide that all the dialogue can be recorded as wild sound. For instance, if you have two people walking arm in arm across a meadow, you might shoot them from behind in such a way that they become two tiny figures on the landscape, and take cinematic liberty to allow the audience to overhear what they are saying to one another.

Just as filming your movie on one or two major sets can be a great benefit to your lighting, this same strategy can greatly reduce the hassles of recording good sound. During preproduction all your locations should be scouted not just for ease of lighting but for ease of recording. The degree of cinematic effectiveness of a given scene is always the result of compromise between the director's vision, the cameraman's vision, and the practical considerations imposed by the lighting and sound conditions.

REHEARSING 'WELL TO SAVE COSTLY TIME ON LOCATION

Preparation is the key to efficiency. As soon as you've finalized your cast, bring them in for a cold reading of the script, all the way through from start to finish. This will start everyone out on the same wavelength. It will give the actors a chance to learn how the director is thinking about certain things before their own concept hardens in their minds. I say this because sometimes when actors rehearse on their own without any guidance or input beforehand, they get used to delivering the lines in a certain style, which may not be what the director wants, and then the delivery becomes so ingrained that it is impossible to shake.

But nipping potential problems in the bud is not the only reason to have a script run-through. Getting cast and production people all together in one room is a great ice-breaker. It ignites enthusiasm and builds confidence by letting everyone see that each person involved in the project is capable, talented, considerate, and excited about the prospects for success.

You should insist that actors learn their lines before they show up for each day's shooting. And you should thoroughly rehearse dialogue and action before rolling the camera. While the rehearsal is taking place, the cameraman, sound man and crew should stay on the set instead of wandering off somewhere for a coffee and doughnut. As the dialogue and action are being refined and finalized, it will become clear how the setup needs to be lit and miked. It drives me crazy when I spend an hour or two rehearsing actors, getting their marks down and their business with the props down, and then at the moment I'm ready to shoot, the lighting man comes in and starts tinkering with lights, or the sound man starts figuring out where to boom his mike, as if it's the very first time the necessity ever dawned on him. Lots of shooting time is lost that way, and it's a loss that can be avoided if the key personnel always stay on top of their jobs.

MAINTAINING ESPRIT DE CORPS DURING LONG HOURS

When people get tired or discouraged, they're more likely to wander away for coffee and doughnuts. Tiredness can't always be prevented, but one way of preventing discouragement is to keep everybody convinced that they're making a good movie. All the points discussed in this chapter contribute toward that end. If you're thoroughly prepared before you come out of preproduction, you won't be scrambling and scurrying so much during production, and that will afford everybody the time and luxury to exercise their creativity. If your shots are well lit and well miked, the cast and crew know it when you screen takes with them, and it will give them the impetus to keep on working hard.

That doesn't mean you should overwork them. However, keeping to a tight, efficient, businesslike schedule is usually much better for morale than letting everything unfold lackadaisically. If you allow too many loose ends, the whole ball of yarn starts unraveling. If someone becomes disgruntled or starts slacking off, others may soon give way to resentment and bickering. To guard against this, you should be sensitive to people's needs and fair in mediating their complaints or differences. Give them a break whenever you can afford it. Beer and pizza during screenings of your footage doesn't cost much and it's a great morale booster.

But despite your best efforts there may be people who start out great guns and then fall to pieces. If talking to them doesn't help, you may have to get rid of them, or they may quit on their own, putting you in a bind and forcing you to find a suitable replacement. Take care of these personnel problems as expeditiously as you can. Not everyone can take the tough grind, and it's better to find out who can't take it earlier instead of later. Keep your own attitude upbeat and keep on plugging. Shooting schedules are always grueling. It's the nature of the beast. Even on big-budget productions everyone is always going without sleep and busting hump 18 or 19 hours a day, trying to put as much as possible on the screen for the money.

Your ultra-low-budget production may require even more sacrifice. But at least the shooting schedule's short. And at the end of it you're going to have your movie in the can, and the toughest part will be behind you and almost nothing will be able to stop you from going all the way

25

How to Avoid Getting Raked over the Coals

THIS CHAPTER WILL focus on key points you need to understand when dealing with agents and distributors, if you intend to let others promote and sell your movie. In the next chapter we will discuss how you can distribute your own movie, in case that is the route you elect to take. Even if you are distributing yourself, chances are pretty good that your efforts might cover only certain markets (U.S. home video, for example) and so you will still need to negotiate agenting and distribution deals for the other markets around the world.

Once you have a finished movie to sell, everything you've put into it is on the line. Now you're going to find out how well your work will be received, both artistically and commercially. The kind of promotion and distribution your movie receives will have a tremendous impact on your career. In order to help you make that impact as positive as possible, in this chapter we will cover:

- The Rights you are Looking to Sell
- The Rights you are Hoping to Keep
- The Commissions you should Expect to Pay
- Key Deal Points in Distribution Negotiations.
- Warning Signs.
- Realistic Profit Expectations.

THE RIGHTS YOU ARE LOOKING TO SELL

If your movie has theatrical possibilities, you will probably do best by offering worldwide distribution rights to a single distributor. In fact, you will have a very tough time getting a distributor to make a heavy investment in 35mm blowup, prints and advertising for a theatrical run, if you refuse to allow him the opportunity of recouping those costs from the worldwide market.

The reason for this is simple economics. You'll see why when I give you a few facts about the distribution of the 1990 remake of *Night of the Living Dead*, which got a major national release by Columbia Pictures. The picture opened in 1,700 theaters, which meant that 1,700 35mm prints had to be pulled at a cost of about $2,000 each or $3,400,000. National advertising cost roughly another $1,600,000 a total P&A investment of about $5,000,000. The movie held for two weeks in the theaters and took in about $6,000,000.

Great! A $1,000,000 profit, right?

Wrong. Most of that money went to pay the exhibitors. And what about the $4,500,000 it cost to produce the movie? It still needed to be recouped. Our major domestic release, because it wasn't a huge hit at the box office, left us about $5,000,000 in the hole.

Where does the distributor stand a chance of recouping all that money? The answer is: in the rest of the worldwide markets, and that is why most distributors won't tackle a major theatrical release unless they have worldwide rights to fall back on. Even a small theatrical release, where the distributor pulls about thirty prints and uses them to work a few large metropolitan areas in order to gain exposure and notoriety to maximize ancillary sales, can cost as much as $500,000 to $1,000,000. The distributor cannot justify that kind of investment in a picture for which he owns just domestic theatrical rights.

THE RIGHTS YOU ARE HOPING TO KEEP

However, if you have a very good movie that you and the distributor believe in strongly, you may be able to get away with offering him all domestic distribution rights, hanging onto all

266

foreign rights for yourself. When I say "all domestic distribution rights" and "all foreign rights" I mean theatrical, television, cable, pay-per-view and home video, and any other rights in those respective territories.

When you make a very low-budget movie there is always a chance that lightning may strike and someone may offer to distribute it theatrically, but I wouldn't hang my hat on that possibility. The overwhelming likelihood is that the movie will have its greatest value in the home video market, with perhaps some television, cable and pay-per-view sales here and there. With this kind of picture, it is quite normal to offer United States home video rights alone to domestic distributors. That means that, if you choose to, you can generally own the other territories, and can either make separate deals in each foreign country or can make an overall deal with a distributor whose business is to work all the foreign markets. As I mentioned before, that's what happened with us when we made *The Majorettes*. We sold domestic home video rights to Vestron and foreign rights (including theatrical) to Manson International, and between the two deals we got paid enough advances to cover our production investment.

THE COMMISSIONS YOU SHOULD EXPECT TO PAY

If you use an agent (otherwise known as a producers' representative) to help you land distribution deals for your movie, the standard commission is ten to fifteen percent. It does not come off the top of the movie's total gross, it comes only out of your share, because the agent is representing just you, not the distributor. You must pay your agent his agreed-upon percentage of any advances and any royalties you receive.

Many agents want to collect the money and then pay you, but you should insist on having it the other way around. You touch the money first; then you make the payouts. This keeps you in the driver's seat where you belong, and helps the agent remember exactly who is buttering his bread.

Sometimes the line between "distributor" and "agent" can get rather blurred. Manson International Pictures called itself a distributor, but it was really more of an agent in my book, when I came to understand how it operated in the foreign territories. Basically, Manson sold *The Majorettes* off to distributors in each country; and the buyers took care of marketing the picture inside their respective countries, not Manson. But Manson collected a 30% fee off of all the money our movie brought in. If we had had the know-how and contacts to sell each of the foreign countries ourselves, we could have kept all of that money.

Instead, what it boiled down to was that we were paying Manson 30% of each foreign dollar, and out of what remained we still had to pay our agent 15%. So it didn't take long for our share of the money to be cut almost in half.

You can see that it behooves you to negotiate on your own as much as possible, as long as you feel capable of handling the negotiations. The time to use an agent is when you feel that he can open doors you can't, or when you believe that his expertise will result in a much better deal than you could negotiate on your own.

In the case of *The Majorettes*, even though we ended up paying some hefty commissions, as I described above, I still believe that we made the right move when we hired a good agent. He was honest and diligent and kept us thoroughly informed at each stage of the marketing process and the dickering process, and he had years of experience in the distribution business, so that his knowledge and connections proved invaluable. Because of working so closely with our agent during the months that it took to land domestic and foreign deals for *The Majorettes*, I learned a great deal that is still helping me today.

The beautiful majorettes from *The Majorettes*.

KEY DEAL POINTS IN DISTRIBUTION NEGOTIATIONS

Although distribution contracts (especially those involving world-wide rights) often run 30 ro 40 pages in length, the key deal points make or break a deal, and once they are in order, the fine points will eventually be ironed out through perseverance and legalistic tedium (usually to the accompaniment of sizable attorney fees). The key deal points are as follows:

1. The term of the contract.
2. The rights to be assigned.
3. The advance to be paid by the distributor.
4. The sharing of profits.
5. The obligations of the distributor.
6. The obligations of the producer
7. Performance and reversion clauses.

For a major theatrical or home video distribution deal, the distributor will want a ten to fifteen year term. This seems like a long time, but you must realize that he will have to make sub-distribution deals in the various markets, and he needs to have an extended right to make those deals because they don't happen overnight. Distribution agreements for U.S. home video rights often have a much shorter term, generally about four years.

You don't want to give up the rights to your picture for an excessively long period, but you also do not want to make the distributor feel that his stake in the picture is going to be too short-lived. He's only going to give his utmost on your behalf if he has a powerful enough reason to do so.

Of course the more rights that you give up, the more you can justify asking for a huge advance. I mentioned that we sold home video rights to *Midnight* in perpetuity for $65,000. But even though Vidmark went on to make a small fortune with our picture, I still think we made the right decision at the time because $65,000 was a big chunk of money to us.

The rights to be assigned to the distributor by the producer are usually spelled out in considerable detail, even if you are assigning all rights. To cover the point up, down and sideways, the clause will list "worldwide domestic and foreign theatrical, network television, syndicated television, pay-per-view television, cable television, home video, DVD...and on and on..." up to "any and all formats or means of production or broadcast already in use or to be discovered in the future anywhere in the universe." I'm not kidding: rights clauses often cover the universe; these distributors really want protection.

As we discussed earlier, you may want to hang onto some rights for yourself, and if so you want to not only omit those rights from the clause listing what rights you're giving up, but then list them in a special clause covering the rights you are reserving. Go to great lengths to protect yourself in this regard, because when deals pop up sometime in the future and there is new money at stake, the distributor will try very hard to claim all that is due him and then some, if you don't have him properly nailed down.

If you are to be paid an advance, there must be a clause covering the total amount, the breakdown, and the due dates of payment(s). There may be a partial payment upon signing, and a further payment upon delivery of the film elements and all attendant material that the distributor requires.

A follow-up clause should spell out your percentage of profits and the basis for determining it. The best kind of deal for you is to have a percentage of the gross, but that kind of arrangement is hard to come by; especially for a first-time producer.

The standard theatrical distribution contract is one where the producer and distributor split profits 50/50 after the distributor recovers his advertising and print costs. When you have this kind of deal, allowing the distributor to recover his expenses before you get paid anything, you must try to limit the amounts and categories of expenses that can be recovered. For instance, you don't want to be paying the distributor's office overhead: his secretaries, telephone bills, etc. And you can put a ceiling on the dollar amount he's allowed to spend for P&A without having to obtain your written consent.

In contracts for home video distribution, the producer usually gets about 15% of the jacket price on each unit sold. But there are also deals based on gross revenue. In video sell-through distribution, the jacket prices are low, usually around $10 per unit, and so the producer is usually offered about fifty or sixty cents per unit. This sounds low until you realize that the distributor has to wholesale the tapes at a big discount, so that he usually only receives about $4.50 per unit, and out of that he must pay sales commissions and advertising, packaging, duplication and shipping charges.

Many other obligations of the distributor should be covered in your contract besides the term, the rights, and the payments of advances and percentages of profit. It is often desirable to get him to commit to exactly how much he will spend on P&A. You don't want him to overspend, but you also don't want him to give your picture a token release and drop it like a hot potato if it fails to catch on.

Of course the producer has obligations as well, most of them centering around "delivery." You must commit to delivering to the distributor by a specified date all the necessary picture and sound elements for mastering, printing and/or duplicating your picture. You must also deliver items such as an acceptable M&E mix; a copy of the script; a dialogue script for dubbing into foreign languages; and photos, synopses, bios, and other material to be used in press books and ads. If you can't fulfill the delivery clause, your contract may be null and void. But there are also ways that a contract may be voided if the distributor fails to perform. To guard against having your movie tied up with a distributor who can't properly exploit it, you can push for a reversion clause that requires him to return certain rights to you if they don't yield agreed-upon dollar levels within a specified time period. In the case of *Heartstopper*, when we made a deal with a foreign distributor we had a country-by-country list of dollar amounts we expected him to achieve in each country and this list was incorporated into the contract. So that you can graphically see what I'm talking about, a partial list of this sort might read as follows:

UNITED KINGDOM	$50,000
FRNACE	$40,000
GERMANY	$30,000
NETHERLANDS	$10,000
THAILAND	$ 2,000

As it turned out, with *Heartstopper* the distributor did not reach the levels we wanted, and we reclaimed all the foreign rights to the picture.

Most video distributors are very willing to incorporate reversion clauses. Their philosophy is that they will release each title with a certain amount of promotion, and if the video stores are interested the orders roll in, and if they're not interested the sales will rapidly hit their highest level and then decline to a pittance. Therefore there is little debating over exactly when a picture is "used up." Once it has been milked, the distributor doesn't mind giving it up for dead and not wasting the space in his catalogue. The name of his business is quantity not necessarily quality, and he has other fish to fry.

But your picture is all-important to you, and you may wish to keep on plugging with it. So it will be to your best interest to make sure your contract contains a reversion clause.

WARNING SIGNS

After your contract is in effect, the first warning sign that the distributor may not live up to his promises is when he takes too long to get your movie into release. This usually means that he's giving other movies the major part of his attention and/or that he's in a poor cash flow position and can't afford to do your movie justice at the present time.

Usually you'll want to stick with it anyhow. Even if you could land another distributor, you've already used up several months or more selling and negotiating and making delivery, and if you start the process all over again it may waste more time than simply waiting for the distributor to spring into action. Another warning sign is when you don't get statements and checks on time. Or when the statement is incomplete. Or when the check is for less than it's supposed to be.

When that happens, it's generally best to jump on the distributor right away. Go in with your attorney and auditor if you can afford to. Even if you can't afford to, do it anyhow. Sometimes it's the only way to keep a distributor reasonably honest.

When one of my movies went into release some years ago, I didn't receive the very first statement on time, and I immediately used my right to audit, even though I could barely afford to pay the auditor. The distributor was very upset with me, but I got the statement and the check, and he never missed a reporting period afterwards.

REALISTIC PROFIT EXPECTATIONS

We always read about movies making millions and millions of dollars, but this is show business, and just about everything is exaggerated. For one thing, the box office grosses get most of the public's attention, but the distributor is lucky to get a third of the box office take, and out of that he must pay for P&A. Then he must pay the producer—you. You are on the bottom. You are not likely to get rich.

Home video sales of B-movies don't generally go through the roof either. While an A title like *Terminator* may sell hundreds of thousands of units, when a B title like *Leprechaun* sells 50,000 units it's considered an enormous success.

But the good news is that when you make a movie for $10,000 or less, you don't need to sell many units to break even, make a small profit, and go on to make yet another movie. So there's no excuse for you not to start building your career by doing what you love to do.

26

How to Distribute
Your Own Movie

IN THIS CHAPTER we will cover the basic steps for distributing your movie on your own. Later, in the interview section of this book, the distribution process will be covered in much greater detail, and from a personal point of view. You will learn the various ways to successfully market your ultra-low-budget movie, and you will gain insight and perception that will enable you to adapt certain methods to your own purposes.

Whether someone is distributing your movie for you or if you are distributing yourself, many of the necessary tasks remain the same. These tasks include:

- Making ads, filers, trailers, press kits and sleeves
- Utilizing press releases
- Holding special screenings
- Finding buyers and sales outlets
- Making delivery and collecting money

ADS, FLIERS, TRAILERS, PRESS KITS AND SLEEVES

Since you are a movie maker, you will be able to make your own trailer for your movie just the same way that you made the movie itself—by using your own skill, ingenuity, and money-saving shrewdness. You'll have good clips from the movie and its sound track to work with. If you don't think you're so hot at writing copy or narration, get someone else to do it. Work just as hard polishing the trailer as you worked polishing the movie itself. Remember that a good trailer can sometimes sell even a bad movie.

You should also be able to put together an excellent press kit on your own. It ought to contain the following:

1. A synopsis of the movie
2. Brief profiles of the producer, director and stars
3. Press clippings
4. Good stills
5. Artwork, fliers or video sleeves
6. Anything else that is eye-catching and pertinent

You may be able to produce ads, fliers and video sleeves on your own, or you may require help, depending on your training and abilities as an artist or layout man. Again, if you took good stills during production, half the battle will be already won. Most distributors and video store owners say that photos from a movie sell it better than artwork ever will. But this opinion is not carved in stone. Sometimes there is no single photo that will do a movie justice, and trying to employ a photo montage clutters up the design of the package or ad.

Once you have your artwork elements produced and laid out, you have to find a printer to crank out ads, filers and sleeves in large quantity. This is a matter of exploring and obtaining competitive bids.

As you can see, this is a quite small amount of money to pay in order to have it within your grasp to distribute your own movie. But if you need to pinch pennies even more, there are many ways of doing so.

For instance, you may be able to get by with black-and-white promotional material and sleeves. Or, if you absolutely must have color ones, perhaps you can begin your marketing effort with much smaller quantities. In general, printers who are going to do a color run refuse to set up and go to press on orders of fewer than a couple thousand at a time. But . . .

Today there is the alternative of making color copies. These only cost about a dollar apiece. Many times if I need a filer or a video sleeve in full color, I have it run off in a small quantity at a copy shop with a color copier. Color copies of a video sleeve design can be inserted into "slipcover" style hard plastic DVD boxes, and they look slick enough for just about any customer.

Another "plus" to the notion of making color copies of your ads and sleeves is that you will be able to hold off on the cost of color separations. Later, if sales are brisk or if your finances improve, you can decide to spring for the whole kit-and-kaboodle.

UTILIZING PRESS LEASES

Whether you are distributing on your own or still looking to sell to a distributor, you can and should start sending out press releases as soon as they are ready. The media attention you garner for your movie may stir up a distribution offer that you just can't refuse, or if you still want to distribute yourself, it will prime the public to become buyers and renters of your movie.

Perhaps a better phrase for "press release" is "media kit." You don't send it only to newspapers and magazines but also to radio and TV stations. This is particularly true once you have "screeners"—the first dubs of your movie—to accompany your mailing. Any media coverage, especially good reviews, will help you in your sales effort.

HOLDING SPECIAL SCREENINGS

If you cannot yet afford to have screeners made, you can invite media people and potential buyers to special screenings. Hold them at your own studio, if you have adequate space. Or rent a banquet room at a nice hotel. Your choice of a screening facility will depend on your finances, but you should of course strive to have a comfortable, attractive place that will make a good first impression.

You don't need to show your shot-on-video movie on a tiny TV screen. You can rent or borrow a big projection-type screen which will almost give the impression that the movie is being shown in a full-size theater.

FINDING BUYERS AND SALES OUTLETS

Lists of movie and video distributors are published by trade publications such as *Variety* and by magazines catering to movie fans, such as *Fangoria*. There are also lists in the Yellow Pages, especially the ones for New York and Los Angeles, where most film distributors are located.

Your media kit and screeners will be essential tools in the hunt for a distributor, or in the event that you choose to distribute your movie yourself. Here is a list of the chief methods employed in self-distribution:

- Uploading a screener to Withouthabox.com (a submission service for film festivals)
- Mailing promo material and screeners to video stores
- Taking ads in magazines
- Mailing ads and fliers directly to potential customers
- Selling to movie fans at conventions and other events
- Making deals with small distributors or agents to handle markets you cannot cover yourself.

There are about 44,000 video stores in the United States, and if each of them bought just one copy of your movie, you'd be rich.

But how can you afford to reach out to them to even make them aware that you have a movie to sell? Assuming that your direct-mail package (not including a screener) costs you about twenty-five cents to produce, and the postage and envelope cost seventy-five cents, then you are going to have to spend $44,000 to reach every store by direct mail. You cannot afford to do so. Furthermore, even if you could afford it, it would be a wasted effort. The major chains are generally not going to buy anything from a one-shot small time moviemaker and distributor. That means that you must aim for the "mom-and-pop" operations and the specialty stores. This cuts down on your market, but it also cuts down on your expenses.

One way of approaching the problem is to start out small, working the video stores near your home. Conveniently, they will be listed in the Yellow Pages. Let's say you select thirty of them that you feel might be your strongest potential buyers. Mail your fliers and screeners to them—or, to save money, mail just the fliers with a letter offering to send a screener upon request. Visit as many of the stores as you can in person. Some of them won't buy; but others might buy more than one DVD. This effort should give you a small income base to work from.

You might decide to use this stake to take your first ad in a magazine. You could place a half-page or even a full-page ad for around five or six hundred dollars. A full-page ad in *Fangoria* costs about $2,500 but it has a circulation of 200,000. You get a big bang for your bucks. And if you have made a horror flick, you will be reaching out directly to fans who go for horror in a big way.

Direct mail is also a good avenue for reaching your kind of fan. You can buy all or just a sampling of a movie magazine's mailing list. Or you can start building your own mailing list by signing people up yourself. How?

Well, one of the best ways to find potential customers is by meeting them in person at movie fan conventions and similar events. You can find conventions in major cities all over the United States and Canada. Check them out on the internet!

Filmmakers' associations, schools, and clubs of various kinds may welcome you as a guest speaker once you've achieved the notoriety of making a movie. When you go to give a talk or put in a personal appearance, bring some of your videos to sell. You may be able to get your movie screened at independent film festivals or at fan conventions or club meetings. This will of course stimulate interest among buyers and result in sales. You don't have to, and probably shouldn't, handle these gigs on your own. Bring your partners with you, let them bask in the limelight. If you have a good-looking starlet in your movie, bring her along to help attract attention. Dress up your booth with posters, stills and any other eye-grabbers you can think of. And if you have items to sell or give away, such as T-shirts, mugs, toys and other gimmicks with your logo on them, you can use them to help publicize your movie and produce revenue.

Don't forget to use these events as opportunities of signing people up for your own mailing list. As your list grows and begins to produce sales, you'll be building a highly valuable resource: a "bank" of customers who have already bought from you and will therefore be most receptive to your future offerings.

Once you have the ball rolling, you may able to hook up with agents or distributors who can help you cover markets you cannot cover yourself. For instance, once a small dealer sees that you are having a measure of success with your movie in your local area, he may realize that it would benefit him to carry it in his area, so you may be able to work out a deal whereby you supply the product and take a piece of the action. You also might be able to get an agent to handle cable, foreign or specialty stales for you. It might surprise you how many opportunities exist, if you will only be on the lookout.

MAKING DELIVERY AND COLLECTING MONEY

Once you have gotten product orders from any source, you must deliver the goods promptly. Otherwise the orders might be cancelled. Even if the customer doesn't cancel this time, he might not order from you ever again. In this business, it is best not to extend credit unless you have to. Too many stores go out of business—or they try to stay in business by not paying their debts. Therefore, you might want to adopt a C.O.D. policy. You will make fewer sales that way, but the ones you do make will put dollars in your pocket instead of a sheaf of "receivables" and a passel of headaches.

Another wise practice is to sell on a non-returnable basis only. All sales are final. With the exception, of course, that you must agree to replace damaged goods.

If you should be fortunate enough to land a big deal involving the purchase of thousands of units by a major chain, you will have to extend credit because they don't operate any other way, and they have the clout to command compliance with their terms. They will also insist on being able to return all units that don't sell. Therefore, you will have to cope with the realization that you may ship 2,000 units, which looks like a hugely profitable deal until 1,500 damaged or unsalable DVDs are returned to you, and you're stuck with the tremendous duplicating and packaging costs.

If you handle your little distribution setup energetically and wisely, you may prove that small movies can produce big results!

Part VI
INTERVIEWS

"I want to constantly to be looking for what is miraculous in the world around me. For me the best part of the creative process is when I feel as though I'm a witness to something, and I'm simply trying to find the words to describe it."

– Clive Barker

"It's very important to anybody who wants to make a career doing movies to remember that it is the film *business,* so if you have a love of the creative process, you still have to take care of the business end . . . it's important to have both sides of the equation represented. Otherwise you're at the mercy of whoever happens to be in charge . . . and you'll always be a hired gun."

– Wes Craven

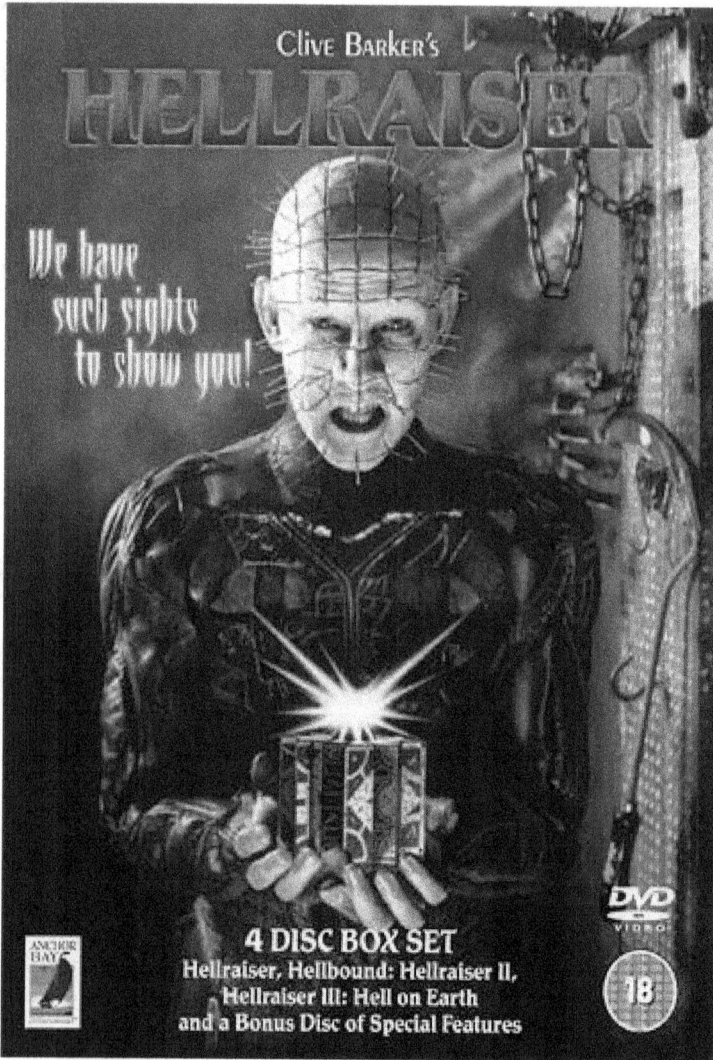

Clive Barker's *Hellraiser*—Anchor Bay Box Set Cover.

27

Clive Barker

Multitalented **Clive Barker** is an artist, an illustrator, a novelist, and a stage and film director. He splashed onto the literary scene in 1984 with the first of his *Books of Blood*, marvelous collections of novellas and short stories which caused Stephen King to say that Clive was "the future of horror." His novels, *The Damnation Game*, *Weaveworld*, and *The Great and Secret Show*, have all been best sellers, and the first two movies that he's directed, *Hellraiser* and *Nightbreed*, have firmly established him as a star in his chosen field of fantasy and horror.

As a person who writes, paints, draws, and makes movies, how do you balance all those activities and make time for them?

Well, they are all part of the same process: that of putting into concrete form something which previously has only existed in the imagination. Writing is very solitary of course while movie-making requires hundreds of people—nevertheless what you're trying to do is make real something which began in your mind. And I use all kinds of cross-referencing between the media I deal with, to get my creative juices flowing. I keep a dream diary, for instance, and I very often draw in that diary, as a way of making a kind of thumbnail notation of something in my dreamscape. A sketch may stimulate something in a novel. Also, a line of something that I write may stimulate a sketch. So, it's a two-way street.

My daily life is real simple. I'm interested in making books, making paintings, making movies. I don't have a family, I don't have animals. I have practically every part of my life looked after by other people. I figure I was born into the world to make things. To be a professional imaginer. That was what I was born to be, and that's what I had the conviction I should be from quite early on, even though I had gotten my Ph.D. because that's what Mom and Dad wanted me to do. It was my belief that I would just work until such time as what I did made money. It took a lot longer than I thought it was going to. So right through my twenties I had no money in my pocket, and it didn't matter to me hugely, I guess, because what I was doing was the only thing I really wanted to do.

I want constantly to be looking for what is miraculous in the world around me, and then making reports on what I see. For me the best part of the things which are going on in my mind are in turn fueled by what's going on in the world outside me. I couldn't make my books if I were locked in a cell, because what starts me going are things that I see or feel—the way the sky looks or the sun looks or the way a child cries, the way a child laughs—in other words, the stimulus, the raw material for the imagining has to be the real world.

Do you believe strongly in the supernatural aspects of your imaginings?

I have a very strong sense of the world as haunted, and it's not just we human beings who are doing the haunting. My great hero is William Blake, the English poet, mystic, and painter. I believe, as did he, that our imaginations are evolutionary tools (though he wouldn't have used that vocabulary) which we are not even beginning to use fully because we don't quite know what to do

286

with them yet. But they have the potential of helping us see how the cosmos works.

That's sort of what *The Great and Secret Show* is all about, isn't it?

You're absolutely right. It's very much a celebration of mind, and I think one of our problems as a species is that we have come this incredibly long distance toward civilization in such a short time, but we're still locked into a very physical assessment of the world. We are still overly preoccupied with solid reality, and it's not actually the way forward. The way forward is mind, which is fluid and complex.

Nowadays we're more materialistic than we ever were before. I don't know that I would have been very comfortable living in 1780 London when the streets were a good deal less safe than they are now, but on the other hand you couldn't waste your life in the pursuit of a second Porsche, because there wasn't the first one to have. It must have been an easier place to be alive, an easier place to imagine the world reconfigured through the processes of mind, than it is now, because we're simply so distracted, not just by solid reality, but by the junk that the technology puts in our hands.

People seem to think that if they move and talk and act as though every moment of their lives is filled, they can distract themselves from a profound wretchedness, which is essentially a religious emptiness. And the only way that kind of emptiness can be filled in my estimation is through the imagination.

In his great prophetic books, William Blake talks of angels and devils inhabiting exactly the same world that Blake himself is living in. His day-to-day emotional experiences, his sense of achievement, his sense of frustration, his sense of loss—all of that is part of what makes him imagine this richer, brighter, more metaphorical world. So I don't want to give the impression that I'm locked up in an ivory tower having a kind of dream trip without relating to the world outside, but rather that the world outside is fuel for the dream trip.

And your movies are very much a part of that trip, right?

I've always seen the movies as being part of a whole parcel of ways in which ideas *get* to people. For instance, we now have a highly successful comic book investigating the worlds of *Hellraiser.* We have two highly successful *Nightbreed* comics. And those are very important to me, because they're ways by which the characters run on in various ways, making further explorations of worlds I've created on the screen. So now other artists and storytellers can use the raw material available in those movies to weave their own dreams and nightmares.

We also have plastic models of some of my creations, which is a pleasure to me. I built my Dracula and Frankenstein models as a kid, and painted them with luminous paint so they could stand guard over my bed. So it's wonderful now to have the plastic *Nightbreed* models coming out, and a new generation having my inventions as local gods.

In *Hellraiser* one of the most striking characters was of course Pinhead. Did he originate in your dream diary?

Well, Eclipse Comics has just published a book called *Clive Barker, Illustrator,* and it contains about 150 illustrations—and some of the drawings were just scraps of paper with vague sketches, and some were more elaborate—but one of those pages contained the original drawing of Pinhead. And God knows where that drawing came from. It wasn't in a dream. But it came from somewhere in my psyche. I probably drew it around the time that I wrote the story because *The Hellbound Heart,* upon which *Hellraiser* is based, contains quite a specific description of Pinhead. The whole geometry of him, the scarification of his face, the pins driven in at each intersection of the lines, and the kind of priestly garb which the Cenobites wore in *Hellraiser* were also described. So really there was quite a solid jumping-off place for Pinhead. But I don't know where those images came from. Maybe it's great that I *don't* know. It's one of the secrets of the psyche.

Did you delve into your psyche once again for the ideas behind *Nightbreed*?

Well, on an elemental level, the idea of a "mythology of monsters" which *Nightbreed* aims to became about simply because I've always loved monsters. My horror stories are full of strange creatures of various kinds for which we often have very ambiguous feelings. I mean, they are not like the creature in *Alien,* for whom we feel only repugnance. Hopefully we're intrigued with them, and maybe even feel some sympathy.

Hellraiser had already set the stage because it had done quite well at the box office and on tape, and it had become this strange phenomenon, the cult film—the kind of thing that only 3 percent of the world likes, but *they* like it really obsessively. I went out on Halloween night in Los Angeles and saw guys whom I didn't know dressed up as my characters, so I guess I knew that somehow the image of Pinhead and the other images from the movie, like the box which opened the door to hell, had found their way into the public consciousness. And I suppose I felt, well, that's pretty neat, I kind of like that. So I wanted to do it again. I wanted to make another quirky, strange movie.

What I mean is that *Hellraiser* and *Nightbreed* are both modestly budgeted, strange pictures which aren't really mainstream pictures. There's something slightly ragged about them which I like—they're not too slick. I'm not a great fan of slick filmmaking. I like the quirky personal stuff. My favorite horror movie of all time is *Bride of Frankenstein,* which is a very strange, quirky picture with weird digressions, really—characters who are humorous and campy and strange, and then of course this wonderful love affair in the middle. So I like offbeat projects as opposed to the super-slick Hollywood projects. I've always preferred the quirky.

With all this stuff tumbling through my mind, I fastened upon a short novel that I had written, entitled *Cabal,* and I took it to Joe Roth, who's now head of 20th Century-Fox, but at the time he was the creative man at Morgan Creek. And Joe liked the story hugely and said, "Let's make this into a movie." So I did a couple of drafts of the screenplay for what eventually became *Nightbreed.* And then Mark Frost, who is the co-writer of *Twin Peaks,* came in and gave me a hand, which was immensely useful. I then did a final pass at it, and we set the movie up. We shot it here in England because that's where we had shot *Hellraiser,* and all my special effects team were here, and it was a very straightforward process from novel to screenplay, and from screenplay to screen.

In your screenplay, how clearly did you indicate what the creatures would be and how much of the creation of them happened sort of after the fact between you and the special effects guys?

In the script, the impressions of the monsters were extremely vague, and that was because I knew I was going to direct it. And I knew from the experience with *Hellraiser* that my special effects team were going to be the kind of guys that I was going to be able to really jam with—like a jazz session for monster-making. I could tell them, "Okay, we've gotta come up with all these monsters. I'm going to draw some stuff that I want to see on the screen, and you guys can draw some stuff that you want to see and that you feel capable of making within our time frame and financial framework, and then let's just all get together, come over to my house, and we'll all get drunk and throw the drawings back and forth." It was like mix and match for monsters, you know? And it was a great way to work because you know special effects guys—they very seldom get a chance to express their *own* desires. They are often pushed by producers and directors into being very mechanical. So I enjoyed telling them, "Okay, I *don't* want something super-slick. I want something weird and offbeat and haunting. Let's make some stuff that doesn't look like somebody else's stuff."

We see many movies that are pastiches or homages or rip-offs of the aesthetic from which a very successful movie has been created. It's very depressing. So I'm very keen on saying to the special effects guys, "Look, we've seen all that before. Let's not do that. Let's do something different." And for me the best way of communicating with these guys is not to write it down but to draw it.

What kind of filmmaking experience did you have before making *Hellraiser* and *Nightbreed?*

The second day I was ever on a film set was the first day of principle photography on *Hellraiser.* When I think back on it, I still get cold chills. If I had thought too hard about it at the time, I might not have done it. There was a kind of value in just going in there and saying, "Okay, I'm gonna do this. I need a swift education." The director of photography took me through the lenses that first day, and my art training helped me with compositions. Since it was my screenplay, if an actor was going to come to me and ask what the meaning of something was, I was likely to know the answer. I was protected in lots of ways, surrounded by people who were just a joy to be with.

The theater experience—and I'd worked in the theater during my twenties—is also a collective experience. The director of a show is less powerful in the theater than in a movie because once he's directed the show the actors can actually go away and do it any way they like—you can't just go up there on stage and stop them. So there is this sense that you've got to give actors room to do what they want to do, within limits, obviously. You've got to share your anxieties with them, you've got to share your vision with them, but you've also got to allow them to contribute and trust their contribution when it's been given.

There was an interesting thing that happened when Charlie Haid came on set for *Nightbreed* for the first day. He's a very self-assured guy, you know—he's got this great booming voice, which is wonderful—and we'd been shooting for about two weeks, and he said to me, "How do you want me to do this?" And I spoke to him about it, and somebody made a remark to the effect of, "Are you gonna do it that way, Charlie?" And he came out with a great quote from *Moby Dick.* "There's only one God in heaven and only one captain of the *Pequod.*" And I said, "What do you mean by that, Charlie?" And he said, "You're in charge!" And I think that's right. I mean, in the front office the producer is in charge, and he's making the money decisions and on his neck the ax will fall if the money isn't calculated properly. On the floor, I'm in charge. And I will listen to absolutely any voice that is raised, and at the end I will assess the ideas offered, and if I choose to use none of those ideas and it's my conception that goes forward, then I will expect everybody to knuckle under, because finally my name is going to go on the screen as the director.

But of course the agonizing thing about studio politics is that very often the people who put their finger in the pie are people whose names will never appear on the screen. And you've got this wretchedness going on where people who are really just paid to have an opinion are interfering with the creative process. And if you're the director, you get slammed by the critics, and you can't tell every critic one by one, "Well, you see, I was actually overruled by three idiots in ties."

I think the problem I find as somebody who does several things—writes and paints and makes movies—is that I'm not so clever or informed in the area of movie-making as I am in writing books. I've written eleven books and only made two movies. And that does put me at a political disadvantage because I don't know the ins and outs of the Hollywood game. For instance, when I took *Nightbreed* to 20th Century Fox, they started to get anxious about it because it wasn't the kind of film they thought they were going to get. The monsters were the good guys and that made them very uneasy. They didn't know what to do with it. I was very naive and very trusting and thought all these people meant me nothing but good. But I'm getting wise. I've gotten wise to all the things which go on in publishing because I've been working in it now for eight years and I know the ins and outs, the pitfalls, and so on. But with movies I'm still learning. I'm moving to Hollywood in eight weeks, though, and I'm looking forward to moving because I've got some good friends out there. Now that I'm learning the rules, the game is going to be a lot more fun.

Wes Craven's *A Nightmare on Elm Street* movie poster.

28

Wes Craven

Wes Craven has written and/or directed some of the most successful chillers and thrillers of all time, including *The Hills Have Eyes, Last House on the Left, Swamp Thing,* and *The Serpent and the Rainbow*. His Freddy Krueger character, infamous villain of *Nightmare on Elm Street* and its many sequels, is one of the most memorable and scariest supernatural villains in movie history.

You were teaching a writing course at Westminster College, and somehow got sidetracked into a filmmaking career, and the same kind of thing happened to me when I left a high school teaching position to start working with George Romero. Was your career switch as unplanned as mine was?

I think it must've been. I was raised in Cleveland, Ohio, and went to Wheaton College outside Chicago, majoring in literature and minoring in psychology. I really had no plan, because nobody in my family had ever gone to college before, and a large part of my life through those years was very improvisational. At that point my option was pretty much to teach English in high school, but I had heard that there was a graduate of Wheaton College, named Elliot Coleman, who was now running the writing seminars at Johns Hopkins, so I wrote him a letter and sent him a bunch of poetry and short stories that I had written at Wheaton, and I got a full scholarship. There was no money in my family, so I wouldn't have been able to go to graduate school without financial help. I hitchhiked out to Johns Hopkins without money, and they gave me a small allowance for living expenses, and I went to those wonderful writing seminars. That was really a great year in my life because there were only about twelve people in the class, and Elliot Coleman was a Baltimore poet and Joycean scholar—a very eccentric and wonderful man. He knew all the great poets of the age of T. S. Eliot, and had hung around with those guys, so I thought I was extremely lucky being exposed to all his wonderful ideas and anecdotes.

Within a year I got a master's degree, and the wonderful thing about the seminars was that you didn't have to write a thesis, you could make a movie, or write a novel, or write short stories or poetry. So I wrote a novel. And at that time I still had no idea about cinema whatsoever. I was very much wanting to be a writer. But when I turned in the novel for my thesis, Coleman made a comment that stuck in my mind—he said, "This would make an incredible movie, it's so cinematic." And I actually thought it might be an insult, and asked him if he meant it was shallow, and he said, "Oh, no, it just shows a very visual imagination."

In Baltimore a few months later I married my college sweetheart on the spur of the moment, and I was actually selling coins at the rare coin counter in Hutzler's Department Store—with no plan whatsoever for my life. My wife was pregnant. And I had routinely put my name in a file at a teaching placement bureau, and September had come and gone and I hadn't gotten a job. So it looked like I was gonna be a rare coin salesman for some undiscernible length of time. And just when I was trying to resign myself to that, I got a phone call that this English teacher at Westminster College in Pennsylvania had fallen dead of a heart attack on the first day of classes, and could I come and teach? I said, "Okay, starting when?" And they said, "Tomorrow." So I literally got on a plane and went to Westminster and stayed up all night learning what I was going to do the next day—which was a wonderful preparation for the film business.

I only taught a year at Westminster, because it was a very conservative college, and I was ready to kick up my heels, so to speak, so the next year I went to Clarkson College in upstate New York to teach. It was there that I bought a camera on the spur of the moment just to make home movies.

But it happened to be a 16-millimeter camera, and as soon as I had it on campus students saw it and said, "Let's start a film club." So we started making little films, and that was the beginning of my making movies.

You mentioned in a previous interview that you were raised in a strict religion. How do you think that may have influenced the kind of work that you do?

I'm sure that some of the intensity of my films comes from the fact that I came from a background of very great containment. And I've noticed that there are people in very shocking forms of art who came from a similar background. Alice Cooper, for example, came from a fundamentalist background and I believe that Sam Kinison was a preacher at one point. So it does seem to give you sort of a running start on raising hell when you're raised to be very proper and good. I think coming from a broken family had a lot to do with it, too. Since I was the youngest, I heard all the family stories and was sort of an observer, and the witness becomes the writer quite often. And I grew up in a tough section of Cleveland. There was violence in the street a lot of the time, and most of the schools I went to were quite violent and confrontational. I think I was sensitive to violence, because it was so much denied by the culture at large, and I was intrigued by the things that were denied by my religious background.

I'm interested in getting across to people how projects are developed and sold. So is there anything you could say along those lines about your current project?

Well, I'm currently in preproduction on *The People Under the Stairs,* and it's one of two sorts of films that I seem to do when I write them myself. That is, sometimes someone says they'd like a movie—for instance, in the case of *Last House on the Left* or *The Hills Have Eyes*—and I go out and try to find an idea. *Last House* was my modern adaptation of Ingmar Bergman's medieval tale, *The Virgin Spring* and *The Hills Have Eyes* resulted from a week I spent in the Forensics Department of the New York Public Library, where I discovered an account of a savage family that lived in England in the seventeenth century. It's such a phenomenal story or legend that it made a remarkably good contemporary tale also. There was a district between London and Scotland that was considered haunted because travelers kept disappearing, over several generations. Nobody could figure out exactly what was happening until a husband and wife on horseback were attacked by what the husband described later as a half-naked group of savages. His wife was dragged off her horse and killed, and the man barely managed to escape with his life. He returned to London and told the story in such detail that they mounted an expedition. But they found nothing, not even the horse. And then just as they were leaving, one of the dogs in the search party discovered a hidden path along a bluff over the sea, and started barking. They followed it down and found a large cave inhabited by a family of feral people who had not only gone wild but were cannibalistic. The remains of victims were even discovered pickled in barrels of seawater. The irony was that the searchers dragged the whole family back to London and executed them in the most horrendous way—breaking the men on the wheel and burning the women.

I thought, "My God, there's so much *in* that—it's just so incredible that people could actually go wild and become cannibalistic." And it also appalled me that when they were caught, they were punished in just as uncivilized and hideous a manner. So I took the anecdote and adapted it, out of a source that I found in my research.

I read a tremendous amount and subscribe to all sorts of magazines, newsletters, newspapers, and so on—and many of my story ideas come from my reading. For instance, back in 1979 I clipped out two newspaper stories, and three years later one became *Nightmare on Elm Street,* and almost twelve years later the other one became *The People Under the Stairs.*

The first story was about young men who were having severe nightmares and were not willing to sleep again. They would try to stay awake for a day or more, and when they finally fell asleep they would die in their sleep—apparently from suffering another, even more severe nightmare.

The clipping stayed in my drawer for about a year, till I completed *Swamp Thing.* Then I decided I would write a spec script for a change, and it became *Nightmare on Elm Street.* But then it languished for three years, with nobody thinking it was any good, until finally New Line Cinema got money to make it.

Another example with an even more extreme half-life is *The People Under the Stairs.* The article I clipped was about a house that was burglarized in a very nice neighborhood. When the police went to investigate, they discovered that the parents were away at work. Still, they heard sounds and went in with guns drawn, and discovered at the back of the house two or three rooms that had been sealed off and were inhabited by teenage children who had never been outside! There was a big furor about it, and I clipped the article then, and wrote the first act of a drama about a young apprentice to two burglars who agrees to burglarize a house because his family is starving, but when they enter this house both the experienced burglars end up dead within five minutes, and the boy, hearing the returning owners, flees even deeper into the house and discovers these children, and is trapped with them and has to plot an escape. So that first act sat in a drawer for literally twelve years, and when I owed Universal a second picture, after *Shocker,* I dragged it out and wrote it into a full script, and we're all very excited about it.

So a lot of what I do comes out of stories that I've either heard or read about that I've felt would make good movies. I have a four-picture deal for horror pictures with Universal, and I have an option to do a non-horror picture between each one. So I did *Shocker,* and between that picture and *The People Under the Stairs* was *Night Visions.*

Is there any particular film of yours that you consider your favorite or your best?

I think the purest ones are the ones I've written myself. Although I put as much of my style as I can into the other films, like *Deadly Blessing* for example, which was a project for which I was given a script but did a humongous rewrite, I still don't feel as close to them as I do to the ones I've written from scratch. I feel closer to the concepts that I come up with myself because they're more personal.

Has *Shocker* succeeded in creating another Freddy-type character and spawning sequels and so on?

It started off as a psychodrama of a serial killer and it turned into something in some ways quite surreal and almost comedic, so I think there may have been too much of a switch in gears in it. I thought it would be a wonderful basis for a series of sequels, exploring all the electromagnetic crannies that a man could get into. Universal has remained sort of indifferent to it, but I still hope to executive produce a sequel to *Shocker* eventually—I think there's a lot of rich material as yet unexplored with it, but it didn't get the phenomenal response that the film about dreams did with Freddy Krueger.

I have found, especially as I mature and my personal life becomes very rewarding, it gets harder and harder to stay on the point of horror, because horror is a very painful place to really be. I found with *Shocker* I wanted to be happy, I wanted to do a film about coming out of the darkness and into a sort of triumph that included humor. I didn't want to quite be in that totally dark place where I'm gonna have to be with *People Under the Stairs,* and I've sort of resolved myself to go back into that dark place and deal with it.

I really like horror and I think it's really been good to me, and I've been able to do films with a great amount of variety within the genre, but I got into horror coincidentally. I set off to be a filmmaker, and the first time I got an opportunity to make a film, somebody said, "We want a scary film." In my *Twilight Zone* episodes I've successfully handled love stories and comedies, but if you mention Wes Craven most people automatically associate it with scariness and shock and terror. There are themes that I'd like to deal with that are not dealt with in the usual horror film. Horror is a very powerful and very primal medium, but in my case it's a matter of constantly putting myself back in the first five to seven years of my own life and trying to deal with those feelings, because I think that's where the rich bed of humus, if you will, for horror really is—in one's early family experiences. But as one matures, one also has adult experiences—of love or raising children, or many other things that do not get so easily expressed within the genre. I love the genre, especially when it's done with originality and gets away from just slash and gore, but it nonetheless is in some ways restrictive. And as an artist I don't like to be restricted.

Are there any films out right now that you feel have been able to deal with some of these other elements—love or romance or whatever—while still being considered horror?

I think there have been some key films that have been in the area of "plastic reality" or "rubber reality" that I talk about sometimes. *Time Bandits* was an astonishing film, breaking free of the normal boundaries of time and distance. Also, Ken Russell's film *Altered States* explored semi-horrific and yet beautiful and ecstatic areas of human existence. And *Alien* was a wonderful film in the sense of a monster film that had real human nit and grit to it and was about adults.

I find now that there's sort of a ready acceptance in the film community for hiring me to do thrillers, so I think that will probably be the next likely step for me. I think if violence is treated in movies, it should be treated within a realistic context. I get turned off by pictures where the violence is removed from the human juncture. I think there's more power in peeling back one person's fingernail than in 2,000 machine-gun deaths. Violence needs to be treated as something that's deeply personal. In *Texas Chainsaw Massacre,* for example, the violence was very one-to-one—there weren't that many deaths, but each one was excruciatingly experienced. And that at least carries a certain sense that a single life is something significant, and if it's going to be ended or interfered with by another person, it's a horrendous occurrence. Whereas if you blow away fifty or a hundred people in a big shoot-em-up, pretty soon the audience loses its capacity to *care.*

It's possible to expand your horizons in this business, but you really have to jump fast if you get an opportunity, or even sometimes you have to generate the opportunity on your own. After *The People Under the Stairs,* I'm going to make a concerted effort to do something as far away from horror as possible in order to break that lock-set of "Wes Craven means horror." If I don't

302

succeed in finding a project that will take me on in that capacity, then I will sit down and write my own script. That's what I did with *Nightmare on Elm Street,* and it worked. That was a big gamble, and I thought it would do the job for me immediately, but instead it took three years, and put me in terrible financial shape. So it can get very scary when you make those kinds of career moves, but it's absolutely essential when you reach certain points to realize that you must stop and go off in another direction come hell or high water. It gets scarier as you get older, too, and don't have as much recovery time.

Does your agent help you make these kinds of career moves? And what about the current practice of using business managers in addition to agents? Do you work that way?

I think it's just axiomatic that you have to do it yourself. You have to generate the interest yourself, and then the agent will follow along and help with the deal. I have a person who takes care of my finances for me. But so many people are taking cuts already that if there's one more cut I might as well not even get up in the morning and go to the set. My business manager takes six percent off the top. Uncle Sam takes God knows how much off the top. So does Social Security. The guilds both take one and a half percent off the top. My lawyers take five off the top. And my agents take ten. So just with agents, lawyers, and business manager we're talking better than twenty percent off the top. But there don't seem to be many alternatives.

I made one arrangement, however, that has worked out very, very well. Marianne Maddalena was my assistant on *Deadly Friend* and *The Serpent and the Rainbow,* and we struck up a real good working relationship and she impressed me with being extremely bright. So after discussing it with her, I announced that she was in charge of development at Wes Craven Productions.

Now, there was no Wes Craven Productions, it was basically me. But I said, "Let's create this thing, in air."

So she became my head of development, and we announced it in *Variety* and so on, and she started just having lunches and networking with studio people and development people. And the upshot was that she was instrumental in getting me a deal with Universal on a series of films that included *Shocker*. So at that point I said to Marianne, "Why don't you produce it? We'll find a really experienced line producer to back you up."

Well, she just moved right into that and became the front person, and since other people were doing the line producing, Marianne was able to keep in touch with what was going to happen next. She was reading scripts and so on. And then we got one more person, an assistant who was very bright, to read scripts and write coverage. So our work became very anticipatory—now we're not only turning out projects but looking for new projects at the same time.

We were wondering at first how we were going to pay Marianne's salary between pictures, so we snooped around with the help of ICM, and lit a fire under a two-year development deal at MGM Television—for *Night Visions* and an anthology piece called *Nightmare Cafe*—and all that stuff was turned over by Marianne, who then became the producer and got a nice salary out of the overall fee paid to Wes Craven Productions. Because she was a woman and was fairly young, she wouldn't have gotten that opportunity with a lot of people who would have been afraid that no one would take her seriously. But there are people out there who are unrecognized, and will often do a better job than the old established cigar-smokers.

Every year there's another puzzle to solve as to how to keep everybody employed and to keep future projects coming. When you're writing and directing, it's just all-consuming. You need somebody fronting for you in the meantime. With agents, unless you're screaming at them or having lunch with them all the time, they tend to forget you. Even under the best of circumstances, they'll say, "Well, so and so is doing a picture right now, so we don't need to worry about him. Who's the wheel making a lot of squeaks? We'll take care of him first."

It's very important to anybody who wants to make a career doing movies to remember that it is the film *business,* so if you have a love of the creative process, you still have to take care of the business end or find someone who will do that with you. I've found that my most successful films have been ones where I was allied with someone who had a good business sense and a real strong social sense. Producers tend to like to shmooze, and writers and directors are people who like to immerse themselves in the project, and if you do only one or the other, then I think you're in danger. But if you can get the two things going together, you can be a lot safer and continue to function and create. I think that's the important thing. If you don't have those personal traits yourself, then align yourself with somebody who does. It's important to have both sides of the equation represented. Otherwise you're at the mercy of whoever happens to be in charge at the time, and you'll always be a hired gun.

John Landis's *An American Werewolf in London* movie poster.

29

John Landis

John Landis, who has directed wonderful comedies like *Animal House* and *Coming to America,* has also directed some landmark chillers and thrillers, including Michael Jackson's *Thriller* and *An American Werewolf in London.*

John, this book is about writing, producing, and directing chillers and thrillers, so it's a happy coincidence that both you and Wes Craven are in the book, because he directed a TV movie called *Chiller* and you of course directed Michael Jackson's *Thriller.*

Well, I'm glad to be in the book, and actually I have a question for *you.* I saw *Silence of the Lambs,* and I thought I recognized George Romero. Is he *in* that picture?

Yep, he did a cameo. I also read the book and thought it was excellent.

I enjoyed it, especially Jodie Foster's performance. It's a big hit for Jonathan Demme, who is a terrific guy.

It's been my experience that with very few exceptions—like maybe *Alien* or *King Kong*—in order for a horror film to be a blockbuster hit, it has to be based on a best-selling novel. I'm not talking about low-budget hits like *Friday the 13th* or *Nightmare on Elm Street*—movies which have performed well in terms of what it cost to make them. I'm talking about major successes like *The Exorcist* or *Frankenstein* or *Dracula* or *Jaws* or *Rosemary's Baby.* *Silence of the Lambs* is in this category; it's basically another version of Ed Gein's story (like *Psycho* and *The Texas Chainsaw Massacre);* but it has the advantage of being based on a best-selling novel. Because it has a literary precedent, many people who wouldn't otherwise have gone to see it are flocking to the theaters. It's respectable. It's okay for them to go and see a monster movie, so long as it has been given a certain cachet, otherwise people tend not to be open to these kinds of movies.

Horror movies have always been part of the exploitation genre because if you made them cheaply enough you always knew you'd get a return. Companies like AIP and New World based their existence on that principle. AIP would first make a hard-hitting poster, and then figure out a movie to go with it. The "exploitation" elements they'd always use were beautiful girls and a monster. If you had a picture with a monster in it, and you made it cheaply enough, you were guaranteed a return because there was a solid hard-core audience for monster movies. They were the same kids who bought monster magazines and comic books and went to the drive-in.

But the ideal situation was to try to get a broader audience than that—in other words, to build on the solid audience that goes to see every horror film. This sparked a trend that started in the seventies, when the studios began giving A budgets to B pictures. Movies like *Star Wars* and *Raiders of the Lost Ark* and *Batman* are lavish productions of essentially exploitation product.

The body count in films like *The Terminator* or *Predator* makes me think of them almost as if they're big-budget snuff movies. But if you look at the really great horror movies like *Psycho* or *King Kong* or *The Texas Chainsaw Massacre* or *The Evil Dead,* they don't depend so much on gore. I know people who tell me they wouldn't want to see *Texas Chainsaw* because it's too gory, and yet they went to see *The Silence of the Lambs* and liked it. As I said before, it's almost as if *The Silence of the Lambs* has been culturally blessed, whereas *Texas Chainsaw* is still a little *outré.*

I'm not a big fan of the Grand Guignol sort of stuff, and I think some of the fan magazines get too gruesome. It's not that I'm in favor of censorship, because I certainly think that violence has a place in the cinema. But the photographs that dwell lovingly on horrific makeups cause me to think that I don't really need to see that sort of thing. Sometimes these effects are called for in the context of the movie, but if you dwell on them in close-up in a still photograph they become excessive. I'm not against graphic violence in a film if it's inherent to the plot and necessary to convey feelings or ideas, but I get kind of sick of movies that verge on becoming just splatter films.

It's also interesting that sometimes a picture has to be advertised with a certain luridness, even though the picture itself may not be particularly graphic in its depiction of sex or violence. For instance, the catch-line for *The Towering Inferno* was "Who will Survive?" And the poster was filled with pictures of all the stars. It was as if they wanted people to get excited about seeing Jennifer Jones or Robert Wagner getting burned to death. I mean, that's how it was sold. And I don't think that on a conscious level people went to the movie thinking, "Oh boy, I get to see a bunch of movie stars being roasted," but I do think it might have been part of the appeal of the ad campaign on a subliminal level.

I remember with *An American Werewolf in London* it had a fairly classy ad campaign at first—a poster of two kids looking over their shoulder—-and the picture came out in the U.S. and did okay business, but not great, and so the campaign was changed to just a picture of a big snarly monster and business went up.

It did tremendous business in the foreign territories, but in each country the campaign was different in order to accommodate the different tastes of each particular audience. The Italian poster was quite lurid, I have a copy of it in my office. If you remember, there was a scene in the movie of an audience of dead people in a porno theater, and that's what was illustrated on the Italian movie poster. It was a photograph that was taken on the set of the lead actor, David Naughton, with about twelve dead people in various stages of decay. It's pretty gruesome. They had it blown up to huge proportions and surrounded it with a sort of art nouveau framing, and it was so wild-looking that you could never use it in the States.

I was terrifically entertained by *An American Werewolf in London,* and when I met you at the Horror Hall of Fame I was intrigued by your intention of doing a sequel because I think there's a lot of room to expand the premise in an exciting way.

I agree, and yet I've always refrained from doing sequels. They wanted me to do a sequel to *The Blues Brothers* and *Animal House* and *Trading Places*—but I had reservations. *An American Werewolf* still offers a lot of territory to explore. I actually wrote the screenplay for that picture in 1969 when I was a gofer on a picture called *Kelly's Heroes,* which was being made in Yugoslavia. It wasn't until 1981, after I had already made *Kentucky Fried Movie, Animal House,* and *The Blues Brothers,* that I finally made *American Werewolf.* I only got to make it after such a long time because my other pictures had made a lot of money.

It's so costly to promote a movie now that Hollywood tends to think in terms of "brand names." The financiers are attracted to things that are already established in the public's mind and psyche. And because of home video certain titles and concepts are kept alive for years, and almost take on a life of their own. So you can now do a sequel many years later, taking advantage of the name-recognition factor. There is a relatively recent phenomenon in our business: this idea that the public is ready to recognize and buy something if they already almost know in advance what they're going to get.

When you were directing Michel Jackson's *Thriller,* did you approach it differently from the way you'd approach a feature movie?

Well, I direct everything pretty much the same, except one has to make constant compromises that have to do with time and budget factors. Making a movie is the same process regardless of the length of the finished product. It's like making a building is, no matter how big or small the building—you still have to have a good design, lay a solid foundation, and so on. And the wonderful thing about making movies is that no matter how many technological advances have been made since the days of the "silents," the basic process is still exactly the same. Whether the budget is $100,000 or $100,000,000 the process is the same, too, even though the logistics may be more complicated.

In this business, people get pigeonholed, as if making one kind of movie precludes any ability to make a different kind of movie. In my case, it's fairly easy for me to get large amounts of money to make a comedy, but if I wanted to make a little love story, my backers might hesitate.

The way *Thriller* got started was that Michael Jackson phoned me because he had seen *An American Werewolf in London,* and he liked the metamorphosis of man into beast. He wanted to turn into a monster! I liked the idea of doing a theatrical short instead of just a three-minute music video.

So we approached it on that level. *Thriller* was intended originally as a two-reeler, and so one of the reasons I got involved with it was that I thought I could take advantage of Michael Jackson's huge celebrity to try to get shorts back into the theaters— I actually had a deal that called for a theatrical run. They fulfilled their contractual obligation by playing it for two weeks in Los

Angeles with *Fantasia,* and although it was very successful, they were much more interested in selling records. That's why they put it on TV as soon as possible.

But it was far more effective in the theater—genuinely scary. We had fun doing it because of Michael and because of the great makeup effects of Rick Baker. And of course I enjoyed doing a *homage* to George Romero and *Night of the Living Dead.*

For my book *Making Movies,* I interviewed Joe Pytka, an old friend of mine who directed Michael Jackson in his famous Pepsi commercials, and Joe was tremendously impressed by Michael's talent and dedication.

Well, Michael works hard, and I have tremendous respect for the hard workers in this business. To me, they're the true professionals. I've worked with people like David Bowie, Don Ameche, Ralph Bellamy, Eddie Bracken, and Tim Curry—and they're professional all the way. They're always on time and they rehearse thoroughly and work hard on camera. They have respect for their craft and respect for the audience, and so they feel that the audience deserves to see them at their best. A lot of performers nowadays don't have that kind of dedication.

What was it like working with a megastar like Sylvester Stallone in your picture, *Oscar?*

Well, the picture was a very risky venture because it's a 1930s-style farce, very stylized, and radically different from anything a contemporary audience expects. So it's a very courageous thing for Stallone to have done and for that matter, I'm beginning to think it was pretty ballsy of *me!* (Laughs) We were working from a 177-page script, and the movie is 99 minutes long. It's solid dialogue. You have to remember that Stallone is very talented. He's an Academy Award-winning writer, an excellent director, and an extremely bright person. With *Rocky* and *Rambo* he portrayed characters that have become cultural icons. So, for the first fifteen minutes of *Oscar,* the preview audiences have had to get used to accepting him in a totally different kind of role. He doesn't show his physique, doesn't hit anyone, and nothing blows up. I had to remind the studio that I'm the guy who made the two Eddie Murphy pictures in which *he* doesn't shoot anybody!

Knowing that *Oscar* was going to have so much dialogue as opposed to action sequences, did you do anything in the directing of it to make sure the pace didn't flag?

I tried to emulate the snappy dialogue of the Hollywood farce, like in the Howard Hawks movie *His Girl Friday,* for instance. The dialogue is really fast and crisp. Ralph Bellamy told me that on that picture, they actually rehearsed many of the scenes with a stopwatch. And they just kept doing it until they got it shorter and shorter and shorter. So I used that same technique a couple of times on *Oscar.*

Do you have any advice that you would like to give to the young filmmakers who read this book?

One advantage that new filmmakers today have, and one that I did not have when I was growing up, is that if you really want to, you can actually make a film. With today's recording advancements like digital you can make movies of very good quality, whereas when I was a kid we had to go to 16-millimeter film, which was way too expensive for most of us. But now, very cheaply, you can make a presentable movie. So for the first time, a novice director can really practice his craft.

When you're a writer, all you need is a pencil and paper. And when you're a dancer, you need your feet. And when you're an actor, you need your body. But when you're a director, you need tons of equipment, people, laboratories, and so on, and nobody will give you millions of dollars to go and practice. So nowadays a kid can take his [personal] equipment and go out and make a movie—with good quality sound, even—it's kind of amazing.

It's very important to keep writing. Write as much as you can, and see as many films as you can. Even read comic books—because they're essentially storyboards. People tend to forget to read these days. Maybe television is making us a nation of illiterates. So the best thing you can do is read. And travel, to broaden your mind. And use your experiences to create a film.

But in terms of "film language," the process is pretty straightforward. Filmmaking is a craft. It's very much like carpentry or any other craft, and you just have to learn it. Once you have the craft, the basic tools of film language, you're there. If you gave seven carpenters the same material and the same tools, and told them to build a chair, they'd all do it pretty well. All of the chairs would be well made, but one might be a genuine work of art. So craftsmanship can be elevated to art. And that's what's exciting about film. Like any artistic medium, it offers the opportunity of creating something really worthwhile.

If not profound, a movie can always be entertaining. And that's pretty wonderful.

Joe Dante's *The Howling* movie poster

30

Joe Dante

Joe Dante launched his career by making exciting low-budget pictures like *Piranha* and *Hollywood Boulevard.* He went on to direct *The Howling* and *Gremlins*—box-office hits that transcended the usual restrictions of the horror genre. When he directed *The 'Burbs,* starring Tom Hanks and Bruce Dern, the result was a hilariously unique blend of mystery, suspense and social satire.

You've done several films that are a blend of horror and comedy. Has comedy always been one of your main interests?

I've always believed that horror works better with comedy. The contrast between what's funny and what's terrifying is one of the most interesting things about the genre. My models are the early James Whale pictures, particularly *The Invisible Man,* in which the most horrific moments are followed by moments that are blackly funny. By keeping the audience off guard and getting them to relax, the impact of the terror is emphasized.

I can also relate this to personal experience. One day my wife and I were coming out of a grocery store in the rain, and two guys with guns forced us into our car and told us to drive and park under a bridge. They were going to rob us, and for all we knew they were going to kill us. They tied us up and asked us who we voted for— which I would have found at least mildly amusing had the question been asked in a different context—and then one of the guys in

316

front wanted my wife to turn off the windshield wipers. She hadn't been very well tied, so she reached out and turned them off, and the other guy said, "Oh, no! Look! She's not tied!" It was a very funny thing, but it was also the most terrifying moment of the entire experience, because that was the point where I realized that anything could happen—they could have just flipped and shot us. They took our money and left, and eventually because they were so inept we untied ourselves and went home. That element of absurdity in the midst of something frightening makes it doubly frightening. And to me one of the appealing aspects of working in this type of film has been to juxtapose comedy and horror in that way.

When I took on *The Howling* it was a very straight werewolf script, very faithful to Gary Brandner's novel, and my feeling was that it needed more humor to work as a movie. And in order to make the familiar elements seem fresh, the story needed to be given a contemporary flavor. I didn't want to have the characters going to the library to read about werewolves or saying, "But tell me, Doctor, what is a werewolf?" That kind of thing had already been done to death, and that was why this sort of film hadn't been made recently. The material had dated, and we wanted to recharge it. So John Sayles, Terence H. Winkless, and I came up with our own take on it, by injecting an element of parody or satire.

There's a line in *Dracula* where Van Helsing says, "The strength of the vampire is that no one will believe in him." And so I felt that in *The Howling* the characters should live in the same world as we all do. In other words there are werewolf movies on TV, and there are cartoons with wolves in them, and there are various lupine associations that actually are part of our everyday life, and we wanted to ask people to go one step further and believe in the supernatural. And this kind of slant seemed to work very well, because when I finally got to see the picture with an audience1 the reactions were much bigger than I thought they would be and they were all in the right places. They were laughing where they were supposed to be laughing, and they were scared where they were supposed to be scared—as opposed to laughing where they were supposed to be scared—which is a big fear when you're making this kind of movie.

What's the story behind the ground-breaking werewolf transformations in the movie?

Well, early on we decided that we wanted to turn a man into a wolf in one shot, and of course we eventually discovered that this was not going to be possible on our $1,000,000 budget. Rick Baker was originally hired to do the transformation effects, and he worked with us long enough to lay down the basic plan, but then John Landis phoned him and said, "How can you work for those guys? You promised me you'd do *my* werewolf picture!"

So Rick told him, "Well, that was years ago, and you never did it, and I want to do a werewolf movie! So I'm doing this one." And John said, "No, no—I'm doing my werewolf movie *now*. It's called *An American Werewolf in London.*" So Rick told me he had to keep his promise to John, but he would remain a consultant to *The Howling.* And Rob Bottin, who was originally going to be Rick's assistant and was only about twenty-two years old at the time, took on a very large responsibility and came up with air-bladder effects and many other terrific innovations, and they were so successful that they got copied in many other films. In fact, sometimes they were overdone. For instance, there's a picture called *The Beast Within* in which a guy's head is inflated to the point where he looks like a giant Charlie Brown.

Unfortunately, the last scene we shot for *The Howling* was the transformation scene, and we never really got it cut together to my satisfaction. It isn't quite as good as it should be. But of course it was the scene that made the picture and sold all those tickets, so I guess I shouldn't complain about it.

It was the first time I had seen air-bladder effects, and it knocked me out to see that somebody had done a transformation in a first-class way. But it occurred to me that maybe the girl should have been tied down while the man changed into a wolf.

Well, when we were cutting the scene together for the first time, down the hall from our editing room some kids were auditioning for TV commercials, and we called them in and ran this thing on the Moviola for them. And they were suitably impressed, but about halfway through it one of them said, "Why don't she run away?" But our rationale had to be that she was just too scared to move. And I think that if we had had more time we would have been able to make the scene shorter and still keep all the good effects. One nice thing was that we used shadowy lighting, so you couldn't see all the rubber prosthetic work. A lot was left to the audience's imagination.

Do you think it's safer to do horror as humor in terms of a wider market?

It depends on the project. *The Howling* had a lot of humor in it, but it was still very much a horror film. And *Gremlins* started out as a straight horror picture with lots of gore, but as we started working with the material, we felt that the initial concept was awfully limiting. There was much more that could be done with the gremlins than just having them bite people's ankles. So, as the movie progressed—not just in the scripting stage, but in the shooting stage—the satirical possibilities started to outweigh the horror possibilities. We found that the gremlins were much more intriguing when they aped human behavior, and the implied social satire was more interesting than the standard horror elements.

It's basically a classical B-picture story—kids find a bad thing happening in town, try to warn everybody, nobody listens to them, and they have to deal with the problem themselves. It's a very generic premise, and all the rest of it is embellishment. And so we just built on the familiar elements to a point where they became more interesting to us and therefore more interesting to the audience. It became a hit because it was a somewhat unique item at the time, a novelty. The creatures were more amusing and I think scarier because they had character—you could recognize human elements in them. You could sense their minds at work, and that was very important to the film's success.

We knew we were making a very dark fairy tale with impossible creatures in it, so we wanted to create a world around our characters that would help the audience suspend disbelief. We made a conscious decision to make the movie look a little old-fashioned and even *unreal,* so that the gremlins would seem more *real.* And so we shot it on back lots that made our picture look sort of like some old movie that the audience dimly remembered. And because of that I think that the more ridiculous elements of the plot became more believable.

When you were doing these embellishments, to what extent did they originate in the scripting stage? Or did most of them just happen while you were shooting?

The script started taking on a more "fun" tone at first, but there were a lot of horrific moments left in it. And once we started to shoot with the creatures and see the dailies and realize how the creatures played off the actors and vice versa, it just sort of changed our idea of what we were going to go for. The movie became a lot more whimsical than we expected.

I like to have the writer on the set because, if things aren't working I don't want to run roughshod over his material and change it all around without consulting him. *Gremlins* was almost entirely a product of Chris Columbus's mind (in fact it was written purely as a writing sample). Steven Spielberg liked it and wanted to make a low-budget horror film out of it. He originally envisioned making it nonunion in Utah and using real snow and so on, but as we started to develop it we realized it was going to cost a lot more than a low-budget horror film. Then it became apparent that we would have to broaden it somewhat, because we couldn't make a picture that expensive for just the horror market. Often, while the gremlins were "down," or broken (pretty often), we would think of new gags and ways to keep the picture interesting for ourselves, because it does get to be very grueling making a puppet movie—it takes a long time, and it's technically complicated, and there are lots of storyboards that you've thought up months in advance, and it's tough to deviate from them on the spur of the moment unless you can think of a way to do it economically.

When you start out making a movie, you have an idea in your head, but then as you shoot the movie it's almost never exactly the movie you envisioned, and what you have to do is perfect the movie it's becoming. After getting the production going, Spielberg had to leave to direct another film, so he wasn't around for the creative decisions that happened during filming. He didn't see the picture until it was completed. It was quite different from what he expected, and he professed to be pleasantly surprised.

In *Fangoria* magazine, Christopher Lee had some nice things to say about working with you—that he would never hesitate to work with you again because you understand and appreciate actors so well. And I had the same impression when I saw *The 'Burbs*. It seemed as if there must've been a lot of good fellowship between you and the cast.

Well, it was a happy set. The actors are the people who are up there on the screen, and that's who the audience comes to see. You might have splendid special effects but if the actors don't look like they believe in what's happening, then the special effects fall flat on their face. To me, working with actors *is* the most fun thing about making movies. They constantly surprise you and come up with things that you didn't think of, or point you in a direction that's better. Sometimes the opposite is true; sometimes an actor will come to you with an idea that isn't very good, but then you don't have to use it, do you?

It seems to me that if you don't want to encourage a creative atmosphere on the set, then everybody's just going through the motions. Because the thing that makes movies work is the combination of interactive egos. I can't think of very many actors that I've ever worked with that I wouldn't want to work with again. And I don't think there are very many who wouldn't work with me.

How did *The 'Burbs* come about?

It came about because I had been working on a picture called *Little Man Tate.* I was going to make it for 20th Century-Fox, and it was not a genre picture at all, it was a sort of comedy-drama. And because I refused to cast a forty-year-old actress in a twenty-year-old part, they canceled the picture. I didn't have another project lined up right then, so I thought, "Great, my filmography is going to have a two-year gap in it, and people are gonna think I was in a detox center or something." But at that moment I was sent a script called *Bay Window* by Imagine Pictures. I said I'd make the picture, but only if we could make it right away, like in *six* weeks. And they said "Oh, no, we can't do it in six weeks!" And I said we could if we did it on Universal's back lot.

There had been a previous director attached to it who had wanted to do it in a barren, rocky desert in Arizona, and his concept was that the people had all been driven mad by their horrible environment. But I didn't think that was very interesting. I thought it would be much more to the point if they were living in a typical suburban neighborhood. And the studio said, "Fine, let's go ahead and do it." So we rushed into the movie, and because of the writers' strike we had to improvise a lot of it, which was fun because the cast was so bright. The execution of the story was challenging because it never left the neighborhood—everything happened in one little cul-de-sac.

The ending was difficult though, because in the original script the character played by Tom Hanks does his speech about how terrible it was of him and his pals to falsely accuse their neighbors of murder, and then he gets in the ambulance and suddenly the villain is in there with him, gloatingly telling him, "You were right." And the ambulance drives away, and that's the end of the picture. But once they cast Tom Hanks, the studio chiefs said, "We can't kill Tom Hanks—we need a different ending." But since the whole picture had been constructed to get to that one final joke, the supply of satisfactory alternate endings that could be tacked on was pretty low.

In my original ending I had the protagonists not being rewarded; in fact, they were feeling pretty bad about what they had done. But audiences didn't like that. They said, "Hey, we watched this movie for ninety minutes, and we want them to get away with it, we want 'em to be happy." So we shot two more endings, one of which is in the movie, and I got a lot of bad ink from critics who said it was a cynical movie because the central characters were getting rewarded for being vigilantes. And that was not the intention, and it was not the ending I preferred, but it was what we ended up with, and I got raked over the coals for it.

Well, I liked it tremendously, and I can't understand how anybody could get bent out of shape over it. It was a beautifully made and beautifully directed film—an excellent blend of comedy and horror and social commentary. Did you purposely give a straight horror treatment to certain aspects of the movie, even though overall it was a comedy?

Yes, there has to be some real jeopardy in any movie or else people won't be interested in it. Even though the story of *The*

323

'Burbs is silly, the characters in the movie take it very seriously. And the audience has to give them enough credit to think they may be right, maybe there is something awful going on in their neighborhood. But in the original script, it was never explained—the murders and so on. The ambulance drove away, and Tom Hanks was right that something dreadful was going on, but the audience wasn't told what.

One of the shots I liked a lot was the long dolly shot when the explanation about the family that had been killed by the father was taking place. It was a long explanation, but the actors were so good that it didn't get boring. How did you work it out that way?

The first thing you have to do in that kind of setup is rehearse with the actors and figure out how long it's going to take them to say their lines and how far they'll have to walk while saying them. And also, since the neighborhood was like a character in the movie, we thought it would be nice to have them walk toward the house that they were worried about. So we rehearsed it a couple of times the day before, and I figured out what kind of coverage I wanted and where I wanted them to stop, because when you have to lay a dolly track that long it's best to figure it out the day before and have it ready right away on the day you're going to shoot. The actors' timing fell into place pretty quickly. We only had to rehearse once or twice, and we shot about three takes.

All during our filming, the actors would change things as we went along. Tom Hanks likes to give away lines, and he likes to convey certain things with his facial expressions instead of always having to spell it out verbally, so we actually eliminated some of his lines as we went along. And all the actors were very good at working out their cues. And my director of photography was excellent. His name is Bob Stevens, and he did two *Amazing Stories* with me.

324

You mentioned using the neighborhood as a character in the movie, and I thought that was one of the aspects that worked extremely well.

Well, it's a very small neighborhood, full of houses from old movies and TV shows (*Harvey, The Munsters,* etc.), and actually it has trams running through it. The Universal Studios Tour is going on while you're shooting, and even if the trams are far away and coming down from the *Psycho* house, they're so loud that they can still ruin sound takes. Also, the *Jaws* setup isn't too far away, and there's a guy who yells, "Helpl Help! Help!" once every three minutes. When you're finally cutting your movie, it's painful to constantly have to listen for the guy yelling "help" in the background.

I don't like to do ADR (looping) if I can avoid it. It's good for changing plot points or explaining things that aren't clear, but I've never really seen a performance that was improved by it. I've seen sound quality that was improved by getting rid of the noise of airplanes flying overhead or other kinds of interference, but performances don't get any better. If you're lucky, they stay the same. It's very hard to be off-handed in a looping session, so comedy especially suffers when you try to ADR it. Many actors find it hard to duplicate the way they said their lines when they were actually on the set and feeling the character.

How did you achieve the beautifully natural nighttime lighting in *The 'Burbs?*

Night shooting can look awful, and in order to get it to look moody and to have the right colors in it, you must go with people that you trust, and I tend to work with people whom I've worked with before. I know their style, and they know mine. It's important also to go to the video transfer, or else a lot of visual stuff that you've really labored over can get lost on TV or on cassette release. I didn't supervise the video transfer on *The Howling* and it

325

was a disaster. There were scenes that were supposed to take place at dusk that were totally corrected to look like midday, and then there was day-for-night stuff that was corrected to look like daylight. The technicians had no idea what kind of lighting we were going for, and so they just tried to balance everything out. The picture looks terrible on tape. And because I don't even know who owns it anymore, it's hard to track it down and get permission to do a new video transfer.

In *North by Northwest,* Hitchcock shot with a yellow filter in the scene where Cary Grant is chased by the crop-duster; consequently Grant's suit took on a brownish hue even though the true color was blue, but Hitchcock went with that in order to come up with the overall lighting effect he was intent upon. And it worked fine. But when the video transfer was made, whoever did it took all the yellow out of the scene in order to get the suit to be the right color, and now it looks completely the opposite of what was intended when it was shot.

On video, the work of the great filmmakers of the past is often being ruined by technicians who are unaware of or don't care enough about what was intended. So, when you've been fortunate enough to direct a film that you care deeply about, you should stick with it all the way, not just from the scripting stage to the making of the theatrical prints, but clear through the video transfer process-because many more people, alas, are going to see your movie on network television, on cable, or whatever the venue, you'll want everybody to see it at its very best.

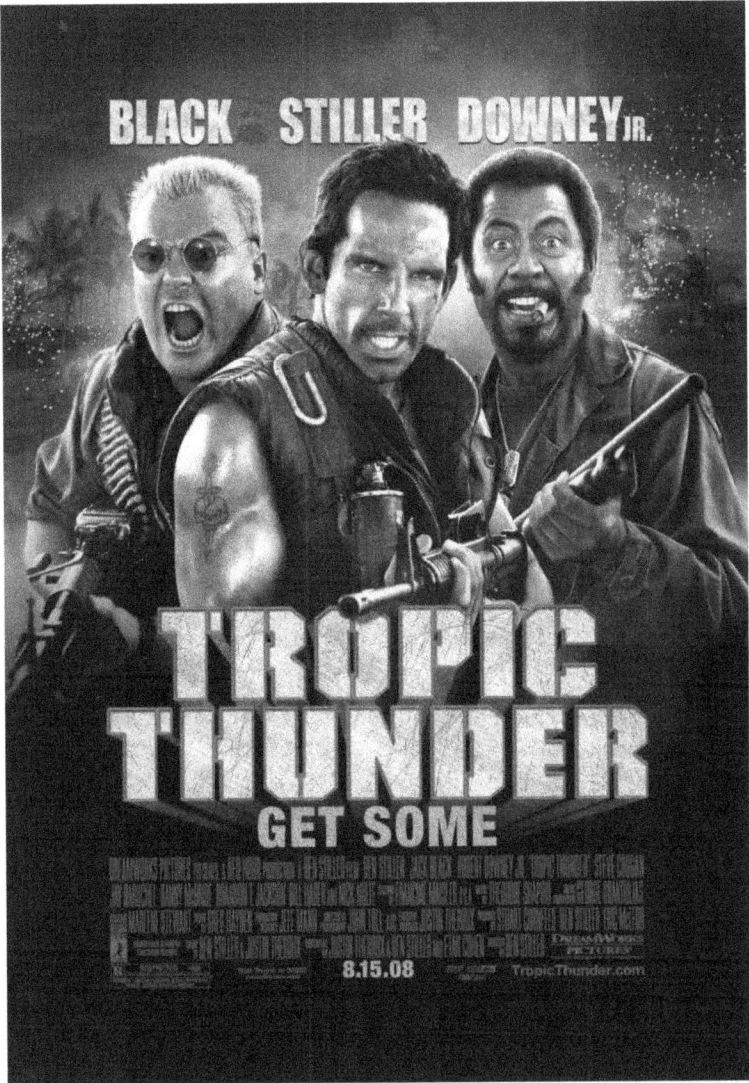

Rick Baker was the makeup designer for Robert Downey Jr.
in *Tropic Thunder;* movie poster pictured.

31
Rick Baker

Special makeup effects wizard **Rick Baker** became known as the "gorilla man of Hollywood" for his work on *King Kong; Greystoke: The Legend of Tarzan, Lord of the Apes: Gorillas in the Mist;* and *Harry and the Hendersons,* for which he won his second Academy Award. Along the way, he also worked on *Star Wars* and *An American Werewolf in London,* whose ground-breaking werewolf transformations earned him his first Academy Award.

How did you become interested in makeup effects?

As a little kid, I was impressed by Dr. Frankenstein, and at first I thought I wanted to be a doctor because he got to make monsters and play with all that great lab gadgetry. But at some point I realized I didn't really want to be a doctor, I just wanted to be the guy who made the monsters.

I was born in upstate New York, but I grew up in a town called Covina, only thirty miles east of Hollywood, where my parents moved when I was only a year old. My dad had a lot of artistic ability, but wasn't able to fully develop it because of always having to get a job to just stay alive, so when he saw that I had some ability, he and my mother both encouraged it and were very understanding.

It's lucky I didn't try to become a doctor anyway, because I'm actually kind of squeamish—I don't like real blood. And although

I've done bloody effects, I don't really enjoy them as much as I enjoy other things that I do. It's pretty easy to get a response out of people with artificial blood, and it doesn't have to be very artistic. But when I was about ten years old and just deciding that I wanted to do this kind of thing for a living, I went through a blood-and-guts period where I liked fooling people with makeup. I was a really shy kid, but when I put makeup on myself it was easier for me to come out of my shell, and it fascinated me that by looking like somebody else you could *be* somebody else. But I wanted to fool people with the makeup, and a little kid as Frankenstein didn't really fool too many people. But the first time I did a cut on my hand and showed it to my mother, she freaked out—I really fooled her! I thought it was great. So pretty soon I was making up every kid in the neighborhood with third degree burns and split-open heads, and they'd go home and scare the daylights out of their parents, and the parents wouldn't let me in their houses again, so I realized that what I was doing wasn't a very nice thing. I saw that the parents were really frightened when their kids came home like that. I still wanted to do something with makeup to fool people, but not necessarily the bloody stuff.

That's how my fascination with gorillas started, which eventually led to my becoming known as the so-called "gorilla man of Hollywood." I wanted to try using makeup techniques to build a real live monster, and the gorilla seemed to fill the bill. But the more I found out about them, the more I realized that they're not monsters at all—they're really quite majestic animals, and not at all like the Hollywood myth. At a very young age I became fascinated with these animals and started building, on a very limited budget, what I could of a gorilla suit. I thought it should be possible to build one that was extremely realistic, but at that time I didn't have enough money.

How did you get your start in films?

329

By the time I was in my teens, I had done a lot of work on my own, and I felt I was getting pretty good, but it was tough to do what I wanted to do on the limited budgets that I could afford. I would mow lawns and save my twenty-five-cent a week allowance, and it would take me months to get enough cash together to buy a quart of rubber to make a mask. So, I wanted to get a job just to be able to buy materials, and I tried to get hired as a busboy or a supermarket bag boy, with no success. And then my father remembered that in one of the jobs he had as a truck driver he was trying to deliver some stuff to a plumbing supply place and went into the wrong building, and next door to the plumbing supply place was a place called Clokey Productions that did stop-motion animation for films like *Cumby* and *David and Goliath*. And I had an interest in stop-motion as well as in makeup, and my dad said this place was near our home and maybe I could get some work. So I went there with a bunch of masks and other stuff I had done, and told them I could sculpt and make molds and I knew a little bit about stop-motion. And I was in the right place at the right time, because they happened to be looking for someone like me. So I went to work for them the next day, during one of my summer vacations from high school. I was hired as a sculptor and mold-maker and foam rubber pourer, and was able to get money to do better stuff, but also I met people there who helped me out in the future.

At about this time, one of the most important events of my life happened, which was meeting Dick Smith, who was my idol—the master of special makeup effects. I thought I'd never get to meet him because he lives on the East Coast, and here I was in Covina, a kid with no money. But because I was born in upstate New York, when I was eighteen and graduated from high school my parents wanted to take me back there to meet some of our relatives. So I wrote Dick Smith a letter, and enclosed photos of stuff I had done, a lot of which was copies of his work. And he sent me an

330

immediate reply that was just great. He said he was really impressed by what I had done and couldn't wait to meet me because he was excited by my work. I thought it was just going to be hello and nice to meet you and good-bye, Mr. Smith, but when I arrived at his house he gave me a notepad, and I was stunned and said, "What's this for?" And he said, "Well, I'm gonna tell you a lot of things, and I don't want you to forget them." So he just started rattling off formulas and all kinds of tricks of the trade and in one day I had pages and pages of notes, and after that my work improved so much that the next thing I did was a hundred percent better than anything I had ever done before.

I kept on corresponding with him and sending him photos of my stuff, and when he was working on *The Exorcist* I got a chance to help out in an emergency because William Friedkin changed the concept of the makeup effects in midstream after Dick already had prepared a lot of the appliances. Dick called me up and said he was in a bind and needed some help, and would I be interested in coming to work with him? Of course I lit up and said I'd be right there. For me, it was like a dream come true. Every day I was learning how the master did his stuff. I actually lived at Dick's house. He came up with another half dozen concepts of what Regan's makeup was gonna look like, and when Friedkin finally picked one, Dick would knock out sculptures and I'd knock out molds, and I'd be running three or four batches of foam a day so we could build up a stock. Sometimes I'd pull a piece out of a mold and he'd almost literally slap it right onto Linda Blair's face.

Did the fact that you had worked with Dick Smith help you land your own film jobs?

Well, the first movie job I ever got on my own actually came through connections I made at Clokey's. It was called *Octoman*, and was a rather terrible movie about an octopus creature. This was around 1971, and I was in my second year at a junior college and didn't even have a shop to work in. I lived with my parents, and there wasn't enough space to build an octopus suit in my bedroom. But a friend from Clokey's, Doug Beswick, had a little shop, and we worked on the film together and made no money, but from that one little film things kind of snowballed, because people who were making low-budget monster movies would hear about me.

What were some of the films that followed *Octoman*?

The next film I did was *Schlock,* which was John Landis's first film. He went to Don Post Studios because he was looking for a gorilla suit, and somebody there said I could make one for him. So that was my early connection with John. I was twenty and he was twenty-one at the time. Again there wasn't much money or time to make the thing, but it was a good experience, and John recommended me to Larry Cohen, and I ended up doing a couple of films for him, including *It's Alive.*

After that, I did a string of low-budget horror films, and then around 1975 I got a chance to do *King Kong.* And it got me a lot of publicity because I was the guy inside the gorilla suit. When John Landis first told me that Dino De Laurentiis was going to do a remake of this great classic, I thought it wasn't a good idea, but De Laurentiis's people were going into it with the attitude that their remake was going to be better than the original because it was more of a disaster movie. I wanted to be involved because of my fascination with gorillas and my hope that maybe something decent could be done, so I showed them some of my gorilla sketches and sculptures, and told them that I was about to start a film called *Squirm*—about killer worms—so they'd have to let me know right away if they wanted me to do *King Kong* instead. But they didn't let me know till after I had already started on *Squirm,* and then I had to finish it up first.

In the meantime, they hired an Italian, Carlo Rambaldi, and said they wanted us both to work together because they thought we were both good. We had different techniques and different ideas, so they asked us both to build test suits and have them ready on the same day to be photographed and compared. I got mine done on time, but Carlo's wasn't ready till a month later. And by that time they had already shot a lot of test footage of my suit and decided it was a lot more like what they wanted King Kong to be. So then we had to rush to make the final suit, and they still said they wanted me and Carlo to work together, but it wasn't a very good working relationship because we had such different styles. Because Carlo was an adult and I was a twenty-four-year-old kid in their eyes, he got to make a lot of decisions that I had to go along with, even though I thought they were wrong.

For instance, while I was doing *Squirm*, Carlo convinced them that he could make a forty-foot gorilla that could be used in the whole movie, instead of using a man in a suit. I said an animated gorilla that huge would never work and pushed them to still make the suit, and they said they'd make it as only a backup because Carlo was a genius and they were pretty sure they'd be doing the whole movie with the giant gorilla. So we knocked out a gorilla suit on a small amount of money while the major part of the budget went into building this giant that barely moved and wasn't even finished until the last week of shooting. So the whole movie was done with me in my gorilla suit.

However, to lure people into the theaters, they wanted to heavily publicize the mechanical monster. So at the last stage of filming they had a big press party where everybody in the world was invited to come out and see this forty-foot wonder, and all it could do was turn its head and move its arms a little bit. They showed the media people some of our footage, shot with me in the suit, and then they showed them pieces of the giant gorilla and told them this was how the movie was being done. But the reporters asked how that could be true, if the thing wasn't even put together yet. So the publicist came up to me and said that a reporter from

Time magazine was gonna talk to me, but I wasn't to spill the beans. But I was sitting there in a gorilla suit, and I said, "What am I supposed to do? Look at me!" So it came to light that King Kong was really Rick Baker in a gorilla suit, and I got a lot of publicity out of it.

After *King Kong* I did a film called *The Incredible Melting Man,* which originally was titled, *The Ghoul from Outer Space.* I didn't want to go from doing a big-budget movie back to doing low-budget stuff, so I gave the producers a bid that I thought was outrageous at the time-something like $10,000—and they said okay, so I went ahead. And then I heard from some friends back at Clokey's about *Star Wars.* The principal photography was already done but George Lucas wasn't happy with the cantina scene and wanted to embellish it. He showed me the sequence that was already cut together, and I thought it was pretty neat, but he wanted to do some new aliens and really spruce it up. I told him I was already working on another film but I could put a crew together and do both films at the same time. There wasn't much of a budget to do the new stuff for Lucas though, because as far as 20th Century-Fox was concerned the movie was already shot and they didn't want to spend any more money, and nobody knew at the time that *Star Wars* was going to be such a megahit. The masks that we did are a little crude, but they worked well because audiences just really loved the concept and bought into it. We made about thirty-five aliens for the cantina scene—things like the cantina band and so on—and our stuff was shot months after the original stuff, but it cut together beautifully.

It's amazing how much of the work in our business gets done that way—on the fly, with very little money—while a great deal of money is often wasted in areas that don't count.

Yes, that's true. But I had a lot of experience working on low-budget independent movies, many of them shot in about ten days, sometimes with only a week to prepare and $500 to spend. All this time, I couldn't wait to work on a real movie, and my first big chance was when *King Kong* happened, and the budget was $25,000,000. And I found out that the guys who made movies in ten days were much more together because they *had* to be. Millions of dollars were wasted on *King Kong* due to poor planning.

Do you have ambitions of producing or directing?

Well, although everybody in this business seems to have that ambition, I'm not interested. I made my own little 8-millimeter movies like most guys starting out, and I enjoyed doing that, but when you're making your own movies as a kid you can make exactly what you want, and I haven't seen a bigtime director yet who's made exactly the film he wants to make. There are always people who have more say about it than the director does, forcing him to cast people he doesn't want or shoot scenes their way instead of his way. So I can see how frustrating it is and what a tough job it is, and it makes me feel that I can be quite happy making rubber monsters.

I've gotten to the point where I can work with people I like, and I feel that I'm good at what I do, so I'm not interested in making my life more difficult. I've gotten credits as associate producer and co-producer on a couple of films, but those were sort of honorary credits because I ended up making a major contribution, although I was not seeking to be known as a producer. For instance, in the case of *Gremlins 2,* I was one of the first people involved, and I did come up with some of the script and story ideas and so on. I enjoy the filmmaking process, and I think that if it could be more like it was when I was a kid and making those little 8-millimeter movies, I might have some yearnings to direct. But seeing what I've seen over the years—directors aging ten years in a year or two while they're working on a movie, or spending years on a project and then getting torn to shreds by the critics—I think I'll stick with my life the way it is.

Joe Dante told me an amusing story about how you were working on *The Howling* but had to go over to *An American Werewolf in London* because of a promise to John Landis.

Well, when I was doing *Schlock* with John Landis, back when I was twenty, he had already written the script for *American Werewolf;* and he told me he wanted me to work on it, and he said he wanted to do a transformation that had never been seen before. He didn't want to do the old lap-dissolve kind of thing. He said that if you were really going through that kind of experience, it'd be painful and maybe full of anguish, and the actor should be able to move around and show those feelings. And he told me I had to figure out a way to do it.

So I had nine years to think about it, because that's how long it took for him to finally get the money and start the movie. I jotted down some ideas and experimented with things on my own, and in the meantime new developments were taking place in the makeup field, and some of them were very useful, and it was fortunate that the concept had a long time to evolve. But once I figured out how to do this elaborate kind of transformation, I was itching to try it, but *American Werewolf* just wasn't happening, so when I got a call from Joe Dante I figured, "Well, here's my opportunity."

But as soon as I started working out my deal with Joe, *American Werewolf* decided it was gonna get made. So I was stuck. Luckily, Joe was very understanding, and I told him I had a very talented assistant named Rob Bottin, who would do an excellent job for him, and I could consult with Rob at the same time I was doing the other picture.

So now you had two werewolf films being made at the same time. Didn't this present some problems?

Well, yeah, because it started to become apparent that *The Howling* was going to come out first, and John Landis was a little upset because he had wanted to do a film with a transformation that no one had ever seen before, and now people were going to be tipped off because Rob and I were using similar techniques. But luckily the two films had two totally different styles. While *The Howling* had shadowy, spooky lighting, for example, in *American Werewolf,* John Landis wanted a normal-looking, brightly lit room for the transformation to take place. And Rob and I were communicating, trying not to do things that looked too similar, but still what really made both transformations work were the three-dimensional heads that changed shape—the fact that you could actually see the heads transform instead of dissolving and changing the makeup on an actor.

Were both movies nominated for an Academy Award?

No, and I don't know why. But the year that I got the Oscar for *American Werewolf* was the first year that there was a special category for makeup. Around that time, makeup effects were starting to become very popular and had caught the public's eye because of films like *Altered States* and *The Exorcist.* So we were lucky in that we had a movie with ground-breaking special effects and we were getting a lot of publicity right when the Academy was deciding to recognize this new category.

After you got the first Oscar, were you able to do more of the kinds of things you like to do?

Well, after *American Werewolf,* I did *Greystoke: The Legend of Tarzan, Lord of the Apes,* but I had already made my deal to work on that film before the Academy Award happened. And by the time I did my next film, *Videodrome,* the Oscar was old news. I'm sure it helped me in a way, but in this business you still have to deal with much the same kind of hassles, no matter what happens.

You never have total creative freedom, and I'm not sure that you should, because filmmaking *is* a collaborative process, and the producer and director and many other people have to have their input.

You got a second Oscar for *Harry and the Hendersons*. How did that job come about?

I was approached by Bill Dear, who directed the film, and he told me he had gotten the script from somebody who was going to do it as a TV series, but he felt it would make a good theatrical movie instead. He said that he thought I was the only person who could do the Harry character the right way, and that I don't just make a rubber monster, I give it a soul, so I was kind of flattered by all that, plus I like making apelike characters, and I was always fascinated by Big Foot, so I really was interested in the project from the outset.

Bill said he was rewriting the script, but he wanted to tie me up in the meantime to do the design of the creature. So we made a deal, and I did some sketches and sculptures, and we were pleased to find out we were both thinking along the same lines. He fell in love with my very first designs. In fact, one of my original sketches, where Harry looked a little different from the final design, was used in the movie as a prop for John Lithgow in the scene where he's supposed to have drawn the creature. From the beginning, Bill wanted John Lithgow to play the part, and he had shown that drawing to John and it helped him make up his mind to be in the film.

What was difficult about making the Harry character was that he had to carry a lot of the movie without being able to talk. So he had to communicate with his facial expressions. And we had a list of seventy-odd expressions that were denoted in the script, and we thought, "Boy, this is gonna be hard to do with a rubber head!" Up to that point most of the rubber mask heads that I did had either limited self-control kinds of apparatus that the actor could work himself by his jaw movements, or else they were cable-controlled. But this didn't give the actors complete freedom of movement—it was all right for close-ups or medium shots, but it didn't allow the actors to move freely from room to room. And in *Harry and the Hendersons* the creature had to walk all over the place and do all kinds of things. So that's why we decided to make a radio-controlled mechanism. And the fact that in most of the Big Foot sightings the creature is described as having a large, pointy head helped us, because our design with the big head gave us the opportunity to put the motors right in there. It worked out quite well.

But I almost didn't get the Academy Award for *Harry* because certain people wanted to disqualify me. You see, most of the Academy members who are makeup artists are *straight* makeup people, making up actors. They don't generally do the special makeup effects that I do. And quite a few of them had been trying to get a makeup award instituted, for many years, without success. And finally, due to the kind of work that Dick Smith, Rob Bottin, and I do, what they had been after did happen, but for them it was a mixed blessing because as the years went by it became obvious that every film that won the award was a special makeup effects film, not a straight makeup film.

So by the time *Harry and the Hendersons* came out, they had made a set of rules that were designed to eliminate any film from consideration that was not a straight makeup film, and they sent us a letter congratulating us that our film was nominated for best makeup, but the letter also said that unfortunately my part of the makeup work wouldn't qualify in the category. My wife was more upset than I was. She said, "You can't just take this sitting down." And I told her I knew all along that this was going to happen. But she said, "Well, who made that decision? How do they even *know* how you did the makeup?" So I thought she had a good point. Who was the so-called expert who had disqualified me? And why would they even consider *Harry and the Hendersons* for best makeup if it wasn't for the creature? After all, the actors in the movie had very little *straight* makeup on them.

So I called up the Academy, and they said they were told by somebody that my work wasn't makeup. And I said, "Who told you that? It's good to know that all it takes is a phone call from an anonymous person to eliminate someone from an Academy Award." I asked if I could at least present my case, and they had me appear before a rules committee mainly comprised of straight makeup people, who immediately said "Well, you admitted you have motors in it, and that means it's not makeup." And I said, "But what about the cosmetic part of it? The whole *look* of the character? The hair work? The sculpture? All of it is part of a makeup artist's job. The only difference is I had to move it with motors because of the size of it." And they said, "You admitted it again. You said 'motors.' You're eliminated."

So I explained once again that John Lithgow is a big man and the director wanted the creature's head to be at least twice the size of John's head when they were seen in close-up together. If I had made huge rubber appliances and glued them to an actor's face, the actor couldn't have moved them enough to show any expression, and the film would have been a failure. I shouldn't be eliminated for Academy Award consideration for doing my job in such a way as to make the film successful.

They sent me out of the room and voted on the issue, and I squeaked by by one vote. It made a lot of them mad when my nomination was considered. And it made them even madder when I won.

You mentioned before that your parents were very supportive when you were starting out. Have they gotten to enjoy your success?

Oh, yes, very much so. They've gone every time with me to the Academy Awards and so on. They're quite proud. In fact, it used to embarrass me, because my dad would carry around a briefcase full of pictures of my stuff, and he'd show it to anybody who would have a look. If he'd go on a plane trip somewhere, everybody on the plane would know about my career.

What's the high point of your career at this point?

I'd have to say it's working on *Gorillas in the Mist.* I had spent my life up to that point making gorilla suits, and yet I was never able to make the kind I really wanted to make. Most movies don't want real gorillas, they want a Hollywood gorilla like King Kong. But I had followed Diane Fossey's life, and when she was murdered I was devastated. When I heard that the movie was being made, I very much wanted to do it and felt I was the right person to do it. They wanted to film real gorillas as much as possible, and they also wanted to use actors in gorilla suits. And I was very much against this at first. I said, "You'll never be able to mix fake gorillas with real ones and cut them together in the same scene. If you do the whole movie with fakes, people will accept them and believe in them. But if you cut from one to the other, the real one will make the other one look phony."

They went ahead and shot some real gorilla footage, but they couldn't get enough of the right kind of stuff to make the scenes work. So my staff and I made the best suits we were capable of, and we kind of outdid ourselves, because as it turned out, the fakes were able to mix with the real gorillas and most people don't even suspect.

I always wanted to go to Africa and see these animals in person, and I'm happy that I was able to do that. It was something I felt I was born to do. It was a thrill just to be able to sit three feet away from a 460-pound silver-backed mountain gorilla out in the wilds of Africa. And I really wanted people to know the story and to realize that there are only about 300 of these majestic animals alive today, and with the woman who had been their savior now dead, they may cease to exist. I felt that the film was important, and I thought it could help bring the problem to the public's attention, and I was grateful for whatever chance I could have of helping to save the mountain gorilla.

*"All Hollywood corrupts; and absolute
Hollywood corrupts absolutely."*
Edmund Wilson.

*"A life in pictures is a lousy way
to make a hell of a living."*
Newsweek

Appendix 1
Sample Pages from
Heartstopper / The Awakening
Novel Outline, Novel, and Screenplay

THE AWAKENING OUTLINE

Sample Pages

Benjamin Latham, age fifty-five, is a physician living in Hanna's Town, Pennsylvania, during the years immediately following the Revolutionary War. A former Tory, now that American independence has been won he doesn't think that the new nation will succeed. He finds the notion of democracy—as put forth by Jefferson, Adams and Franklin—to be totally preposterous. He uses his wealth and position to keep him aloof from the "dregs of society" who, as he sees it, are going to have more say-so than they deserve in the affairs of the United States that the former thirteen colonies are supposed to be.

Like other physicians of his time, Benjamin Latham "bleeds" people when they are ill. His secret is that he sometimes drinks the blood that he takes from his patients, particularly if he can persuade those who are not seriously sick, or not sick at all, to submit to being bled. Like Countess Elisabeth Bathory, of whom he has read, Benjamin Latham believes that drinking or bathing in human blood contributes to longevity, good health, and youthful appearance.

One day Benjamin bleeds a young maiden from the village, and she catches him drinking her blood. Horror-stricken, she runs from the house and tells her parents what happened. A magistrate is summoned, a formal complaint is made, and Dr. Latham is arrested and tried for witchcraft. He is accused of practicing vampirism. Since he was a Tory during the war, he is disliked by prominent villagers, and those less prominent are anxious to curry favor by furnishing testimony corroborating the charges against him. He is convicted and hanged. As he is placed in his coffin, a necklace of garlic is tied around his neck and a stake is driven through his heart. He is buried at a crossroads. The garlic, the stake, and the burial at a cross-shaped location are all measures designed to prevent the vampire's body from rising up again.

Two hundred years pass. Benjamin Latham molders in his grave, worms devouring his flesh. The cloves of garlic slowly turn to green, powdery mold and disintegrate to dust. The coffin becomes waterlogged and rots to pieces. The stake decays and falls through its cage of bone.

New flesh begins to grow on Benjamin Latham's skeleton. Lying under the earth, he is reshaped into a handsome young man, in the perfect image of himself when he was twenty-five years old. But he is not alive, not yet ... not quite. He has no awareness of his existence.

The crossroads are a talisman powerful enough to prevent life from being breathed into the vampire. The shape of the cross remains a guardian against the creature's rebirth. But by the 1980s what was once a rural crossroads is part of a suburban highway network. And a new shopping center is going to be built on the site, with a system of intertwining roads and access ramps.

When the pavement is ripped up, building foundations are laid, and new road patterns are surveyed and created; the old crossroads cease to exist. The last obstacle to the rebirth of the vampire is removed.

Benjamin Latham rises from his grave, with the help of a bulldozer that overturns tons of dirt, partially excavating him from the earth.

He awakens and crawls out of the mud. Naked and befuddled, he creeps into the surrounding woods, while the bulldozer crew is breaking for lunch. Hiding in the foliage, he watches the men and the huge beast-like machines as they start up again—it is his first shocking exposure to modern technology. He tries to orient himself. He knows that he should be dead. Is he dreaming? Or did somebody work a spell on him that caused him to go mad?

He remembers that he was accused of being a vampire, an accusation he refuted because it was pure poppycock so far as he was concerned. He never bit into anyone's neck with long fangs. He never slept in a coffin, not till he was hanged. He was *not* a vampire, not in the supernatural sense. He had occasionally drunk blood, as one might take medicine. He never believed that drinking it would make him immortal—but maybe it had. Here he is, a young man again, when he ought to be dead. There has to be some explanation.

***

NOTE: Later in our story, when Benjamin researches records of his trial in 1785, he reads about the disposition of his corpse— the necklace of garlic, the stake in the heart, the burial at the crossroads. In a flash of insight, he realizes that the charms must have worked in the opposite way they were intended; instead of preventing the vampire from rising, they made Benjamin *into* a vampire by preventing an essential part of his spirit from leaving his body. Thus, the vampire was created by superstition.

Peering through foliage at the bulldozer crew, Benjamin figures that he must be on the earth, but it can't be the same earth he was familiar with. The men are dressed strangely; their machinery is awesome and scary. Puzzling it all over, he gets careless and is spotted. Three of the men chase after him, figuring he is a "flasher." He runs naked through the woods in a frantic chase, frightened out of his wits, and he finally gets away.

He hides. Then, when he dares, he starts making his way out of the woods. He crouches behind some shrubs and peers out at the fenced-in backyards of a ticky-tacky suburban housing area. Clothes are hanging on a line. Benjamin is able to steal garments and puts them on, solving the problem of going about naked. He comes across a child, a little girl, playing in a backyard sandbox. The girl says, "Hello, mister," and giggles because he doesn't have any shoes. He starts asking her questions, pretending it is a game, when he is really trying to find out what time and place he is in. (Earlier, in the woods, he saw his reflection in a pond; so he knows he has been reincarnated as a young man, while he still has the thoughts and memories of his previous age, which was fifty-five.) The little girl, Stephanie, age six, finds his appearance, mannerisms, and speech patterns funny and strange. She is friendly and trusting though, and fetches him an old pair of sneakers from her father's garage. He finds himself desiring her blood—in a way that shocks and revolts him, because the urge is more animal, more ingrained, than before. As his need for her blood overpowers him, he frantically tries to think what to do about it—he can't "bleed" her. His solution is to make her cut herself "accidentally" on a piece of glass in her sandbox, then he sucks her wound. His desire for the fluid is so ravenous that he almost can't make himself stop; he muffles the girl's screams and keeps sucking, then forces himself to pull away. To his horror, Stephanie goes into convulsions and dies, even though he doesn't think he took enough blood from her to kill her. Did she die of shock? Or is there something about him that is poisonous now for other human beings? *Is* he a human being? He flees the scene, lost in panic, bewilderment, and terror at what he has become.

348

But the startling thing, the thing he wishes he could deny, is that the taste of blood has made him feel strong, refreshed, keenly alive, in a highly sensuous, virile way. He walks the streets of suburbia, trying to get all this together and come to grips with himself. What to do and where to go next? The sense of well-being that he got from drinking Stephanie's blood is paradoxical in that he still feels revulsion and remorse over her death. The thought strikes him that maybe she will come back to life, as he did, and he regrets that he couldn't stick around to find out.

NOTE: The theme of the newly made vampire coming to grips with his evolving nature will be an important theme in the novel, and will be carried through his experiences in his new world. Benjamin is not the kind of vampire that needs to return to his coffin at dawn; he can exist quite well in daylight or darkness. He doesn't know if he is immortal or not, but suspects that he may be (this is analogous to an ordinary man's wonderings about immortality).

He doesn't want to have to kill for blood—when he was "bleeding" people, he wasn't permanently harming them. But he can sense that his desire for blood is more animalistic, less intellectual, than it was in his previous lifetime. He doesn't want to grow accustomed to killing. He wants to preserve a bond with mankind because, unless he can find other vampires, he is going to have to live among men—and he dreads being estranged from them . . . and being hunted by them.

Another major theme of the novel will be the confrontation of the eighteenth century with the twentieth century—America's childhood with her middle age

349

THE AWAKENING NOVEL

Sample Pages

1

The earth was heavy on his chest and limbs, but his grave was shallow and the dirt was loose. He began to claw his way out. They had hanged him, but somehow he had not died. He remembered the jerk and snap of the rope, the blinding pain, and nothing after that. They must have buried him unconscious, thinking he was dead. But the noose hadn't broken his neck. He still had air in his lungs. The shallow, loosened earth must have enabled him to breathe just enough, his need for air reduced while he was in a coma, like Indian fakirs he had read about, who could let themselves be buried for days on end. He had survived, he had cheated death. He pulled himself up, his body rising through clods of moist yellow clay. He hadn't opened his eyes yet; unused to anything but darkness, they hurt even with the lids shut. By the rough feel of dirt and stones against his skin, he could tell that he was nude. The gravediggers must have stolen his clothing and his good leather boots. And they must have decided to save his coffin for somebody else—as if his remains didn't deserve to be treated with modesty and respect. Well, their penny-pinching had saved his life. He could hardly have clawed his way out of a nailed-shut pine box.

In a half crouch, he brushed his thighs and calves, rubbing the dirt off with his hands, awakening the good tingly sensations of muscular living flesh. He opened his eyes slowly, and they hurt till they got used to the light. Tears coursed down his cheeks. He blinked. He blinked again, trying to convince himself of the reality of his surroundings.

He was standing amid a vast expanse of torn-up, devastated ground. Weeds, stones, and even trees had been plowed and uprooted to completely clear an area of at least two acres all around. Would his executioners have ordered all of this dug up, in order to obfuscate his exact place of burial? He'd put nothing past them. Their minds were in the Dark Ages. They had convicted him of sorcery and vampirism, and were so terrified of him that they had talked of driving a stake through his heart, stringing cloves of garlic around his neck, and burying him at a crossroad. They wanted to make sure he stayed dead. How ironic that their noose hadn't even strangled him sufficiently as he twisted and dangled in front of their superstitious fear-maddened eyes. His feet sank in and it was hard to walk, till he groped his way to firmer ground. Squinting against the bright sun, he held out his arms and felt the hot rays on his skin, convincing himself that he was flesh and blood. He touched his neck, wondering why it didn't hurt, why the rope hadn't even left any burns. Perhaps his coma had had a healing effect. Benjamin Latham was still alive, up from the nameless grave to which he had been unjustly consigned. But he had no time to revel in his rebirth. He must find some clothes to wear. He must get away from here in all haste, lest his enemies spot him and finish the job they had left undone.

Benjamin made his way toward a patch of woods that was still intact, at the edge of the devastation, and hid in a thicket of trees and weeds. He didn't know exactly where he was. Which direction was Hanna's Town? The sun was straight up in the sky—giving no clue as to where it had risen or where it would set. He couldn't get his bearings, couldn't tell east from west. Surely they wouldn't have buried him far from the outskirts of town, the site of the jail and the gallows. Yet, nothing looked familiar. He thought he might have been able to recognize a landmark or two, if the acreage around his grave hadn't been so rudely and utterly denuded.

Maybe the townspeople had taken the time and trouble to disguise and obliterate all this place, as a substitute for burial at a crossroad—which was supposed to confuse the spirit of a risen vampire so it wouldn't know which way to go to return home. Benjamin scoffed at the superstition. He wasn't a vampire. But for the moment he was surely lost, and his joy at surviving the noose was beginning to be eroded by desperation.

Taking another look around, he suddenly realized what was so odd about the woods where he was hiding. The trees were all *young*—he could tell from the thinness of their trunks and branches. Where, in the vicinity of Hanna's Town, was there any substantial growth of new forest? Nowhere. The answer seized him with unreasoning panic. Where *was* he? He couldn't be near Hanna's Town, for it was a frontier settlement, carved out of ancient wilderness. Nothing had lived there but Indians and animals until a few years ago.

He wondered if they could have carted him far away to bury him, a hundred miles or more, back toward Philadelphia where some of the forests were younger. But then why hadn't he regained consciousness during such a lengthy journey? No. He must be close to home. Maybe he'd realize it soon. His ordeal must have disoriented him, confounding his five senses. It would be wise not to make a move till he got himself under control. He might stumble into the arms of his persecutors. His freedom would depend on keeping his wits about him. Even if he could get away he'd have to struggle and scheme to make a new life. Everything he had owned was gone. His home and all his possessions had been burned to the ground. The crazed mob had destroyed his medical supplies and equipment—the "wicked tools of the vampire sorcerer."

When he first heard the shouts, the clattering hooves, and the pounding of fists on his cabin door, he thought they were coming to tar and feather him because he was a Tory. He had no intention of running from them. Since the start of the Revolution, he had lived with the possibility that they might turn on him this way, and had resolved to face up to them with a showing of courage and dignity. They ought to be ashamed of themselves.

They ought to skulk away with their tails between their legs. They *needed* him here. He was their only doctor. And he was a skilled Indian fighter, from his experience in the French and Indian War. Out here in the wilds of Western Pennsylvania diseases and tomahawks were more to be feared than redcoats.

Maybe his neighbors hated him for being against independence from Great Britain but they still ought to be grateful for the lives he had saved last summer when Shawnees had attacked Hanna's Town, murdering settlers and burning their log houses. They hadn't called him a Tory traitor when he was loading and firing his musket alongside the best of them, and giving medical care to the wounded while screaming savages were beaten off from the fort. When times got tough, they accepted Benjamin Latham as a damned valuable member of their frontier community, regardless of his loyalty to King George.

He figured he could make them see the light of reason, by reminding them of all the good he had done, and then see if they still wanted to tar and feather him and ride him on a rail. Coming to the front of his cabin, he took his time lifting the heavy wooden bar out of its iron brackets. Let them wear some skin off their knuckles, let their voices go hoarse from yelling and swearing. It might sober some of them up and blunt their cowardly "patriotism."

When he opened the door, they pounced on him, pummeling him to the floor and binding him in coils of coarse hemp. He was knocked unconscious and his mouth was gagged, and he had no chance of defending himself. He came to as they hoisted him onto the bed of a horse-drawn cart, and by that time his cabin had been torched—wild flickering tongues of fire made the faces of his captors look weirder and crazier. Instead of lynching him or immersing him in tar, they dragged him to the jailhouse and locked him inside.

The next morning, before a panel of three judges and a room full of noisy, gawking spectators, he was accused of "bleeding" Patience Rutherford, an indentured servant, sixteen years of age, and of drinking her blood and using it in occult experiments. Patience and her younger sister, Sarah, age fourteen, had sworn out a complaint before a magistrate, in which they said that they had spied on him through his cabin window and had witnessed him drinking the blood that he took from Patience on several occasions, and on other occasions had seen him treating her blood with salts and potions that caused it to separate into three layers, all the while mumbling a charm over this Devil's "work" which caused Patience to suffer "agonizing headaches at night, and horrible contortions of her limbs" so that she could not remember the words to her prayers or even kneel to say them.

Benjamin realized that he could not hope to reason with the pandemonious mob that filled the spectators' benches, gibbering and gasping over the sensationally embellished testimony of the Rutherford girls. But the three judges were learned men, his peers, and he thought that by being candid he could make them understand him. They would see that he was actually an avant-garde personality, much like their hero Benjamin Franklin, whom they revered for his great inventions and his daring experiments with electricity.

After considerable pounding of the gavel and threats to evict some of the more unruly spectators, the judges allowed Benjamin Latham to arise and testify in his own behalf. They listened intently, restoring order as best they could whenever some of his statements provoked the ignorant mob.

He admitted that he had indeed tasted blood from time to time, in order to test the effect of its nutrients upon himself. He made the point that the judges and everyone else in the courtroom tasted blood every time they ate freshly butchered meat—it was what made the meat red. They also tasted blood whenever they licked a cut finger, and no harm was ever known to arise from this universal human reaction to bleeding. As far as the experiment the Rutherford girls had witnessed, the separation of blood into three layers, that chemical procedure had been discovered hundreds of years ago by Hippocrates; Benjamin had been making use of it in order to arrive at a better understanding of the ingredients of human blood, for he believed that by such knowledge many diseases might someday be cured.

He confessed that, as a doctor who liked to keep up with all the latest discoveries of his profession, he no longer truly believed in the efficacy of phlebotomy—the letting of blood for medicinal purposes. He explained that human blood, and the blood of all creatures, did not stay in one place but circulated throughout the entire body, as had been proved by William Harvey, the eminent physician of the Royal Society of London. "If the blood does not lie still in the vessels, but is constantly flowing, then how can we heal a swollen arm by letting some of its blood out of it? It would merely be replaced by blood from other parts of the body." He allowed some time for this concept to sink in, and for the furor to die down.

He went on to say that in recent years he had continued to bleed patients who insisted on it; and he had used this fluid that would have been otherwise discarded to try to learn more about its life-sustaining properties. And, furthermore, he had drunk some of it—at great risk to himself, as some might have thought—since it had come from patients who were ill. But, he had never contracted a disease from any of his patients so treated—a result not to be anticipated if their illnesses had been caused by so-called "bad blood." On the contrary, he believed, though he couldn't verify it as yet, that the small amounts of blood he ingested had nurtured him and contributed to his overall well-being. Through his studies, described in a half-completed treatise that had been burned with the rest of his belongings, he had proved the uselessness of phlebotomy as a medical procedure, and future generations could now be spared its agony, its scars, and its false hope.

Summing up his defense, he gave a quote from the preface of William Harvey's monumental contribution to medicine, *An Anatomical Essay on the Motion of the Heart:* "I only wish, by this work, under God the Creator, to contribute something pleasing to good men, and appropriate to learned ones, and of service to literature." He hoped that his invocation of God would please everyone in the courtroom and convince them that he could not be a sorcerer.

He might as well have saved his breath. The judges had listened to him, giving him their rapt attention, not because he held them spellbound with his cleverness and his obvious innocence, as he had thought, but because they believed in his guilt wholeheartedly and were content to let him expound it in public. In their opinion, he had hanged himself by his own testimony. Their sentence of death on the gallows would carry out literally what he had done figuratively. The fact that he was a "damned Tory" no doubt added to their glee in bringing him to "justice." He was condemned to die at sunrise, on the morning after his trial.

How long ago had he stood wearing the noose around his neck?

Yesterday?

The day before?

A week ago?

He had no idea how long he had been buried. If the stories about the Indian fakirs were true, which he no longer doubted, he might have remained in a trance-like state for an incredibly long time. It would have taken weeks and weeks and a large party of men with their beasts of toil to clear the field he now looked out upon. But maybe it had already been cleared by farmers far away from Hanna's Town. And now it was ready to be plowed and planted. His executioners must have expected his corpse to feed the roots of new vegetables.

But their deepest dread had come true . . .

HEARTSTOPPER SCREENPLAY

Sample Pages

1. EXT WOODS NEAR COLONIAL PITTSBURGH—NIGHT

FADE UP. RAUCOUS NOISE. A ROARING BONFIRE. Men in knee breeches and three-corner hats are tossing armloads of books, herbs, and medicine vials onto the fire. The flickering flames cast an orange glow upon the anguished face of DR. BENJAMIN LATHAM, who is shackled to a tree. Benjamin is strong, handsome, about twenty-five years old.

THE FILM'S TITLE AND OPENING CREDITS ARE SUPERED OVER THIS SCENE.

A big burly member of the mob tosses a pile of leather-bound medical texts into the fire, then steps back, making the Sign of the Cross over himself.

CU of Benjamin shows fear and disgust in his face, but he is trying to control his emotions, in hopes that his calmness and rationality will eventually quell the mob.

WIDE SHOT shows three more men coming out of Benjamin's log cabin with armloads of stuff to be burned. Two of the men toss books and papers onto the fire, but the third man, CONSTABLE FARLEY, comes over to Benjamin and opens the lid of a small trunk.

NOTE: This trunk is very distinctive. Painted on its lid is the healers' emblem (a caduceus): two serpents entwined on a staff. A CU of the velvet-lined interior reveals that it contains vials and beakers of various potions and elixirs in addition to surgical instruments.

Constable Farley comes over to Benjamin and holds up a flask full of a syrupy dark red substance.

CONSTABLE FARLEY
Well, well, well, Dr. Latham—this is human blood, I'd wager!

Two of the mob members, JACOB LATHAM and ISAAC MORSE, start piling dry twigs and kindling around Benjamin's feet. Jacob (who is Benjamin's brother) works with difficulty, since his left arm is only a stump, amputated six inches from the shoulder.

JACOB
May God protect us! It's blood all right, Constable Farley. He drinks it. My wife, Patience, saw him sipping blood and praying to Satan. If he loves the devil so much, let's give him a taste of hellfire! Torch him! It's the only way to free Patience from his evil curse!

BENJAMIN
Have you lost your *mind,* Jacob? You are my brother! Your wife is lying to you to tum you against me!

JACOB
Patience is a good woman! *She* does not lie! You are no longer my flesh and blood. You are possessed, Benjamin. The devil lives inside you, and must be purged!

SHOUTS OF APPROVAL from the rest of the mob. But Constable Farley turns to face them, his hand on the butt of one of the two flintlock pistols stuck in his belt.

CONSTABLE FARLEY

I understand how you men feel, but I can't stand by and let you burn him, much as I might like to. He'll have a fair trial tomorrow morning. Then he'll be hanged until he's dead. That's the punishment prescribed by law here in Pennsylvania, and I'm sworn to uphold it.

MORSE

Benjamin Latham doesn't believe in American laws—he's a damn Tory, loyal to King George! To my mind, that's reason enough to hang him. I say we torch him right here and now, before he works his forked tongue on the judges and tricks them into setting him free.

A CHORUS OF APPROVAL from the frenzied mob, as they surge forward. But Farley draws and fires one of his flintlocks, stopping them in their tracks. When the smoke clears, we see Benjamin Latham in CU as he speaks.

BENJAMIN

There are no such creatures as vampires, and sorcerers are merely deranged men—ordinary human beings consumed by ignorance and superstition. Hear me out—all of you! It's true that I experiment with human blood—blood that comes from sick people who want me to perform phlebotomies— to let the so-called bad blood out in hopes that their diseases might be cured. Normally this blood would be thrown away, wasted, but instead I have been experimenting with it, trying to learn its scientific properties. I believe that many medical secrets are yet to be discovered by these kinds of experiments.

MORSE

There, we have his confession! He admits to sorcery! He worships Satan! Let's burn him before he puts a curse on us all!

The mob starts chanting, the roaring bonfire weirdly illuminating their angry, fear-ridden faces.

MOB

Burn him! Burn the vampire!
Burn him! Burn the vampire!

MOB'S CHANT CONTINUES AND SLOWLY FADES OUT AS WE CUT TO:

2. EXT BACKYARD OF A SUBURBAN HOME—DAY

WIDE ESTABLISHING SHOT of the pleasant-looking home, but CAMERA PANS to reveal that all is not pleasant here today. Many policemen are on the scene. A coroner, ED STANFORD, is bending over the corpse of STEPHANIE KAMIN, a six-year-old child. Her body lies near a sandbox with a sand castle built inside. She's flat on her back, her lifeless blue eyes staring straight up into the sun. Her face is puffy and whitish-blue.

The VOICE of LIEUTENANT RON VARGO, a tall, craggily handsome county detective, intrudes over the shot of the dead little girl.

VARGO

Notice the cut on her finger, Ed?

STANFORD

(picking up the lifeless little hand)

Cut's not too deep, Ron. Not much blood around it, for a fresh wound. Looks like she must've put it in her mouth and licked it clean.

VARGO

How do you think she died?

STANFORD

Hard to say. If somebody choked her, he didn't bruise her throat. Asphyxiation can make the face puffy and blue the way hers is, but so can certain types of snake venom. Another possibility is anaphylactic shock—an acute reaction to a bee sting or spider bite. You can see that the cut finger is swollen twice its normal size, and some of the swelling moved into her hand. If a spider bit her right where her finger was cut, it might've been enough to put a little girl into a state of shock. Extreme fright can paralyze the vagus nerve, stopping the heart.

VARGO

Well, I just finished talking to the parents and some of the neighbors, and I'm afraid we're not dealing with an accidental death here. Stephanie's mother was keeping an eye on her, glancing out the kitchen window to make sure she was okay, and at one point she thought she saw a neighbor kid, Georgie Stevens, sitting on the edge of the sandbox while Stephanie was playing. Except Georgie is a high school senior, and we were able to verify that he didn't cut classes today. He just got home on the bus a half-hour ago.

STANFORD

So who was with Stephanie if it wasn't Georgie Stevens?

VARGO

That's what I'd like to know. Whoever it was, he may have been the last one to see her alive. And he's probably wearing Georgie's clothes. His mother had one of his sport shirts and a pair of jeans hanging outside to dry, and now they're missing. Who'd want to steal clothes off a line? Maybe somebody who had to get rid of a uniform. For instance, an escapee from Laurel State Hospital—one of the psychopaths they're trying to rehabilitate over there. Saving them from Death Row, where they belong.

STANFORD

Well, even if Stephanie was talking to a stranger, it doesn't prove he killed her, right? He could have left, and then she got bitten by something.

VARGO

If a snake bit her, she'd have run screaming to her mother right away. Same thing if she was stung by a bee or hornet. I have a hunch we're talking about a human snake here. Somebody cut her on purpose and poisoned her.

CUT TO:

3. INT. COLONIAL COURTHOUSE—DAY

His ankles and wrists chained and shackled, Benjamin Latham stands in the dock, facing a CHIEF JUSTICE, who looks ponderously stern and dignified in his white wig and black robe. At the witness stand is Jacob Latham's wife, PATIENCE. Pleased to be a star attraction in these proceedings, she plays to the noisy, gawking crowd that fills the courtroom.

The CHIEF JUSTICE pounds his gavel, and the noise subsides to a low murmur. The prosecutor, Constable Farley, clears his throat and scratches an itchy spot under his wig.

                    CONSTABLE FARLEY
So, Patience, tell us what happened when you went to see your brother-in-law, Dr. Benjamin Latham, about the boil that you had on your forearm.

                    PATIENCE
Well ... he took his time examining me ... much more time than was necessary, I thought. I found it embarrassing, but I said nothing. All the while, he was talking about my husband, his own brother, in a most unflattering way. Finally, he remarked, with a smirk, that it must not be entirely pleasant to sleep with a cripple. And he touched his fingers to my . . . to my breast.

                    BENJAMIN
I did no such thing! Please believe me, Jacob! If seduction was on anybody's mind that day, it was—it was not my own.

                    364

JACOB

Liar! Your unholy experiments have made you the pawn of
Satan, and he causes you to covet your brother's wife!

A furor erupts in the courtroom. Isaac Morse has to restrain
Jacob from attacking Benjamin, as the Chief Justice pounds
his gavel.

PATIENCE

When he fondled me, I slapped his face, Jacob! Then he
whined and simpered, begging me not to tell on him, and to
let him treat my boil, as if nothing had happened between
us. Angrily I told him to never again try to lead me into
adultery. Outwardly, from that point on, he behaved with
delicacy and remorse. I let him spread a potion over the
boil. Then he lanced it, using his fleam, and letting the
blood and pus flow freely into a glass beaker. He took the
beaker into the back room of his cabin.

Constable Farley goes to a table, where Benjamin Latham's
doctor's trunk is lying with the lid open, revealing its display of
"evidence." He takes out a fleam (an instrument for letting blood)
and picks up a beaker.

CONSTABLE FARLEY

Is this the same fleam that he used? And is this the type of
beaker that you refer to?

PATIENCE

Yes. He told me to be brave because he was going to have
to draw some blood, and he said it wasn't going to hurt me
much, but he was lying—it hurt a lot!

CONSTABLE FARLEY
Then what happened?

PATIENCE
He cleaned and bandaged the cut. (She holds up the bandaged incision on her forearm, and the courtroom buzzes once again.)

CONSTABLE FARLEY
What happened after that? After you left the cabin?

PATIENCE
An odd feeling crept over me, as if I was not yet free of harm. So, I crept around the side of my brother-in-law's cabin and peeked through the window.

CONSTABLE FARLEY
Was this the first time you had ever spied on Dr. Latham?

PATIENCE
No. I must admit I had done so on two other occasions, because I was scared of him, I did not trust him, and wanted to see what he might be up to. Once I saw him drinking blood that he had purged from my father. And another time I saw him mixing salts and potions into a flask of blood, causing it to separate into three layers.

GASPS AND MURMURS ERUPT from the crowd. The Chief Justice raps his gavel for silence. CU of Benjamin Latham staring pleadingly at his sister-in-law, silently asking why she is doing this to her. She stares right back, giving him a smug, catty smile.

CONSTABLE FARLEY

What did you see through the back window after your boil was lanced?

PATIENCE

Benjamin drank from the beaker! He drank pus and all! Then he wiped his lips and began praying to Satan! He put a curse on me and my husband. For three days and nights we could not sleep, eat, or talk. Our arms and legs were all twisted up and aching as if the devil was trying to twist us and tear us apart. We couldn't do our chores. When we tried to walk, we fell down. We broke out in a rash and fever when we went near our church. We couldn't remember the words to our nightly prayers, and we couldn't even kneel to say them.

On hearing this, the mob goes wild, crying, "Hang him! Hang him! Hang him! Hang him!" The mad chant continues and SLOWLY FADES after we have CUT TO:

4. EXT KAMINS' BACKYARD—DAY

Ed Stanford zips little Stephanie into a body bag, which lies on a gurney, and two morgue men load the corpse into a van.

Ron Vargo is using a rake to turn over the sand in the sandbox.

STANFORD

I'll see you at the autopsy tomorrow, Ron. Can you be at the morgue at ten? Unless you're willing to concede that we're dealing with an accidental death here. Then you won't have to attend the postmortem.

VARGO

The little girl was murdered. Deliberately poisoned. I can feel it in my bones. I felt like this on the day my daughter Kathy was killed, even before I got the call. I can't believe the guy who did it is still on the loose. He should've gotten the chair. But they let him cop a "diminished capacity" plea, and sent him to Laurel State. A damn country dub! Minimum security. He wasn't there three weeks before he went over the wall.

Stanford nods sympathetically.

Just then the rake Vargo's using makes a sharp CLINK. He glances meaningfully at Ed Stanford. Then, wielding the rake quite gingerly, he tries to expose whatever made the clinking noise.

CU of the rake sifting the sand till we catch a glimpse of something shiny and green.

Vargo kneels and uses his pocket handkerchief to fish out a jagged fragment of glass. He holds it up for the coroner to have a look.

VARGO

This has to be what cut her, Ed. How much you want to bet the lab guys will find some kind of poison on it?

A LOUD RAPPING SOUND starts and CONTINUES INTO NEXT SCENE:

5. INT COLONIAL COURTHOUSE—DAY

The Chief Justice is RAPPING his gavel. Benjamin Latham has risen to his feet. But he's still chained and shackled.

CHIEF JUSTICE

Benjamin Latham, you have waived your right to a lawyer, so it is up to you to speak in your own defense. I warn you that anything you say may be used against you. You are at the mercy of this court, which is sworn to uphold the laws of God and of mankind.

Benjamin slowly turns around, making eye contact with everyone in the court, but particularly with Patience and Jacob.

BENJAMIN

Last summer, when the Shawnees attacked Hanna's Town, I took good care of the wounded, saving many lives—including yours, Jacob.

JACOB

What you took was my left arm, *Doctor* Latham! And now you are trying to take my wife!

MORSE

You're not only a Tory but a butcher!

PATIENCE

You wanted your own brother to be a cripple!

BENJAMIN

If I hadn't taken the arm, then blood poison would have taken your life, Jacob. I was doing my sacred duty as a physician even while the screaming savages were being beaten off from our fort. Nobody berated me then for my political views—I was considered a damned valuable member of our community.

MORSE

That was before we found out you were a vampire—or before you became one, by drinking the blood of God knows how many of us!

SHOUTS OF APPROVAL from the mob, till the Chief Justice quiets them, pounding his gavel.

CHIEF JUSTICE

I warn you! I will have order in my court! The stock and pillory are waiting for those who disagree!

The noise subsides to a low murmur, and Benjamin continues. . .

Appendix 2

Sample Distribution Agreement
Sample Investor Agreement
Sample Free Lance Player Contract
Sample Release Form

DISTRIBUTION AGREEMENT

This AGREEMENT made and entered into the_____day of _____ between

_____

(hereinafter referred to as "OWNER OF MASTER") and _____

_____

(hereinafter referred to as "DISTRIBUTOR") .

WITNESSETH

WHEREAS, OWNER OF MASTER is the owner of original audio- visual programs entitled:

_____

(hereinafter referred to as "Programs"; and

WHEREAS, OWNER OF MASTER grants to DISTRIBUTOR certain rights to distribute the Programs, and DISTRIBUTOR accepts from OWNER OF MASTER the rights to distribute the above mentioned Programs subject to the terms and conditions of this Agreement;

NOW THEREFORE, in consideration of the promises and of the mutual covenants and agreements hereinafter set forth, the parties agree as follows:

1. *Definitions*: for the purposes of this Agreement the following words have the following meanings:
   a. "Master": A professional duplication of an original recording of the Programs, whether on magnetic tape, disk, or any substance or material that is primarily used in the manufacture of video cassettes or videodiscs or both, as further defined in 7 (A).
   b. "Work": Videocassette tapes, digital video discs, or on demand broadcasts containing the performances embodied on a Master.
2. *Distribution Rights*: Worldwide.
   a. OWNER OF MASTER hereby grants to DISTRIBUTOR the exclusive rights, during the term of this Agreement, to manufacture, distribute, and sell video cassettes, digital video discs, on demand broadcasts of the Programs to the Home Video Rental Market, Sell-Through Market, Premium Market, Sponsorship Market, and Catalogue Market. OWNER OF MASTER hereby represents and war- rants that all rights granted herein to DISTRIBUTOR are and will be free of and clear of liens and other restrictions of any kind.

INITIALS _____

373

b. OWNER OF MASTER further represents and warrants that no claims relating to any prior use or exploitation of the Programs exist or are pending or threatened against OWNER OF MASTER. OWNER OF MASTER further agrees to indemnify and hold DISTRIBUTOR harm- less from any claim, suit or other action alleging facts that are inconsistent with the above warranties.

c. In addition, OWNER OF MASTER states that he has not distributed the Programs nor any part thereof prior to the date of this Agreement in the Home Video Market, Premium Market, Sponsorship Market or Catalogue Market.

3. *Terms*

a. The term of the Agreement (the "Term") shall be that period of time beginning from the date hereof and terminating _____ years from the date hereof. DISTRIBUTOR shall return the Master (s) within sixty days following the expiration or other termination of this Agreement, after which time DISTRIBUTOR reserves the right to sell any returned or future returned Works and existing inventory from its warehouse, for which it shall continue to account to OWNER OF MASTER for sales and any royalties pursuant to the accounting provisions hereof.

b. It is understood that DISTRIBUTOR has the right to enter into a sublicense agreement granting to any third party the rights granted to DISTRIBUTOR here- under, at any time prior to the expiration or valid termination of this agreement. The original Term hereof can be extended past the original termination date, but only with respect to the sublicensed territory it includes, and with written acceptance of such extension by OWNER OF MASTER.

c. In the event the DISTRIBUTOR fails to pay royalties or properly report to OWNER OF MASTER as provided in section 6 of this Agreement in any calendar quarter, OWNER OF MASTER may give written notice to DISTRIBUTOR of OWNER OF MASTER'S intent to terminate this Agreement due to such failure, and DIS- TRIBUTOR shall have thirty (30) days from the date of the receipt of such notice to cure any such failure to pay royalties or properly report. If DISTRIBUTOR fails to cure, OWNER OF MASTER may terminate this Agreement immediately.

d. DISTRIBUTOR reserves the right to cancel any Programs by giving OWNER OF MASTER thirty (30) days written notice.

4. *Royalties:*

a. In full consideration for all the rights, warranties, representations and agreements granted and made by OWNER OF MASTER:

i. From sales to the rental Market, DISTRIBUTOR shall pay to OWNER OF MASTER royalty rate of _____ percent (_____) on one hundred percent (100%) of Gross Revenue as defined below.

INITIALS _____

374

ii. From sales to the Sell-Through Market, Premium Market, DISTRIBUTOR shall pay to OWNER OF MASTER a royalty rate of _____ percent (_____) on one hundred (100%) of Gross Revenue as defined below.

iii. "Gross Revenue" shall mean all revenue earned by, credited and paid to DISTRIBUTOR in respect of actual sales and uses of the Work(s), including without limitation except as stated in paragraph iv below, revenue from sales, rentals, and any other use or exploitation of the Works permitted hereunder.

iv. For purposes of calculating royalties on sales from direct response television marketing, fifty percent (50%) of the revenue earned by and paid to DISTRIBUTOR in respect of such sales shall be included in Gross Revenue.

v. "Gross Sublicensing Income," as used herein shall mean any royalties which have been earned by DISTRIBUTOR in respect of actual sales of the Work(s) by a sub-licensee and of which DISTRIBUTOR has received payment.

vi. DISTRIBUTOR shall not assign or delegate any of its obligations hereunder pertaining to the payment or accounting of monies to OWNER OF MASTER.

5. *Copyright*
    a. OWNER OF MASTER retains all copyrights and other proprietary rights to the finished Programs. Nothing herein shall be construed to transfer any of said rights to DISTRIBUTOR.
    b. OWNER OF MASTER shall be responsible for placing the following notice at the end of the Programs on each Master provided to DISTRIBUTOR:

    "Copyright (year of creation) (copyright holder's name). Distributed by (DISTRIBUTOR) under license from (OWNER OF MASTER). All rights reserved."

    c. It is understood and agreed that DISTRIBUTOR is the sole author and owner, for purposes of copy- right, of all artwork created by DISTRIBUTOR (except for any elements thereof provided by OWNER OF MAS- TER) for packaging of the Work(s) and for any promo- tion and advertising materials used in respect of the Programs.

6. *Materials*: The following material must be delivered to DISTRIBUTOR:
    a. An acceptable Master.

INITIALS _____

375

b. Photography and/or other materials or information readily available to OWNER OF MASTER and necessary, in DISTRIBUTOR'S sole judgment, for DISTRIBUTOR to produce sleeves/packaging for the Work(s).

c. A copy of the Copyright Registration from the Library of Congress or a letter from OWNER OF MASTER stating that the title has not been registered with the Library of Congress, if true.

d. Master and all other materials required to be delivered under the terms of this Agreement are due no later than ten (10) days from the date OWNER OF MASTER receives signed Agreement. If this due date is not met, DISTRIBUTOR, in his sole and absolute discretion, may terminate this Agreement.

7. Governing Law: This Agreement is entered into in (state) _____ and shall be governed by the laws of that state.

AGREED AND ATTESTED BY:

OWNER OF MASTER   DISTRIBUTOR

_____   _____

_____   _____
Signature & Title   Signature & Title

INITIALS _____

INVESTOR AGREEMENT

This AGREEMENT by and between _____
(hereinafter referred to as "Producer") and _____
(hereinafter referred to as "Investor" do hereby set forth and intend to be legally bound by the
following terms and conditions:

WITNESSTH:

1. Investor shall provide the sum of _____ toward the production
    of _____ motion picture(s) entitled
    _____

    and henceforth referred to as the "Product."

2. Investor shall recover production costs of _____
    from first proceeds deriving from sale or distribution of the Product. Any monies
    remaining shall be defined as "Net Profits."

3. The first _____ of Net Profits shall be paid to the Investor. Thereafter,
    any Net Profits shall be shared on a basis of _____ percent to the Investor and
    _____ percent to the Producer.

4. All monies owed to Investor by Producer shall be paid within fourteen days of receipt of
    same by Producer. Supplier shall be entitled to and shall receive from Producer full and
    complete statements of income and copies of statements from distributors necessary to
    validate the timeliness and accuracy of payments.

5. The Investment shall be spent essentially according to the Production Budget attached to
    this Agreement. The Producer will give his best efforts to assure that the Product is
    produced in a timely and cost-effective manner and that the Product matches or exceeds
    the quality of other Product of similar budget.

6. The Producer will employ _____ in the role of
    _____.

7. The screenwriter and director will be _____
    _____.

INITIALS: _____

8. The Producer will be responsible for securing distribution and marketing and merchandising contracts for the Product, and will use his best efforts toward those end. However, because of the risky nature of the entertainment business, there can be no guarantee by Producer as to how much money the Product will earn or that it will produce any Net Profits.

9. This Agreement shall be construed and interpreted pursuant to the laws of the Commonwealth of Pennsylvania.

10. This Agreement represents the full and complete understanding between Producer and Investor, and shall be binding not only upon Producer and Investor but upon their heirs and assigns, in perpetuity.

ATTEST:

_____
Producer

_____
Investor

INITIALS: _____

FREELANCE PLAYERS CONTRACT

This agreement made this _____ day of _____ (year) _____ between (company name) hereinafter called "Producer" and hereinafter called "Player", do hereby set forth and intend to be legally bound by the following conditions. These conditions extend also to the heirs and assigns of both "Producer" and "Player."

WITNESSTH

1) *PHOTOPLAY, ROLE SALARY AND GUARANTEE:*

   Producer hereby engages Player to render services as such in the role of _____ in a photoplay, the working title of which is now (company name) at the salary of $_____ per day or $_____ per week. Player accepts such engagement upon the terms herein specified. Producer guarantees that it will furnish Player not less than _____ day(s) or _____ week(s) employment; however, Player's work days or weeks may not be consecutive and player will only be paid for actual days or weeks on camera.

2) *TERM:*

   The term of employment hereunder shall begin on or about _____ and shall continue thereafter until the completion of the photography and the recordation of said role. If in the judgment of the Producer, for any reason, the Player fails to perform his role satisfactorily, the Producer has the right to terminate employment of the Player at any time during the production of the photoplay at which time wages will also terminate.

3) *PLAYER'S ADDRESS:*

   All notices which the Producer is required or may wish to give to the Player may be given either by mailing the same, addressed to the Player at

   _____

   or such notice may be given to the Player personally, either orally or in writing.

4) *PLAYER'S TELEPHONE:*

   The Player must keep the Producer advised as to where the Player may be reached by telephone without unreasonable delay. The current telephone number of the Player is

   _____.

5) *FURNISHING OF WARDROBE:*

   The Player agrees to furnish all modern wardrobe and wearing apparel reasonably necessary for the portrayal of said role; it being agreed, however, that should so-called "character" or "period" costumes be required, the Producer shall supply the same.

379

6) *PLAYER'S WORKWEEK:*
   The Player's workweek shall consist of five (5) nine (9) hour days or a total of forty-five (45) hours.

7) *PLAYER'S WORKDAY:*
   The Player's workday shall consist of nine (9) hours.

8) *TERMS OF WAGE PAYMENTS:*
   The Player agrees to defer _____ % of wage payments specified under Paragraph 1 of this FREELANCE PLAYERS CONTRACT. Such deferments shall be paid by the Producer from first monies derived from the theatrical release of said photoplay. The Producer may, at his discretion, pay all or any portion of the deferred wages before release of the completed photoplay.

9) *RIGHT TO USE PHOTOGRAPHS:*
   The Player grants all rights to the producer to use any photographs, still pictures or motion pictures that may be taken in connection with the above mentioned photoplay. The Player agrees that the Producer's "right to use photographs" extends also to cover any advertising, promotional or publicity purposes, and also extends to the producer's heirs and assigns.

10) *SCREEN CREDIT:*
   The Producer agrees that the Player will receive full name screen credit on each release print which is made.

11) *PLAYER'S SOCIAL SECURITY NUMBER:*
   The Player's Social Security Number is _____ .

_____

For the Producer

_____

Player

_____

Witness

_____

Witness

380

TALENT, SERVICES AND ADVERTISING RELEASE FORM

_____
City & State

_____
Date

For value received, I agree and consent that _____ (company name) and its nominees and assigns may use any motion pictures, still photographs, videotape recordings, magnetic tape recordings, optical recordings, taken of _____ on _____ or any reproduction thereof, in any form, style or color, together with any writing and/or other advertising and/or publicity material in connection therewith, including the use of my name, as they may select.

I understand that my talents and/ or services and any related advertising and publicity materials are to be used in connection with _____ (company name).

This consent and release is given by me without limitations upon any use for projection, playback, reprints, rerun, broadcast, telecast, or publication of every kind, including the advertising and publicity connected therewith. I also agree that the originals and copies therefrom shall be and remain the exclusive property of _____ (company name) or its nominees and assigns.

I am over eighteen (18) years of age. If subject is under 18, a parent or guardian must sign this form on behalf of the minor.

_____   _____
Name   Social Security Number

_____   _____
Address   Phone

_____   _____
City and State   Witness

381

For more information on John Russo,
his books, movies, and official merchandise,
please visit:

www.TheJohnRusso.com

ABOUT THE AUTHOR

With twenty books published internationally and nineteen feature movies in worldwide distribution, John Russo has been called a "living legend." He began by co-authoring the screenplay for NIGHT OF THE LIVING DEAD, which has become recognized as a "horror classic." His three books on the art and craft of movie making have become bibles of independent production, and one of them, SCARE TACTICS, won a national award for Superior Nonfiction. Quentin Tarantino and many other noted filmmakers have stated that Russo's books helped them launch their careers.

John Russo wants people to know he's "just a nice guy who likes to scare people"—and he's done it with novels and films such as RETURN OF THE LIVING DEAD, MIDNIGHT, THE MAJORETTES, THE AWAKENING and HEARTSTOPPER. He has had a long, rewarding career, and he shows no signs of slowing down. Recently his screenplay for ESCAPE OF THE LIVING DEAD was made into a five-part comic book released by Avatar to great acclaim; it made the Top Ten of Horror Comics nationally and spawned two graphic novels and ten sequels.

Russo's recent novel THE HUNGRY DEAD, was published by Kensington Books. He is also slated to direct two movies: a remake of his cult hit, MIDNIGHT, and a brand new take on the "zombie phenomenon" entitled SPAWN OF THE DEAD.

Russo's latest novels DEALEY PLAZA, THE ACADEMY, THE AWAKENING, and LIVING THINGS are published by Burning Bulb Publishing. His short story CHANNEL 666 appears in THE BIG BOOK OF BIZARRO.

His popularity among genre fans remains at a high pitch. He appears at many movie conventions each year as a featured guest, and he considers his appearance at the Orion Festival, hosted by Kirk Hammett and METALLICA, one of the highlights of his career.

ALSO AVAILABLE:

HOW TO MAKE YOUR MOVIES LOOK PROFESSIONAL

Written and Narrated by
JOHN A. RUSSO

HOW TO MAKE YOUR MOVIES LOOK PROFESSIONAL - JOHN A. RUSSO

HOW TO MAKE YOUR MOVIES LOOK PROFESSIONAL - JOHN A. RUSSO

John Russo's filmmaking books, lectures, seminars and workshops have paved the way to success for many famous professionals and hundreds of young, aspiring filmmakers! NOW HE WANTS TO HELP YOU JUMP-START YOUR CAREER!!

HOW TO MAKE YOUR MOVIES LOOK PROFESSIONAL is a 44-minute audio book that lets John Russo deliver his lessons to you personally, in his own recorded voice, just as if the two of you are sitting in the same room -- or vehicle.

John Russo will elevate you above all those who think they are filmmakers just because they can point a camera and press a button. He will teach you all about blocking, screen direction, pacing, composition, camera angles and much more!

Learn how to become a true professional by listening to the man who has written, produced or directed 20 feature movies in worldwide distribution, including
MIDNIGHT, THE MAJORETTES, HEARTSTOPPER and
NIGHT OF THE LIVING DEAD.

Burning Bulb
PUBLISHING

www.BurningBulbPublishing.com

COMPACT
DISC
DIGITAL AUDIO
CD-R FORMAT

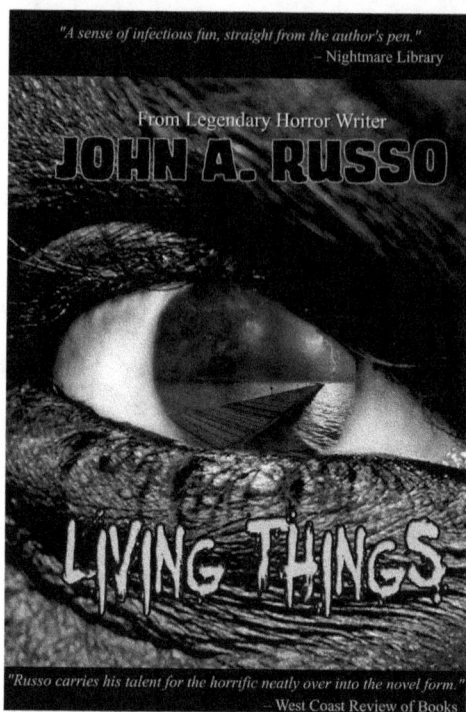

LIVING THINGS

Beneath the shimmering Miami sun sprawls one of the Mafia's biggest empires, a glittering world of lavish beachfront mansions, neon-painted nightclubs, beautiful women, expensive cars—and absolute control over the state's billion-dollar drug trade. But, one by one, its ganglords and henchmen are falling prey to a new rival. His powers are fueled by monstrous ancient rituals; his hellish undead legions slaughter mobsters and innocent citizens alike, his unholy lust for power is virtually unstoppable.

Now a burned-out ex-detective and a brilliant anthropologist must enter a gruesome, nightmare world to fight this master of malevolence and illusion. Their time is short, their weapons few, and they face an ultimate, terrifying choice - annihilation or the loss of their souls to the eternal torment of those who never die. . .

www.TheJohnRusso.com

Burning Bulb
PUBLISHING

You've just read the book, now watch the movie!

"The most unique vampire story since 'SALEM'S LOT."
- George A. Romero

Hanged as a vampire, he's back with a thirst for justice.

HEARTSTOPPER
A FILM OF TERROR BY JOHN RUSSO

DIRECTOR'S CUT

BASED ON THE AWAKENING BY JOHN A. RUSSO

A Thinker Productions Presentation

Starring KEVIN KINDLIN, MOON ZAPPA, TOM SAVINI, JOHN H ALL TOMMY LaFITTE.

Special Appearance by MICHAEL J. POLLARD.

Director of Photography JOHN RICE. Original Music by PAUL McCOLLOUGH.

Executive Producers CHARLES A. GELINI & ROBERT A. DONELL.

Associate Producer LAUREN Z. WYSE. Line Producer RAYMOND LAINE.

Producer CHARLES A. GELINI.

Written & Directed by JOHN RUSSO.

© 1989 Thinker Productions, Inc.; Director's Cut © 2014 Movie Emporium, Inc. All Rights Reserved

Available on DVD and VOD at

www.TheJohnRusso.com
www.BurningBulbPublishing.com

Burning Bulb
PUBLISHING

"The most unique vampire story since 'SALEM'S LOT."
- George A. Romero

From Legendary Horror Writer
JOHN A. RUSSO

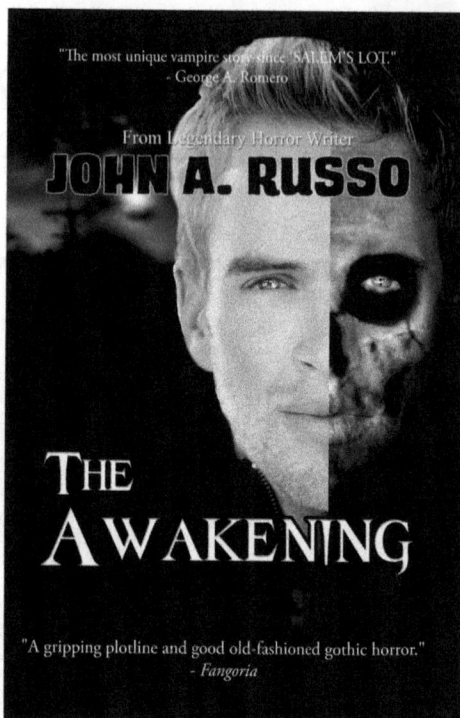

THE
AWAKENING

"A gripping plotline and good old-fashioned gothic horror."
- *Fangoria*

THE AWAKENING

For two hundred years, he has rested. Now he rises. Now he will be satisfied. Nothing can stop him. No one can resist him.

Benjamin Latham is young and handsome, his eighteenth-century mind wakened to a bizarre twentieth-century world. And there is the need deep within . . . an animal need, frightening, murderous, unholy . . . a vital need that must be fed.

And with his need comes a power over men and women to do his bidding, to quiet his dark craving . . .

Until the murders begin. And the inquiries. All suggesting the same hideous truth.

Now Benjamin must find a sanctuary: a lover, a partner, a friend. Someone who can share his darkness. Someone he can lead to . . . The Awakening.

www.TheJohnRusso.com

Burning Bulb
PUBLISHING

"THE BLAZING SADDLES OF SEX SATIRES!" - GEORGINA SPELVIN

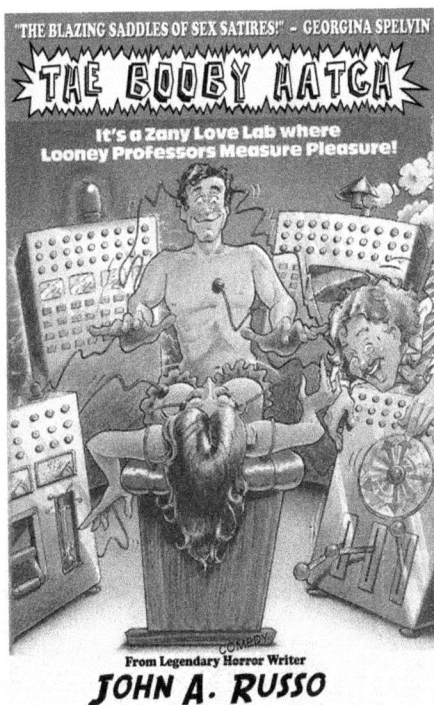

THE BOOBY HATCH

It's a Zany Love Lab where Looney Professors Measure Pleasure!

From Legendary Horror Writer
JOHN A. RUSSO

THE BOOBY HATCH

With NIGHT OF THE LIVING DEAD, John Russo helped blaze a path in the horror genre that has never been equalled. In this hillarious erotic novel, he blazes a path through the wild, zany Sex Revolution of the 1970s.

Sweet, innocent Cherry Jankowski works for Joyful Novelties, where she tests sex toys ranging from the ridiculous to the sublime. But she can't find love or peace of mind and her efforts are hampered by a Peeping Tom, an exhibitionist, a cross-dressing boyfriend, a quack psychiatrist, and even her own product-testing partner, Marcello Fettucini, who can't get it up anymore and is scared of losing his job!

www.TheJohnRusso.com

Burning Bulb
PUBLISHING

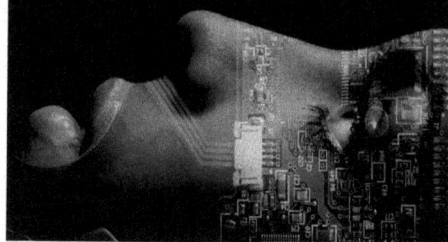

Bright little children, at school and at play,
until their minds are stolen away...

A Novel of Terror by

JOHN A. RUSSO

THE ACADEMY

THE ACADEMY

The Academy. It's every parent's dream, turning their little darlings into geniuses, superachievers, perfect little children.

And if there's a problem, the Academy fixes that too. It's a simple operation. Just a little device. Then a teeny pink scar on a tender little skull . . .

One boy knows the secret. Now he wants his mind back. But it's much, much too late. Too late for anything but the ugly feelings. The bad feelings. The messy sexy feelings. The knife-cold hatred, the murderous rage, for total, screaming, blood-drenching revenge . . .

www.TheJohnRusso.com

Burning Bulb
PUBLISHING

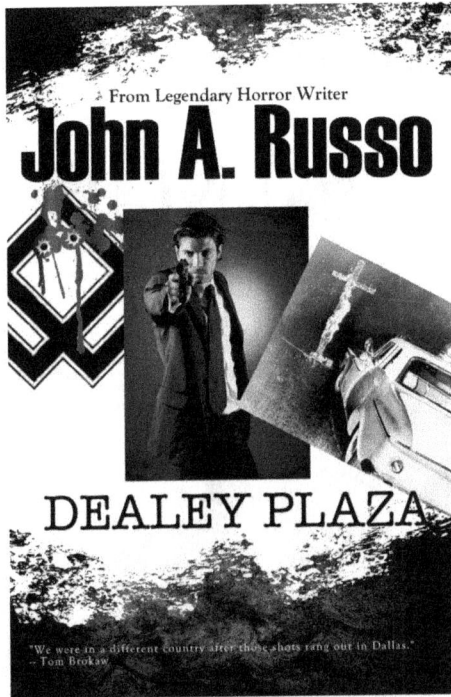

From Legendary Horror Writer
John A. Russo

DEALEY PLAZA

"We were in a different country after those shots rang out in Dallas."
~ Tom Brokaw

DEALEY PLAZA

From legendary horror and suspense writer JOHN RUSSO comes a harrowing tale where no one is safe!

Dealey Plaza is one of the most notorious places in America, and when youthful conspiracy buffs go there in 1964 to stage their own reenactment of the Kennedy Assassination, four of them are brutally murdered ~ the first victims of a hate-filled legacy that continues for four more decades.

The survivors of that long-ago Dallas trip, each of them now icons of the American way of life, are about to be honored ~ or killed.

Who will live and who will die? Will it be country-western star Lori McCoy? Her loving husband? Her scheming ex-husband? Or the case-hardened FBI agent and longtime friend who risks his life trying to protect them?

www.DealeyPlazaBook.com

Burning Bulb
PUBLISHING

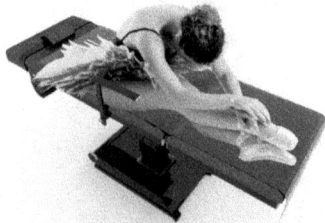

From Legendary Horror Writer
JOHN A. RUSSO
L I M B
to
L I M B

LIMB TO LIMB

SUCH A PRETTY GIRL . . .
Tiffany Blake was a beautiful long-limbed dancer with a glorious future and the backing of a rich benefactor. Then a monstrous accident severed her leg at the hip.

SUCH A COLD, CRUEL KNIFE . . .
And now her fellow dancers are disappearing without a trace. One by one they fall victim to a dark and deadly pattern of evil – caught by the bloody, brutal logic that would have them pay with their lovely bodies for the cruel fate of another . . .victims of the sadistic madman whose flashing knife will make them writhe a gruesome new dance.

www.TheJohnRusso.com

THE MOST FRIGHTENING MOVIE EVER MADE IS NOW A NOVEL!

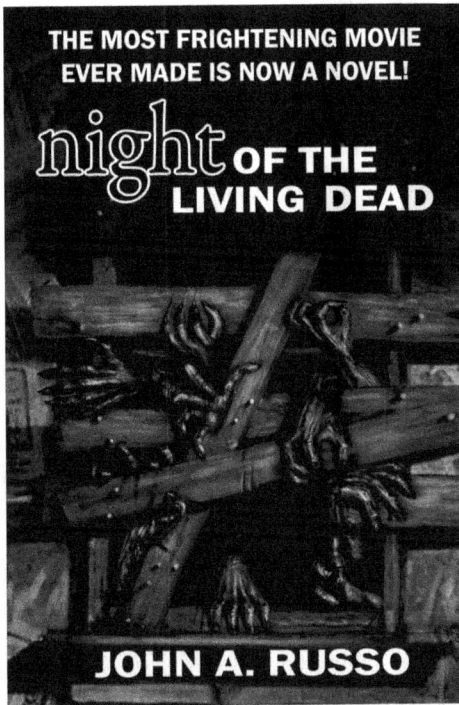

night OF THE LIVING DEAD

JOHN A. RUSSO

NIGHT OF THE LIVING DEAD

Why does **Night of the Living Dead** hit with such chilling impact?
Is it because everyday people in a commonplace house are suddenly the victims of a monstrous invasion? Or is it because the ghouls who surround the house with grasping claws were once ordinary people, too?

Decide for yourself as you read, and the horror grips you. All the cannibalism, suspense and frenzy of the smash-hit move are here in the novel.

www.TheJohnRusso.com

Burning Bulb
PUBLISHING

RISE OF THE DEAD

AN EARTH-SHATTERING ANTHOLOGY OF ZOMBIE TERROR

Featuring Stories By:

John A. Russo   Tyson Blue   E.L. Stice   Nelson W. Pyles

Andy Rausch   Stephen Spignesi   R.D. Riley   Zakary McGaha

David J. Fairhead   Gary Lee Vincent   David C. Hayes   Rachel Montgomery

Paul Victor Wargelin   David F. Walker   William Vitka

Rich Bottles Jr.   Douglas Brode

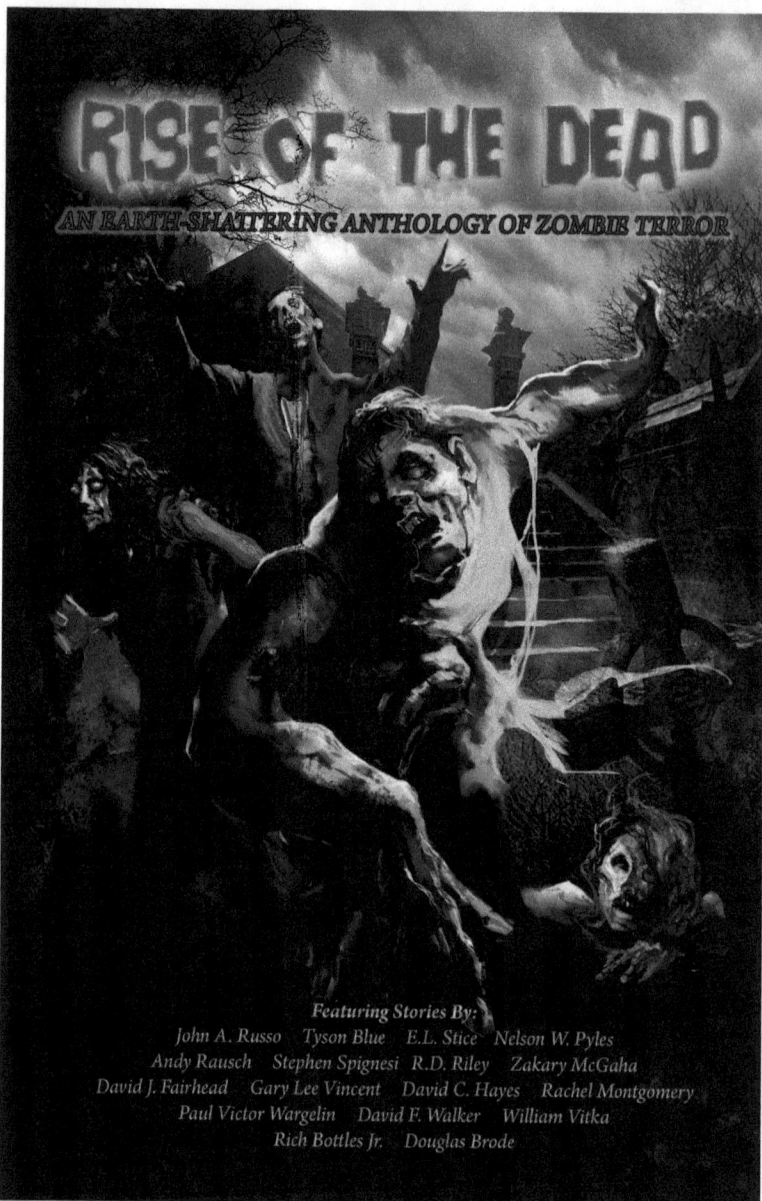

RISE OF THE DEAD - a collection of seventeen
tales of unspeakable zombie terror. Featuring a foreword and
short story by John A. Russo!

www.TheJohnRusso.com

Burning Bulb
PUBLISHING

OTHER GREAT TITLES FROM

Burning Bulb
PUBLISHING

WWW.BURNINGBULBPUBLISHING.COM

ANTHOLOGIES
BIZARRO AND TRANSGRESSIVE FICTION

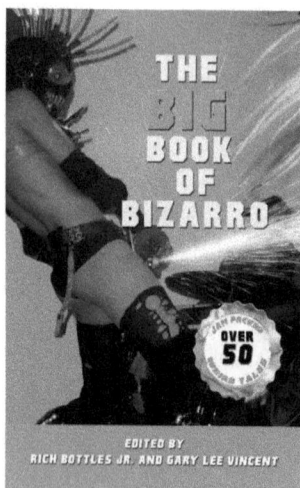

THE BIG BOOK OF BIZARRO

The Big Book of Bizarro brings together the peculiar prose of an international cast of the most grotesquely-gonzo, genre-grinding modern writers who ever put pen to paper (or mouse to pad), including:

NIGHT OF THE LIVING DEAD horror writers John Russo & George Kosana; HUSTLER MAGAZINE erotica contributors Eva Hore, Andrée Lachapelle, & J. Troy Seate and established Bizarro genre authors D. Harlan Wilson, William Pauley III, Wol-vriey, Laird Long, Richard Godwin and so many more!

From Alien abductions to Zombie sex, The Big Book of Bizarro contains OVER FIFTY STORIES of the most outrélandish transgressive fiction that you'll ever lay your capricious and curious hands upon!

WARNING: This book may be one of the most controversial and dangerous books you'll ever read.

WESTWARD HOES

Nine outlaw writers rode into town from obscurity to pen nine tantalizing tales of horror and fantasy, and leaving once they branded their own personal marks on the weird western genre and became living legends of the American Frontier experience.

Like drunken Indian scouts, the writers fervidly tracked down and captured the Western genre, tore off its fashionable veneer and ravished its exposed essence.

So belly up to the bar with your favorite soiled dove and enjoy perusing these thrilling tales of Old West debauchery, danger and desire; compiled by the publisher of The Big Book of Bizarro and featuring the bizarro novella Big Trouble in Little Ass by Wol-vriey.

Burning Bulb
PUBLISHING

ANTHOLOGIES
BIZARRO AND TRANSGRESSIVE FICTION

THE BIG BOOK OF BIZARRO SPECIAL KINDLE EDITIONS

HORROR COLLECTION
EDITED BY
RICH BOTTLES JR. AND GARY LEE VINCENT

SCI-FI & FANTASY COLLECTION
EDITED BY
RICH BOTTLES JR. AND GARY LEE VINCENT

EROTICA COLLECTION
EDITED BY
RICH BOTTLES JR. AND GARY LEE VINCENT

OTHER AWESOME COLLECTIONS

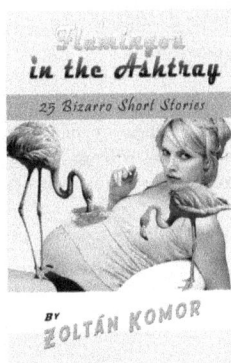

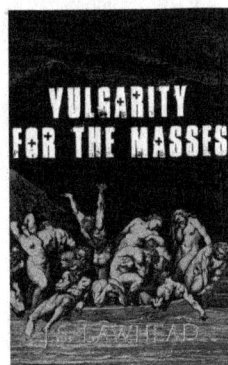

THE FILING CABINET OF DOOM
SEVENTEEN Bizarro Short Stories
MADELEINE SWANN

Flamingos in the Ashtray
25 Bizarro Short Stories
BY ZOLTÁN KOMOR

VULGARITY FOR THE MASSES

Burning Bulb
PUBLISHING

GARY LEE VINCENT'S
DARKENED
THE WEST VIRGINIA VAMPIRE SERIES

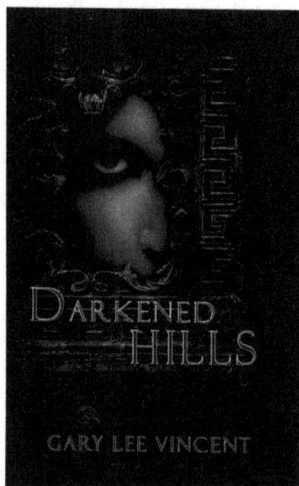

DARKENED HILLS

When evil descends on a small West Virginia town, who will survive?

Jonathan did not start out his life to become a rambler, it just worked out that way. William was a troubled youth with something to hide. Both were from Melas, a small town tucked away in the West Virginia hills... a town where disappearances are happening more and more frequently.

After the suicide of a wanted serial killer, the townsfolk thought the nightmare was over. But when a centuries-old vampire is discovered they find out the hard way it's just getting started. Dark secrets can only stay hidden for so long and when the devil comes to collect, there will be hell to pay. Can Jonathan and William find a way to stop the vampire before it's too late? Find out in *Darkened Hills!*

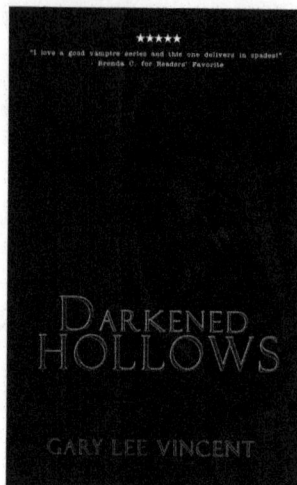

DARKENED HOLLOWS

In the heart-stopping sequel to the award-winning *Darkened Hills*, Jonathan and William must return to West Virginia to face possible criminal charges stemming from their last visit to the damned town of Melas, where both had narrowly escaped the clutches of a vampire seethe.

And as livestock start mysteriously getting murdered with all of their blood drained, worried farmers are searching for answers - leaving the local Sheriff and his deputy racing against time to learn the cause before a more violent crime is committed.

WWW.DARKENEDHILLS.COM

GARY LEE VINCENT'S
DARKENED
THE WEST VIRGINIA VAMPIRE SERIES

DARKENED WATERS

When the world goes to hell, the chosen must arise!

As Talman Cane orchestrates a flood of epic proportions in this third installment of the *Darkened* series the towns of Melas and Tarklin are caught completely off guard by the deluge. Hell-bent on finishing what they started, the evil brothers return to the lunatic asylum to take care of the witnesses and add to the ever-growing army of the undead.

Aided by Lucifer himself and the insane vampire demon Legion, the stage is set to channel all of the forces of hell to come forth. In an all-out race to survive, Jonathan, William, and Amanda soon discover they are up against impossible odds as Lucifer opens the Gateway to Hell, ushering in the zombie apocalypse and the End Times.

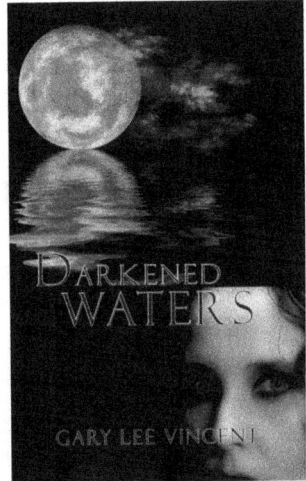

DARKENED SOULS

Melas and the Madison House are about to be rebuilt.
True evil is about to be reborne!

Young ex-priest and vampire-killer William is drawn back to the West Virginian town that almost killed him, where his vampire arch-enemy Victor Rothenstein still stalks the earth.

The town of Melas lies destroyed after the battle of the End of Days. But why is wealthy Jackie Nixon so eager to rebuild it using the bone dust of murdered souls?

Terrible evil has visited before, but the Gateway to Hell is about to be reopened in a horrific climax. And this time – it's personal.

WOL-VRIEY
BIZARRO AND TRANSGRESSIVE FICTION

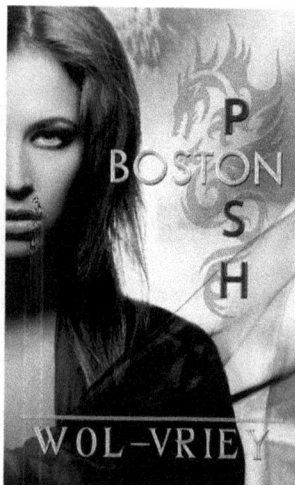

BOSTON POSH

In 2028 AD, the USA is a nation ravaged by hungry dragons and dinosaurs. In Boston, Massachusetts, private eye Bud Malone is hired to rescue a kidnapped heiress. But nothing is as it seems.

Malone works to unravel a tangled web involving Boston Chinatown, a 200-year-old woman with a 9-year-old body, white robots, a human-liver-eating psychopath, a golem, a porcelain dragon, and a snake goddess with a crush on him. There's also a woman obsessed with chicken sex. Then Malone meets Posh Lane, a gorgeous call girl who's desperate to quit her pimp.

Romantic sparks ignite between Posh and Malone, but Posh's past suddenly catches up with her in a BIG way. To save Posh, Malone agrees to run a quest for Earth's new rulers, the Forks. But, Malone has no idea that agreeing to the Fork's odd request will send him on the weirdest trip he's ever been on in his life.

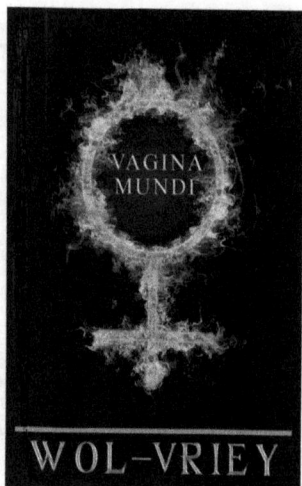

VAGINA MUNDI

Rachel Risk is a professional thief with super-strong hair that can stretch like tentacles to manipulate objects. Ashley Status has both a digitally augmented brain, and 'muscle-purses' in her arms and legs in which she stores inflatable objects—cars, guns, rocket launchers, etc.

When Raye is framed as the fall girl in a jewel robbery, the pair flee Chicago's vengeful robot gangsters and take refuge in the Hotel Bizarre, where the gorgeous 'vagina singer,' Femina, is performing for a week.

But the Hotel Bizarre is even stranger than its name suggests, and very soon Raye and Ash are involved in an deadly adventure, a struggle for survival the likes of which they'd never imagined possible—with loads of deviant sex, drugs, music, and violence at every turn. And just what is the old woman in the skin desert really doing with all those cats glued to her walls?

Vagina Mundi—a Bizarro Hymn in praise of WOMAN!

Burning Bulb
PUBLISHING

WOL-VRIEY
BIZARRO AND TRANSGRESSIVE FICTION

VEGAN VAMPIRE VAGINAS

The biggest bank heist in US history. And Tom Palmer can't remember pulling it off. And no, this isn't your standard case of amnesia. After a one-night-stand gone horribly wrong, Boston salesman Tom Palmer wakes up with a vagina implanted in his left hand. Then his day gets worse.

Tom is transported across space-time to a nightmare version of Boston, one where the Bizarro virus has transformed half the population into cannibals. Worst of all, Tom discovers that in this new Boston, he's the infamous gangster Pussypalm, wanted for robbing the Federal Reserve Bank of Boston a year ago. He also learns that the vagina in his hand is prophetic, i.e. it talks . . . after sex.

With 130 people left dead during his bank heist and six billion dollars missing, Tom knows he's living on borrowed time. It is in his best interests not to remember anything. Because once he does . . .

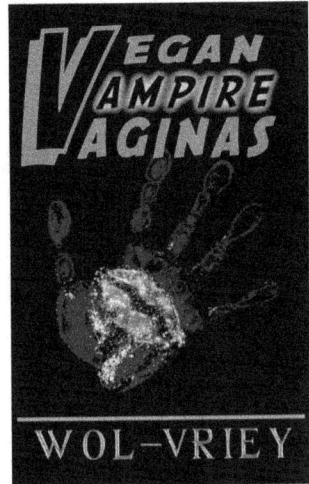

VEGAN ZOMBIE APOCALYPSE

In the post-apocalypse worlderness, zombies rule the earth. They're allergic to meat, and brains literally make them explode. Zombies now eat blood potatoes, parasitic tubers grown in the flesh of humancows corralled in maximum security farms. Two fugitives meet in the ancient ruins of Texas. The first is Soil 15-f, a woman-cow who's escaped her farm a week before she's due to be killed and her blood potato crop harvested. The second fugitive is Able Kane, former head necros food technician, now sentenced to death for heresy. But Soil is no ordinary humancow.

Unknown to herself, she's the vegan zombie agricultural revolution, and the zombies desperately want her back. And the necros equally desperately want Able Kane dead. He's fled with a forbidden discovery which will reshape the world for the worse if used. And Able is just hardheaded/misguided enough to use it.

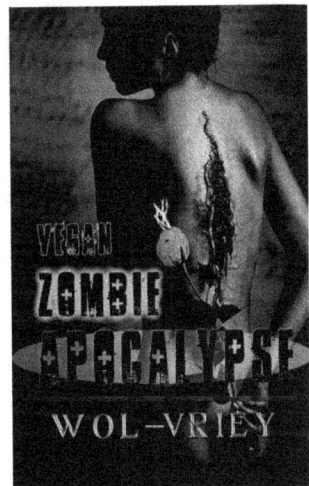

Burning Bulb
PUBLISHING

WEST VIRGINIA-THEMED HUMORROROTICA
BY RICH BOTTLES JR.

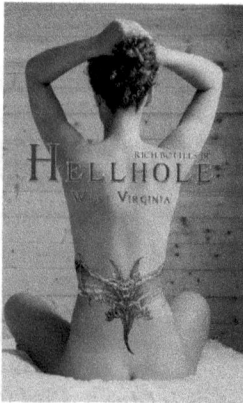

HELLHOLE WEST VIRGINIA

From the heights of Mothman's perch high atop the Silver Bridge in Point Pleasant to the depths of Hellhole Cavern in Pendleton County, evil lurks within the shadows as the sun sets upon the haunted hills and hollows of West Virginia.

Bizarro author Rich Bottles Jr. blows the coffin lid off horror genre clichés with this tour de force cast of Eco-friendly vampires, beach-yearning zombies and sex-starved she-devils.

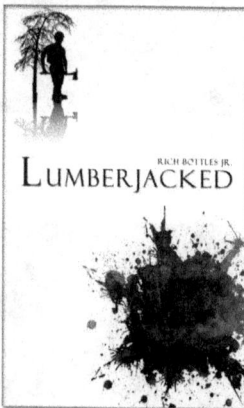

LUMBERJACKED

If you are easily offended or do not possess a truly depraved sense of humor, this story may not be the light summer reading fare you desire. As for the four feisty female freshmen stranded on top of West Virginia's third highest mountain, they have no choice but to experience the sick, twisted debauchery and perverted mayhem described deep inside the tight unbroken bindings of this horrific missive.

Lumberjacked takes the reader to a nightmarish world where character development and aesthetic integrity are prematurely cut short by the swinging axes of maniacal lumberjacks, who are hell bent on death and destruction in the remote forests of Appalachia. And at the climax, when paranoia crosses over to the paranormal, Lumberjacked makes Deliverance look like a family raft trip down the Lower Gauley.

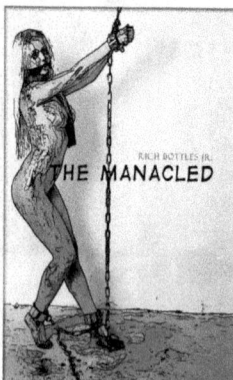

THE MANACLED

What happens when twin brothers lease out the former West Virginia State Penitentiary with the false purpose of filming a documentary on supernatural phenomena, but their true intention is to make a pornographic movie?

Chaos ensues as the disturbed spirits of murdered convicts, along with the reanimated dead from the neighboring Indian Burial Mound, take their vengeance on the unwary and undressed trespassers.

Zombies, ghosts, mobsters and porn collide in this bizarro tale from horror author Rich Bottles Jr.

Burning Bulb
PUBLISHING

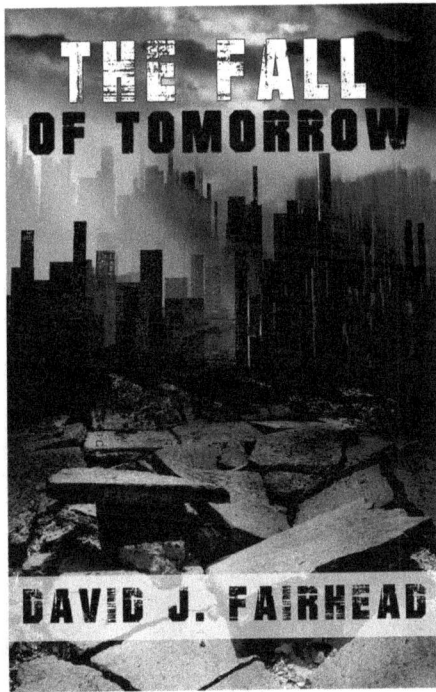

THE FALL OF TOMORROW

Hopelessness... How do you protect your loved ones when Hell itself opens its insidious mouth?

Horror... Nightmarish Creatures invade your world and there is nowhere to hide.

Blood... How long can you hold out before they come for you?

Pain... Where do you run to avoid being eaten alive by monsters with a voracious appetite for your flesh?

Screams... While you selfishly run for your own life.

Questions... Who is to blame? Where did they come from? How many people survived...and how does the human race find the means to fight back?

THE FALL OF TOMORROW is man's last tale of desperation told by those that are striving to salvage some hope against a ravenous bastion of evil beasts bent on ruling our world.

"David Fairhead writes compelling stories that offer very human characters and very inhuman monsters. There is no subtlety in Fairhead's imagination - he is simply dying to scare the hell out of you."
- Nelson W Pyles - author of DEMONS, DOLLS AND MILKSHAKES

Burning Bulb
PUBLISHING

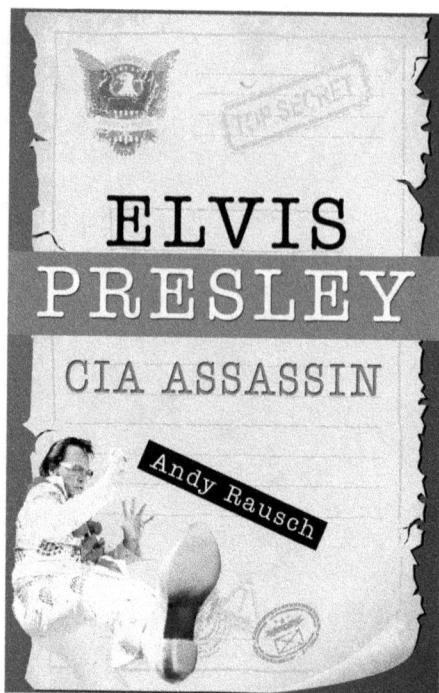

ELVIS PRESLEY, CIA ASSASSIN

"I can guarantee you. Read this book and you'll never look at Elvis the same way again!"
~ Douglas Brode, author of ELVIS CINEMA AND POPULAR CULTURE

SOON TO BE A MAJOR MOTION PICTURE

In 1970, singer Elvis Presley secretly met with President Richard Nixon. This new comedic novel imagines that Presley became a Central Intelligence Agency operative, eventually moving up through the ranks to become a skilled assassin.

Presented in an oral history fashion, the book tells us about Presley's secret transformation by the people who knew him best.

Did he fake his death in 1977? Was Presley involved with the Watergate scandal? The Iran hostage crisis? Communicating with aliens?

Read this book to find out the answers to these and many more questions.

Burning Bulb
PUBLISHING

MAD WORLD BY ANDY RAUSCH

"*Mad World* is dark, twisted, no-holds-barred fun."
—Jason Starr, author of *Bust*, *Slide*, and *The Max*

EVERYONE'S PLAYING AN ANGLE IN THE CITY OF ANGELS

Mad World tells the stories of a black hitman who doubles as a university professor, a Catholic priest who longs to be a gangster, a would-be author from Kansas, a gay phone sex operator who claims he's straight, a group of rich twentysomethings playing a deadly game of life and death, a vicious Mafia boss, and a sleazy Hollywood movie director. As each of their stories intersect, the body count piles up and the action comes nonstop in this tense, white-knuckle thriller by first-time author Andy Rausch.

"A wild ride. If you like it gangster, *Mad World* delivers."
—Daniel Birch, author of *Get Some*

Burning Bulb
PUBLISHING

BLOODLETTING

A TALE OF REVENGE

ANDY RAUSCH

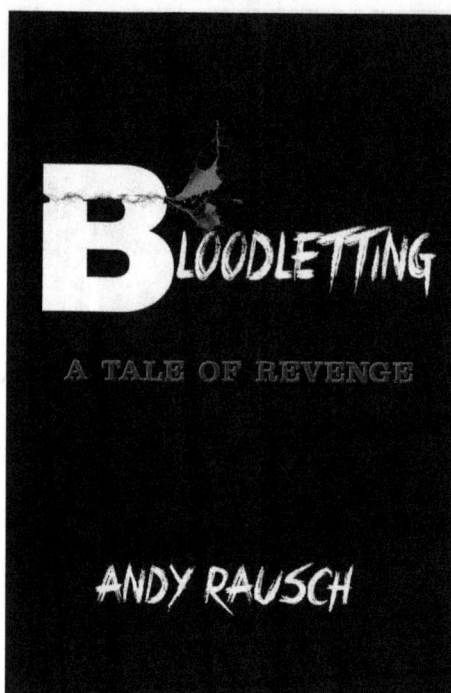

BLOODLETTING: A TALE OF REVENGE BY ANDY RAUSCH

"Relentless... Addictive... The kind of nightmare you don't want
to wake up from."
—Heywood Gould, screenwriter of *Rolling Thunder*

He was just an average Joe. But when he finds his family held at
gunpoint by merciless thugs, he's told he must murder a Mafia
chieftain if he ever wishes to see his loved ones again.

Against all odds, Joe keeps his end of the bargain, but the criminals
don't. Now at his wits end, Joe is pushed beyond his breaking point
and forced to exact bloody revenge against those who've done him
and his family wrong in this powerful and violent novella by author
Andy Rausch (*Mad World*).

"Andy Rausch has a tight noir style that combines gritty, realistic drama
with a cinematic flair that makes for a powerful, compelling (somewhat
Stephen Kingesque), authentically visual reading experience."
—Stephen Spignesi, author of *Dialogues*

Burning Bulb
PUBLISHING

www.ingramcontent.com/pod-product-compliance
Lightning Source LLC
Chambersburg PA
CBHW062357090426
42740CB00010B/1311